From Borneo
to Lockerbie

From Borneo to Lockerbie

Memoirs of an RAF Helicopter Pilot

Geoffrey Leeming

Pen & Sword
AVIATION

First published in Great Britain in 2013 by
PEN & SWORD AVIATION
An imprint of
Pen & Sword Books Ltd
47 Church Street
Barnsley
South Yorkshire
S70 2AS

ISBN 978-1-84884-765-1

Typeset by Concept, Huddersfield, West Yorkshire.
Printed and bound in England by CPI Group (UK) Ltd, Croydon, CR0 4YY.

Pen & Sword Books Ltd incorporates the imprints of Pen & Sword Aviation,
Pen & Sword Family History, Pen & Sword Maritime, Pen & Sword Military,
Pen & Sword Discovery, Wharncliffe Local History, Wharncliffe True Crime,
Wharncliffe Transport, Pen & Sword Select, Pen & Sword Military Classics,
Leo Cooper, The Praetorian Press, Remember When, Seaforth Publishing and
Frontline Publishing.

For a complete list of Pen & Sword titles please contact
PEN & SWORD BOOKS LIMITED
47 Church Street, Barnsley, South Yorkshire, S70 2AS, England
E-mail: enquiries@pen-and-sword.co.uk
Website: www.pen-and-sword.co.uk

CONTENTS

LIST OF MAPS

LIST OF PLATES

ACKNOWLEDGEMENTS

Although the majority of this book has been written from personal memory, aided by my accumulation of Pilot's Flying Log Books, I am indebted to the many friends and former colleagues who have rummaged through their own memories and attics to provide me with their own recollections, corroborating or correcting my version of the events portrayed here. Long-forgotten photographs and maps have also been unearthed in the process. I am particularly grateful to Mike Ramshaw for his detailed memories of our shared time in the Far East and to Bill Gault, Brian Canfer, Martin Cocksedge and Dave Lloyd for their additions and corrections to my memories of the numerous rescue missions we undertook together in Scotland.

My thanks go to the renowned nature and adventure photographer, John Beatty, for generously allowing me to reproduce the image displayed on the jacket cover and other photographs within. I am also grateful for the detective work of Lee Barton of the Air Historical Branch of the Ministry of Defence and of Stewart Blair of Cumberland News Media in tracking down elusive photographs in their respective archives, and to Alan Macgregor, Rick Atkinson, Chris Gibbons, Robin Bryden and Bob Geddes for sorting through their own photographic collections for me.

I am very happy to acknowledge the issue of an Open Government Licence (*see* http://www.nationalarchives.gov.uk/doc/open-government-licence/) by the Crown Copyright Unit of the Ministry of Defence for use of the many RAF photographs shown in this book.

A big thank you is due to my wife, Marian, for her unfailing support and sound advice during this project, as well as for her necessary good humour during some of the tenser moments of its evolution.

My foremost thanks, however, must go to Martin Middlebrook, without whom this book would still be a distant and, probably, unfulfilled dream. His enthusiasm in overcoming my procrastination and subsequently his significant guidance and advice as my editor during the writing of this book have proved invaluable.

INTRODUCTION

'Have you thought of writing this down?'

There were four of us. Mary and Martin Middlebrook were guests at our home at Trearddur Bay overlooking the sea in Anglesey, where Marian and I had put down our roots during my last posting at nearby RAF Valley. We had all known each other for more than fifty years since our early days at Boston in Lincolnshire. Marian had been my childhood sweetheart. Mary was Marian's cousin. Martin was her husband. His youngest brother, Peter, had been one of my best friends at Boston Grammar School.

We had dined well and were relaxing with talk of former days. Martin, a much-published military and aviation historian, was interested in my flying career and soon I had embarked on my 'war stories'. With some prompting and occasional questions from Martin, story followed story. Some included incidents of close encounters with fate and distressing circumstances that I had never even told my wife.

I confessed that I had promised to record it 'one day' as a family history for my grandchildren but, for Martin, this was not enough. He urged me to do it immediately and offered to use his contacts to help get the stories published.

I did not set out to write a definitive history of the period between my first operational helicopter posting to a forgotten war in Borneo and my final search and rescue mission following the terrorist bombing of Pan Am Flight 103 at Lockerbie. Nevertheless, history it is, albeit a narrow and very personal account of the intervening events and a tiny fragment of the overall picture.

Through these stories, I hope that the reader may gain some insight into the life of an RAF helicopter pilot and the nature of helicopter operations in an earlier era – one before the ubiquitous presence of media cameramen and reporters in every zone of conflict and at every disaster made such events a regular and familiar feature of current television news and documentaries.

Geoffrey Leeming
Trearddur Bay
Wales
2013

CHAPTER ONE

WINGS

Frequently on first acquaintance most people are familiar with the question, 'Why did you want to . . .?' or 'When was your first interest in . . .?' For me, of course, that question was always about flying, and my answer was quite simple: I had wanted to fly for as long as I could remember. Like most small boys I had flirted with the idea of becoming a fireman or a train driver, or even a high court judge, but these alternative careers were very much fall-back positions to my burning ambition to become a pilot – not just any pilot, mind you, but a Royal Air Force pilot wearing those much-coveted, iconic pilot's wings.

Born and raised in Lincolnshire, 'Bomber County' of the Second World War, I had been surrounded by the sight and sound of aircraft. First the drone of German bombers over Grimsby where we lived during the war, heralded by the unforgettable, mournful wail of the air-raid siren and followed invariably by the crump and rattle of falling bombs. During my school years in Boston came the change to the roar of jets as Gloster Meteors and, later, Hawker Hunters weaved overhead in mock aerial combat. During school holidays, I and my similarly obsessed school friends, Peter Middlebrook and Dale Reynolds, thought little of cycling the 50-mile round trip to the RAF College at Cranwell where, to the irritation of Air Traffic Control, we would haunt the runway threshold adjacent to a minor public road, coming almost within touching distance of the many Percival Provost, Boulton Paul Balliols and de Havilland Vampires based there as they made their low final approaches to land. A glimpse of a smoky trail in the distance towards Lincoln would have us furiously pedalling a further 12 miles to get as close as possible to the new Avro Vulcan delta-winged bombers recently arrived at RAF Waddington.

* * *

Discounting an early experiment when I had leapt out of a tree while hanging from an open fisherman's umbrella, my first flight had been at Cleethorpes. There, at the age of twelve and clutching my five-shilling child's fare, I presented myself alone to be flown by Captain Jim Crampton, who operated a couple of four-seater, single-engined Austers off the beach at low tide. Far from feeling concerned by the stomach-lurching plunges and frequent wing-drops occasioned by the turbulence and air-pockets above the hot sand, I watched, fascinated, as the pilot deftly moved the controls to maintain a steady climb, the small aircraft's movements as it rode the unseen air currents merely emphasising the exciting new medium in which I now found myself. The experience exceeded all my expectations and made me re-double my resolve to be a pilot.

Throughout my schooldays, I and my friends had made regular visits to the fantastic Farnborough Air Show, at that time an annual event. Such was our keenness that we sometimes made the 300-mile round trip in an Austin A40 pick-up truck driven by Peter's father, a local wholesale potato merchant, taking it in turns to travel in the open back of the truck before a spell in the cab to warm up. The sheer magic of the event banished all memories of any discomfort, immediately immersing us in its unique atmosphere – the warm pervasive smell of burning aviation fuel wafting over the large crowds, the announcements and commentaries echoing into the far distance from the Tannoy public address system, the periodic bang as yet another customer was fired up the Martin Baker ejection seat rig but, above all, the thundering, crackling wall of noise of aircraft engines at full power reverberating around the airfield and echoing back from the famous Black Sheds on the opposite side of the runway from the spectators. The test pilots flying the latest proto-type aircraft were household names in that exciting era in British aviation – Neville Duke in the Hawker Hunter, Mike Lithgow in the Supermarine Swift, Roland Beaumont in the English Electric P1, Roly Falk in the Avro Vulcan and a host more. We followed our heroes' careers and exploits as avidly as others followed those of film stars and pop idols. Part of the RAF's contribution to the display comprised fly-pasts by the recently acquired V-bombers and, at Boston, Peter and I had been thrilled to witness a daily low-level fly-past of four Vickers Valiants as they rehearsed in the weeks leading up to the 1955 Farnborough display. Never in my wildest dreams did I imagine that I would be flying those very same aircraft just seven years later.

A family move to Bletchley in Buckinghamshire marked my entry into the Sixth Form and the serious work of Advanced Level GCEs. It also coincided with the publication of the infamous 1957 Defence White Paper from the newly-appointed Minister of Defence, Duncan Sandys. The sweeping and radical policy changes proposed included the end of the manned fighter and bomber, with their roles being taken over by the increasingly reliable anti-aircraft missiles and intercontinental ballistic missiles. It was obvious that the number of pilots required in the wake of this policy would be severely reduced with a corresponding increase in competition for those places remaining. Already uneasy about the appalling RAF accident rates (some 853 RAF personnel had been killed in flying accidents during the first three years of the decade), and worried by what they saw as my diminishing prospects, my parents sought to dissuade me from pursuing my dream and urged me to think of a different career. Mindful of this, and with the end of my school days rapidly approaching, I applied for and, following successful A-Level results, was accepted as an Assistant Experimental Officer with the Ministry of Aviation at the Royal Aircraft Establishment, Bedford, an outstation of the famous Farnborough establishment. This, I felt, would offer me a satisfying alternative career in aviation should my bid to join the RAF fail.

My work at Bedford was on a project examining the low-speed handling characteristics of highly-swept delta-winged aircraft as part of the research towards the development of a supersonic transport aircraft (the 'SST', later named Concorde). The main hangar there was an aircraft enthusiast's paradise, containing many of the amazing aircraft of that dynamic and exciting decade of aeronautical research. These included the sleek, needle-nosed, world record-breaking Fairey Delta FD2, the English Electric P1, forerunner of the Lightning fighter, the dumpy Short SC1 and the Flying Bedstead (the descriptive nickname for the skeletal Rolls Royce Thrust Measuring Rig). These latter two aircraft were the first vertical take-off and landing jet aircraft in the world and led directly to the development of the Hawker Siddeley Harrier jump-jet. I took full advantage of my access to these aircraft, spending many of my lunch breaks sitting in their cockpits indulging in my Walter Mitty-like fantasies. However, despite this interesting and stimulating environment, I was now even more desperate to become a pilot.

I had applied to the RAF soon after my arrival at Bedford and eventually I was invited to attend the Officer and Aircrew Selection Centre at RAF Hornchurch in Essex. A major early hurdle to selection was the formidable medical examination. In this respect I was at an advantage, having only recently successfully undergone the same medical at another research establishment at Boscombe Down, This, along with advanced training in pressure breathing and explosive decompressions in specially constructed chambers, had been to prepare me as a flight test observer for a very high altitude research programme at Bedford. On completion of the RAF medical I was somewhat disconcerted, therefore, to be summoned back later to face a panel of three medical officers.

'You are a very fit young man,' the senior medical officer declared, 'but we're rather puzzled about the number of broken bones you have sustained in your short life – we are concerned that you may have unnaturally brittle bones. Tell us how you incurred these injuries.' Under 'Medical History' on my application form I had listed two breaks to my right arm, a broken right leg, three broken ribs and a broken shoulder blade. Twenty minutes later, after hearing my explanation involving road accidents and rugby injuries, they had revised their opinion to 'accident prone'. As this did not come within their remit, they declared me fully fit. The remainder of the selection process

– a battery of aptitude tests, team exercises and discussions – all proceeded satisfactorily. Six weeks later I was bidding farewell to my colleagues at Bedford and setting off to follow my dream.

* * *

Reporting to the Initial Training School at RAF South Cerney in Gloucestershire on 1 January 1961, I embarked on an intensive and arduous period of officer training. We had been informed early on in our course that we would have the honour of having the Queen to review our commissioning parade. We therefore received the doubtful privilege of hour after hour of additional early morning drill, undertaken under the eagle eyes of Drill Instructors possessed of a well-honed line in sarcastic wit and repartee. All went well, however, and four months later found my course of twenty-six students standing rigidly to attention and proudly presenting arms for the Royal Salute. A sunny late-April day, the almond trees bordering the parade ground in full blossom and the Royal Standard billowing gently on the flagstaff graced a most memorable occasion.

I was now a commissioned officer in Her Majesty's Royal Air Force.

* * *

Basic flying training for those of us destined to become pilots commenced at No. 6 Flying Training School at RAF Tern Hill, near Market Drayton in Shropshire. There we were introduced to our first aircraft, the Percival Provost (later known as the Piston Provost to differentiate it from the new Jet Provost just entering RAF service). The Provost was a 'meaty' aircraft, possessed of a super-charged 550-horsepower radial engine and a host of complications such as separate rpm and boost controls for the engine, as well as manual controls for air intake filters and for regulating oil cooling. This made for an excellent training aircraft and one that demanded the full attention of inexperienced pilots. Together with my fellow course members, I struggled through the first discouraging weeks of learning by heart pages of aircraft checks and bouncing the Provost all over the airfield. Eventually, however, under the expert tutelage of our instructors, we each experienced that most memorable moment of flying one's first solo – in my case after eleven hours of instruction.

The RAF was undergoing major reorganisation of its air bases during this period and it came as a welcome change when we found ourselves moved to Acklington, about 8 miles south of Alnwick in Northumberland. After the industrial haze-laden Tern Hill air from the nearby Potteries and the confined flying area, this was like being let out of a cage. Not only was our 'local area' now huge, stretching from the River Tyne to the Scottish Border, but the visibility was simply amazing in the cleaner air. Also, the scenic

Northumberland coastline was a gift to those amongst us who were still struggling to maintain an accurate check on their precise location while flying. By now we were considered reasonably competent pilots and, after only the briefest dual local familiarisation flight to point out the salient landmarks, we were let loose in our new surroundings.

We were also fairly adept in such advanced manoeuvres as aerobatics and spinning, exulting in the freedom to chase each other around the towering white cumulus clouds as we and our aircraft became one, and our reactions more instinctive. Accompanying all this was the intoxicating cocktail of smells from the engine – raw high-octane fuel, hot engine oil, and the sweet smell of glycol anti-freeze from the radiator every time we turned the responsive Provost upside down.

* * *

In late January of 1962, my course had completed basic flying training and we moved on to fast-jet training. We started at RAF Oakington near Cambridge, before again getting caught up in the RAF's upheavals and being moved to RAF Swinderby, near to Lincoln. Our new aircraft were the single-engined de Havilland Vampire and the twin-engined Gloster Meteor, both training versions of the RAF's very first jet aircraft. The latter was used by our longer-legged colleagues, for whom the limited clearance for their legs and feet during an ejection could have resulted in serious injury. The new course certainly marked a significant change of pace in our training. Now, instead of being carefully prepared for our first solo flights over as many sorties as necessary, that key event simply appeared as the tenth training flight in the syllabus, the assumption being that we would be word-perfect in our checks and fully competent to take a Vampire or Meteor solo after only seven hours of flying instruction. During that time, the four of us selected for 'fast-jet' training had bridged the so-called 'speed gap', the significant jump in performance between the Piston Provost we had recently left and the high-speed world of jet aircraft. As well as allowing us to fly faster than before, the Vampire also introduced us to flying at high altitudes. It was capable of climbing to well in excess of 40,000 feet and it was in these regions that we explored a concept new to us of flight approaching the speed of sound, the so-called 'Sound Barrier' – Mach 1. To us students, these were exciting and sometimes unpredictable excursions towards the limits of controllability – those very same limits with which our schoolboy heroes had battled at the dawn of the supersonic era in similar aircraft barely a decade earlier. Although the Vampire's cockpit was pressurised, its heating and demisting system was rudimentary and a film of ice would quickly form on the inside of the canopy after only a few minutes at height. A small sponge soaked in glycol anti-freeze was supplied to tackle this problem and, after removing it from its leather pouch on the instrument panel, it could be used to rub a tiny, temporary port-hole in the ice through which to view the outside world. This could lead to momentary excitement if the Vampire inadvertently entered a spin during high-altitude manoeuvring.

* * *

In order to qualify for my 'wings', I had to undertake two flying tests at the end of the course – a Final Navigation Test and a Final Handling Test, the latter being a thorough check on all aspects of flying the aircraft, with random practice emergencies being thrown in at intervals by the examiner. In the event, both tests provided more than a sufficient number of real emergencies to deal with. Shortly after taking off in very poor weather for my Final Navigation Tests, my Vampire suffered a series of serious unrelated faults that resulted in my examiner and me just scraping back into Swinderby, short of fuel, without a radio, without any navigation or let-down aids, and an un-identified hammering and heavy vibration on the airframe. Prior to this, we had squeezed down to a very low height in an attempt to re-gain visual contact with the ground and, hopefully, identify our position. Just as my examiner had decided that we were totally lost and ordered me to prepare for ejection, I suddenly recognised a pig farm sited on a disused airfield several miles from Swinderby. I had used this same airfield as a turning point on a recent solo low-level navigation exercise and, by carefully re-tracing this route in reverse, I eventually came upon our home base where we landed with almost nothing but fumes in our tanks. Despite having been technically lost for much of the flight, I was deemed to have passed this test.

The second drama came on my Final Handling Test when one of the main undercarriage wheels broke up as I took off. I wanted to land the Vampire with its undercarriage retracted but, for some unknown reason, my examiner insisted we land with what remained of our undercarriage locked in the down position. We shut down the engine on the final approach to minimise the risk of a fire but the subsequent landing had its predictable consequences. The wheel-less undercarriage leg dug into the runway surface on touch-down, violently twisting the aircraft sideways and shearing off the other main-wheel, whereupon the Vampire skidded to an abrupt stop as both legs cut grooves into the runway, starting small fires beneath the fuselage.

This event occurred on the Friday morning of a 'long weekend'. The RAF had only recently ceased working a five-and-a-half day week, before which Saturday mornings had been taken up by normal working or parades. An occasional weekend starting mid-day Friday was therefore a much anticipated break. The paperwork and initial investigation into our mishap took us well into the afternoon until, with everyone else long departed, I eventually sought out my girlfriend, Marian (later my wife), waiting with her father's car to collect me for the weekend.

'Where the dickens have you been?' was the uncharacteristic angry outburst that greeted me, 'I've been waiting here for over two hours! Why couldn't you have told me you were going to be late?'

'I've just crashed on the runway,' I replied, naively assuming that this simple explanation would suffice to assuage her anger. But no! From where she had been parked, her view of the airfield had been obscured by intervening hangars and she had witnessed nothing of my unfolding drama less than half-a-mile away. We drove off in silence, passing the end of the runway where my Vampire still sat forlornly on its belly, gently simmering and surrounded by fire vehicles.

The following Monday, I successfully passed my Final Handling Test and, with the award of our 'wings' now assured, the four of us on the course anxiously awaited news of our postings. At that time, almost all graduates from the fast-jet flying school went straight to bombers – the V-Force, which was charged with the awesome responsibility of nuclear retaliation in the event of a conflict with the Warsaw Pact. Despite the elite nature of the V-Force and the vast resources devoted to it, we all harboured ambitions to become fighter pilots. Such postings were, however, rare but, when our postings were announced, Tim Webb had won a coveted fighter slot, while Des Sheen was posted to Avro Vulcans, Martin Todd to Handley Page Victors and me to Vickers Valiants.

A week later we were presented with our 'wings' by Air Commodore (later Air Chief Marshal Sir Christopher) Foxley-Norris, a renowned Battle of Britain pilot, before dispersing to our various Operational Conversion Units for final specialised training to equip us for service on the RAF's front line.

Almost two years after starting out on my RAF training and with nearly 250 hours flying experience, I had achieved my dream of becoming an RAF pilot.

CHAPTER TWO

VALIANTS

On 10 October 1962, I reported to RAF Gaydon in Warwickshire to commence an intensive course on the Valiant. As well as learning to fly the aircraft, this course gave me a thorough grounding in its wide range of complex systems – fuel, electrical, avionics and the weapon delivery system in its cavernous bomb bays, which enabled it to drop either a nuclear bomb or ten tons of conventional bombs. Before flying the actual aircraft, several hours were spent in the Valiant flight simulator. This was my first acquaintance with this training aid and I was much impressed by its effectiveness. Although generations away from the comprehensive modern-day simulators, every detail of the actual aircraft cockpit was faithfully reproduced and much care was taken to enhance the feeling of realism. Full flying clothing was worn, oxygen masks connected and the ejection seats treated as if live. By the time I climbed into the Valiant's cockpit for my first flight, I felt that I was entering an environment already familiar to me.

Our busy course was rudely interrupted by a frightening development – on Monday, 22 October, Gaydon moved onto a state of war alert. A Tannoy announcement from the Station Commander ordered everyone to remain on the base and await further instructions. He said that President John F. Kennedy would be making a television broadcast later that evening, and that we should assemble in the various messes to watch it. The Cuban Missile Crisis had just reached a critical phase and the world now stood on the brink of nuclear war. Shocked disbelief was evident all round, from the new chaps like me who, perhaps without thinking too deeply during selection interviews, had affirmed their willingness to drop a nuclear bomb in the course of their duty, to the experienced pilots with at least a tour on an operational bomber squadron behind them. Having participated in numerous regular, realistic and challenging exercises to test and hone their reaction times, these pilots would have been familiar with the measures and preparations now being activated on V-bomber bases all around Britain, and were probably thinking of their recent colleagues making final studies of their assigned targets, while ground-crews carefully loaded the nuclear weapons into the bomb bays of their waiting aircraft. History records the crisis dragging on for a further five days of tense negotiations between the USA and the USSR but, at long last, the merchant ships carrying Russian nuclear missiles to Cuba, the trigger for the crisis, turned back and the world breathed again.

*   *   *

Further delays on the course followed, caused by the heavy snowfalls of the severe winter of 1962-63. Flying eventually resumed in earnest in mid-February and I was soon waiting to hear to which of the ten Valiant squadrons I would be posted. Unique at that time amongst the three V-bombers, the Valiant operated in three additional distinctive roles. One squadron flew from Wyton, near Huntingdon, in the strategic photographic reconnaissance role, another at Finningley, near Doncaster, specialised in electronic warfare and countermeasures, while a further two squadrons, one at Marham, near Kings Lynn, and the other at Honington, near Bury St Edmunds, operated as tankers for air-to-air refuelling.

When the posting finally arrived, I was a little disappointed to find myself assigned to 90 Squadron at Honington flying tankers, rather than to one of the more 'sharp-end' squadrons. However, I soon came to appreciate the number of overseas detachments that this job entailed. I also enjoyed the demanding duties that I had as a co-pilot, responsible for the complete management of the complicated fuel system of a dozen separate tanks and, with their associated pumps, moving over 40 tons of fuel around the aircraft's fuselage and wing tanks while preparing to transfer more than half of it down our 90-foot refuelling hose to a receiver aircraft. Like the bomber crews of the Second World War, the V-Force had 'constituted' crews, meaning that we almost always flew with the same crew members. Our team of Flight Lieutenant Tony Langmead as captain, me as co-pilot, Flight Lieutenant Trevor Ward as navigator, Flying Officer Roger Willson as radar navigator and Master Signaller Geoff Baker as the air electronics operator, soon formed an effective and efficient crew as we roamed throughout the Middle East from our regular overseas operating bases in Cyprus, Malta and El Adem in Libya, and took in such further-flung locations as Karachi, Nairobi and the Maldives. We also participated in long-range exercises, one of which culminated in a Vulcan achieving the record time of seventeen hours and fifty minutes for a non-stop flight from the UK to Perth, Australia. (These long-range flights helped evolve the tactics and procedures that were used to such dramatic effect in Operation Black Buck in May 1982 when, during the Falklands War, a series of bombing raids by single Vulcans was carried out on Stanley Airport and against Argentine positions. This involved each of the Vulcans in non-stop flights of over 7,800 miles while being air-refuelled periodically by a fleet of Victor tankers.)

*   *   *

Approaching my second year at Honington, I got married. This was no whirlwind courtship – I had known Marian since I was aged about six. She was a native of Boston, where I too had lived from the age of three, and we had attended the same primary and junior schools. Later we shared many of the social activities of our early teenage years, engaging in several on-off relationships before my family's move to Bletchley. We stayed in contact and met up again soon after I joined the RAF, at which time Marian was studying at the Royal Academy of Music. My best man at the wedding was Flying Officer Des Sheen, my colleague from training days and now a co-pilot on Vulcans, while Flying Officer Peter Middlebrook, my collaborator in all things aeronautical from my schooldays and now a radar navigator on Vulcans, was a member of the Guard of Honour along with my fellow Valiant crew members.

Shortly after my return from honeymoon, I was selected to undergo an Intermediate Captain's Course back at Gaydon. This short course qualified me to fly the Valiant as First Pilot under supervision and, more importantly, fly from the captain's position in the left-hand seat. This experience also opened up the possibility of a captaincy on the Valiant for my next tour. However, it was towards the end of this course that an event occurred that eventually was to change the whole course of my flying career. On 6 August 1964, a Valiant returning to Gaydon suffered a failure of its wing flaps on one side, causing the bomber to commence an uncontrollable roll. Acting with commendable alacrity, the crew retracted the flaps and proceeded to complete the landing without them. While investigating the failure of the drive mechanism to the flaps, it was discovered that the aircraft had suffered a near-catastrophic failure of its main spar which, in turn, had allowed the wing to flex to such an abnormal degree that the flap drive mechanism on one of the wings had become disengaged. The main spar being the major structural component holding the wings and fuselage together, this aircraft had almost lost its wing. Immediately, all Valiants were grounded pending further investigation and I returned to my squadron to await developments.

*   *   *

Initial inspection of several aircraft, selected as representative of the range of ages of the airframes, seemed to support the logical suggestion that only the older aircraft were approaching this critical condition. As a result, a plan was drawn up to categorise all the Valiants into three groups – the first to be grounded permanently; the second available for operational use only, in other words, war; and the third group allowed to operate normally. All of our squadron aircraft fell into the last category. It should be clarified that the 'age' of the aircraft in this context refers to its fatigue life, simply the recorded wear and tear a particular aircraft has sustained. While there is often fairly close correlation between calendar age and fatigue life, much depends upon the role in which the aircraft has been operated.

*   *   *

The shooting down in May 1960 by a Russian missile of a very high-flying American Lockheed U-2 spy plane flown by Gary Powers had exposed the vulnerability of the V-Force to a new generation of advanced ground-to-air missiles, forcing a major revision of RAF bomber tactics. The Valiant, along with its V-Force stable-mates, was switched from a high-altitude bomber to a low-level role. This was a punishing environment for all aircraft and greatly increased the rate of wear and tear on them. The Valiants employed as tankers had not been exposed to this low-level environment and the assumption was that our aircraft should not, therefore, have been seriously affected. However, the critical failing in the Valiant was in the innovative new aluminium alloy used in its main structure. Unfortunately, this material was now discovered to suffer from a complex form of unstable crystalline corrosion. This led to unpredictable and premature fatigue failures that bore little correlation to the number of hours that the aircraft had flown. In effect, the aircraft were rotting away even while they stood.

We knew little of this development as we embarked on what was to be our final overseas flight, an operation to accompany Gloster Javelin fighters to Singapore, via Malta, Bahrain, Karachi and Gan in the Maldives. Over the preceding year, I had taken part in refuelling Victors and Vulcans for their lengthy detachments to the Far East as part of the general build-up of British forces there to help defend the newly-formed Malaysia against armed intervention by Indonesia, little realising what a profound effect this 'Confrontation' was about to have on my future. Coincidentally, we became involved in a bizarre incident at Karachi. Shortly after departing there in company with several Javelins, we suffered a fire in one of our four engines and turned back towards the international airport from where we had been operating. Transmitting a 'Mayday' distress call requesting an immediate landing, I was amazed to be told that permission to return was refused. I requested a suitable alternative nearby and was again refused. Faced with an aircraft carrying 40 tons of fuel and with an engine on fire, my captain, Tony Langmead, chose to ignore the refusal and we landed at the airport shortly afterwards, accompanied by much verbal haranguing on the radio.

It wasn't until some hours later that we discovered the cause for their extraordinary reaction to our emergency. Landing within minutes of our earlier departure had been President Sukarno of Indonesia, with whose country we were technically at war. This had presented the Pakistani government with a delicate diplomatic situation. This had been exacerbated when the President's aircraft was followed by a stream of large Russian Antonov AN-12 transport aircraft bearing Indonesian Air Force insignia, which landed shortly after us and parked nearby. The British Air Attaché was soon on the scene, expressing great interest in these aircraft with their Russian crews and, more specifically, in their cargoes, which were suspected of containing armaments for use against Malaysia. The damaged engine of our Valiant was eventually replaced by a team of engineers but not before the local water supply in the hotel had taken its toll on two of us, rendering us unfit to fly. A relief crew was sent out while we flew home as the sole passengers in an empty Britannia, which had been diverted to collect us.

Shortly after our return, the full extent of the Valiant's structural problems became apparent and, with no economically viable repair scheme identified, they were all scrapped. It was sad to see the sudden demise of these graceful aircraft, which had been the first of the V-bombers to enter service, the first to be involved in active service (Suez), and the only one to have dropped live nuclear bombs (during the British nuclear test programme).

My 'own' aircraft, XD813, for which I held the inventory and on whose side were stencilled the names of all our crew, enjoyed a brief burst of fame before its final end. The James Bond film, *Thunderball*, being produced at that time included an airborne sequence in which a Vulcan carrying a nuclear bomb is hijacked and ditched off a Caribbean island. The cockpit scenes were, in fact, of my Valiant, the nose section of which had been purchased by the film company. Now, whenever I watch that film, I have a nostalgic moment, recalling the numerous hours I had sat gazing at that very same instrument panel those many years before.

The Valiant's sudden demise proved something of a Godsend for the RAF department responsible for aircrew postings. They faced the dilemma of finding sufficient helicopter pilots to meet the increasing demands in Borneo as the confrontation with Indonesia moved towards greater intensity. A large proportion of former Valiant pilots suddenly found themselves facing a dramatic career change.

Despite my initial protest, I became a helicopter pilot.

CHAPTER THREE

HOVERING AROUND

Towards the end of April 1965 I reported to RAF Tern Hill in Shropshire to join No. 55 Basic Helicopter Course along with a dozen fellow students. The airfield and its surrounding area were familiar to me from my early days of flying training, but the flying itself was now so very different. So different, in fact, that in many respects it was like learning to fly all over again, with new handling skills to be mastered and different instinctive reactions developed. Long-forgotten frustrations emerged as the various hurdles were approached and overcome, particularly the all-important transitions – the changes to and from the hover from forward flight – and, of course, the hover itself. We watched in awe and envy as our instructors effortlessly and accurately demonstrated the required procedures, sometimes even controlling the hovering helicopter with the controls clamped between their knees so as to be able to use both hands to illustrate more graphically some particular aspect of the teaching. The helicopter used for the initial part of the course was the Bristol Sycamore, an elegant-looking, piston-engined design but one that displayed some idiosyncratic handling characteristics. With the application of tentatively applied power, the Sycamore would leap skywards in an excitingly unpredictable manner, at least in our inexperienced hands. The presence of other helicopters taking off and landing in close proximity on the dispersal merely added to the sense of drama and helped concentrate the mind wonderfully. A series of unfortunate take-off accidents signalled its end as a suitable basic training helicopter a short time afterwards.

I was airborne on my first solo flight just ten days after starting flying the Sycamore, experiencing sensations very similar to those on my very first fixed-wing solo. My instructor had taken me to the middle of the airfield for this occasion.

'When I get out, I want you to take off and hold it in a steady hover and then land again,' he said. 'If I give you a "thumbs up", take off again and fly one circuit back to this spot. If you see me near here, do not try to land by me. Just put it down and I will come to you. Do not chase me.'

I acknowledged and waited patiently while he secured all his loose harness straps and closed the cockpit door. Having completed my take-off checks, I carefully pulled up on the collective lever. The Sycamore obligingly lurched into the air and wobbled around uncertainly as I strove to keep it in one place about 10 feet above the grass. After a minute or so of this ungainly aerial ballet, I landed. Mildly surprised, but very relieved, I obtained the authoritative 'thumbs up' and repeated the procedure once more. A further signal from my instructor cleared me to proceed on a circuit of the airfield. As on my first solo in a fixed-wing aircraft five years earlier almost to the day, the first part of the circuit passed in a blur of activity but soon I was on the descent towards the airfield with the most difficult part of the circuit ahead of me – bringing the helicopter back to the hover. I could see the distant figure of my instructor still near to the centre of the airfield and, remembering his injunction not to try to land too close to him, I selected a spot about 20 yards further away. I almost got the Sycamore to a hover but, while struggling to adjust my height, the Sycamore started creeping forward. I arrested the forward movement, only for the height to change. The game was on. Hover ... creep forward ... hover ... creep forward. I suddenly realised I had used up a large part of the airfield in this repetitive futile exercise and, with the boundary fence and trees now getting uncomfortably close, I decided on drastic action. Raising the nose abruptly at the same time as lowering the lever, the aircraft came to an abrupt stop. Before it could start moving again, I stuck it on the ground in one undignified movement. The episode had been akin to being astride a fractious head-strong horse that had only stopped when arriving at the end of its field.

I sat in the cockpit, fuming at my poor performance and waiting for my instructor to catch up with me. I had a long wait. Eventually my instructor, panting and red-faced with exertion after his long walk, climbed back into the cockpit.

'What the hell was that all about?' he demanded. 'I only wanted a normal approach from you, not a bloody charge across the airfield and a quick-stop!' The latter referred to an advanced manoeuvre where a helicopter is brought to a very quick hover from high-speed forward flight, a skill that had not yet appeared on our syllabus. Thankfully, subsequent flights proved much better and I was gradually able to exploit the helicopter's unique ability to land without requiring a whole airfield for the purpose. Slowly, my random gyrations and lurches in the hover gave way to a more steady and stable state as I learnt to coax and cajole the responsive Sycamore with gentle, smooth control movements to do my bidding. As my handling skills developed, I started to enjoy this previously alien form of flight into which I had been pitched with neither choice nor notice.

The course progressed through all aspects of helicopter operations, including landings and take-offs in confined areas. These areas took the form of small cleared areas in nearby woods and looked at first sight to be impossibly small. With growing confidence, however, we course students soon found it possible not only to get into these tight spaces but even to manoeuvre carefully around inside them, always aware of the position of the vulnerable tail rotor in relation to the many obstructions.

Later we moved on to fly the Westland Whirlwind Mark 10, a much more powerful, jet-powered helicopter. On this aircraft we repeated all the lessons learnt on the Sycamore, honing our skills in hovering, coping with limited power and heavy loads and squeezing into ever tighter clearings in the surrounding woodlands. The course also undertook a detachment to RAF Valley, on Anglesey, for a basic search and rescue familiarisation course. Because of its unique abilities and versatility, the helicopter could be called upon at any time to assist in an emergency situation and it was therefore essential that safe standard procedures should be learnt to avoid the many dangers waiting to trap the inexperienced and unwary. Not only did we learn to hover accurately over land and water while performing practice rescues on each other as 'survivors', but the course also included search patterns, rescues from cliffs around the Anglesey coastline, as well as from stationary and moving ships. Another important part of the course was familiarisation with flying and operating in mountainous terrain; the nearby mountains of Snowdonia provided a challenging and scenic classroom for this purpose. I thoroughly enjoyed this part of the course and decided that search and rescue was what I wanted to do.

Returning to Tern Hill, flight on instruments and at night completed our course, and again I found myself anxiously awaiting news of my next posting. Unlike my earlier V-Force posting, this next one could be to any one of a large number of home or overseas locations including search and rescue or support helicopter roles in the UK, Cyprus, Hong Kong, Belize in Central America and Borneo. The latter two postings were in support of the Army who were protecting these two countries, both newly independent from British colonial rule, from armed opposition by neighbouring countries intent on territorial claims. In Belize, the former British Honduras, Guatamala was claiming sovereignty, while in Borneo, it was opposition by Indonesia who objected to the formation of the independent state of Malaysia. Both campaigns were characterised by being undeclared wars and almost totally lacking any public awareness. Of the two, Borneo was the larger campaign and required a regular supply of new helicopter pilots to meet the Army's demands for mobility and supply in largely inhospitable territory. We students also knew very little of the background to the Borneo campaign – the so-called Confrontation (or *Konfrontasi*, as the Indonesians referred to it). A few of our instructors had recently returned from a tour in Borneo and were more than happy to air their war stories in the Officers' Mess bar. There was a vicarious thrill and fascination attached to the thought of active service and also to visiting an area of the world synonymous with the ultimate in remoteness and inaccessibility. The term 'Wild Man of Borneo' had been a familiar one since schooldays and had even featured in Richmal Crompton's 'Just William' humorous short stories. Despite the allure of this mysterious region, I applied for a search and rescue posting and got – Borneo!

Initially, I and several others of my course were posted to 225 Squadron, a Whirlwind unit based at Kuching in Borneo and operating in support of the Army. This was to be a one-year unaccompanied tour and I duly made arrangements for the anticipated lengthy absence from my newly-married wife. We were both philosophical about this turn of events. Teaching employment and accommodation were arranged for her, as was a car for her daily transport. It came as a major shock, therefore, when the posting was changed barely two weeks before my departure to a full, two-and-a-half year tour based in Singapore. Most of my colleagues were delighted, as this meant that they could now be accompanied by their wives. An added bonus for them was that this posting would also attract one of the highest rates of Local Overseas Allowance, an adjustment to pay to compensate for the relatively higher cost of living in various overseas locations. Similarly, my single friends were overjoyed at the prospect of experiencing the magic of Singapore.

I was devastated. Being still under the critical age of twenty-five, I was single in the eyes of the RAF and now faced the prospect of two-and-a-half years on my own in the Far East. There was no provision for accommodation for my wife, nor was there a free place on a trooping flight to get her out there with all the other wives. The two weeks to embarkation passed very quickly, with little being resolved and only the promise that I would do everything I could to get Marian out with me as soon as possible. A miserable October morning witnessed a tearful farewell at the West London Air Terminal, not knowing when we would see each other again. I then joined the large group of excited, chattering families boarding coaches to take us to Heathrow for the long trooping flight to Singapore in a Britannia of British Eagle Airways. Only one other couple on my course was in a similar situation. Flying Officer Mike Ramshaw had married his childhood sweetheart, Rita, during the course and had already departed on an earlier flight to Singapore. This misfortune was to be the basis of a long and lasting friendship and many shared experiences.

CHAPTER FOUR

INTRODUCTION TO THE FAR EAST

I and my colleagues arrived in Singapore in the early hours of the morning, tired and aching after a series of long stages on the trooping flight. As I walked down the aircraft steps of the Britannia at Paya Lebar, the international airport for the island, I was conscious of being enveloped in the hot, humid tropical air, just like walking into a sauna fully clothed. The flight was met by two members of my new unit, 110 Squadron, who escorted us back to its base at RAF Seletar on the north coast of Singapore. Despite the time, it soon became obvious that this was a region that never slept. In every village or *kampong* on the road from the airport to Seletar I saw shops still open and food stalls still plying their trade by the roadside. My sense of smell was assailed by a whole new range of aromas, from the heavy fragrance of the exotic vegetation, the smell of wood smoke, to the less alluring pervasive odour of bad drains. Arriving at Seletar, we were directed to our new accommodation, little more than a hut containing a bare room shared with another five officers and located about 50 yards from the main building of the Officers' Mess. Some of the beds already contained sleeping occupants, anonymous in the dim lighting and cocooned in their mosquito nets. At one point, as three of us groped our way around seeking vacant beds, one of the room's occupants stirred in his sleep, muttering something incomprehensible. From his swarthy appearance and what we took to be a foreign tongue, we were momentarily disconcerted, thinking that we must have strayed by mistake into one of the huts for native workers.

After a late start the following morning, I presented myself at the Squadron Headquarters out on the airfield. To the amusement of my new colleagues I was wearing the standard khaki drill shirt and shorts, monstrosities of a style that had been purchased at great expense from the military tailors during my embarkation leave. These dark, thick, unyielding garments, seemingly unchanged in pattern since the Second World War, contrasted most unfavourably with locally produced uniforms employing much lighter modern materials. I was whisked off down to the local village of Jalan Kayu, a bustling ribbon development along the long straight road leading up to Seletar's entrance gates. There, a local Indian tailor measured me up, promising to

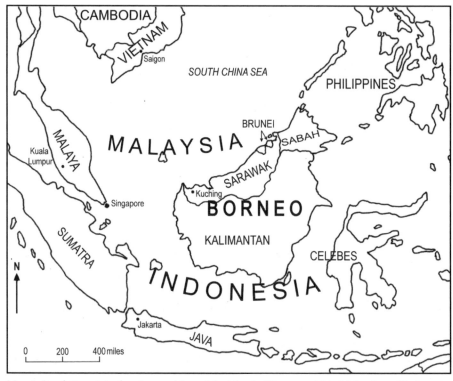

Map 1. South East Asia showing position of the island of Borneo within Malaysia and Indonesia.

have four sets of new uniforms ready for me by the following day. Less satisfactory were the flying suits. The RAF had run out of lightweight tropical flying suits and had let a contract with another of the local tailors in the village. Where they had copied the pattern from was anyone's guess, but they were far too tight, low in the crutch, and fitted with flimsy, fine-toothed zips that jammed and broke regularly. Our aim was to get our hands on the pale-green Australian suits that were far more practical. I eventually obtained just one of these coveted suits, which I washed out every night for the rest of my tour.

The squadron crewroom provided a welcome respite from the constant heat and high humidity. Apart from inside some of the major city stores and restaurants, this was the only air conditioned building I encountered throughout my whole tour in the Far East. It was as if we were trying to prove the point that the British military could cope with any conditions, scorning any idea of comfort as being soft and unmanly and a hindrance to acclimatisation. After the formalities of arriving on my new squadron, the paperwork, the interview with my new Squadron Commander, the allocation of a locker and pigeon-hole, I settled into a routine of regular training flights under the expert eye of the squadron's Qualified Helicopter Instructor, Flight Sergeant 'Chas' Spinks. Although the aircraft flown was the Whirlwind, already familiar to me from my helicopter training, the environment in which I was now operating was markedly different from that in the UK. The high temperatures and humidity adversely affected the Whirlwind's performance, leaving it struggling for power when operating at its maximum weight, while the tiny clearings in the woodlands of Shropshire had suddenly become tiny clearings in the huge Malayan jungle trees, which reached daunting heights of 200 to 300 feet. Intensive training was also undertaken with the Army, for whom we supplied the helicopter training for their newly arrived troops. This was carried out at the British Jungle Warfare School, set in the Malayan jungle at Ulu Tiram, some 15 miles north of the Straits of Malacca between Singapore and the Malayan mainland. This training involved familiarising the troops in rapid helicopter emplaning and de-planing in hostile territory, as well as abseiling and roping drills to enable them to be deployed from a high hover in locations where it was impossible for our helicopters to land.

During this period of preparation for my first detachment to Borneo I, along with other recent arrivals, attempted to get to grips with the local political situation – in other words, why were we there? At no time, either before leaving the UK or since arrival in Singapore, had we received any form of briefing or indoctrination on the situation, a fact that might help to explain the widely different attitudes to the 'war' held by those based solely in Singapore and by those of us who were actively involved in Borneo, an aspect I shall return to later. Prior to our arrival in Singapore, we had only the 'war stories' of our helicopter instructors at Tern Hill to give us an inkling of what was happening in Borneo. These, however, largely dwelt on individual actions or skirmishes and did little to enlighten us on the wider aspects of the campaign.

*   *   *

Before continuing with my narrative, it is therefore worth undertaking a brief examination of the background to this particular conflict and offer an explanation of why, despite the huge amount of personnel and materiel expended over a four-year period, this particular campaign has retained its status as one of Britain's 'forgotten wars', one which, nevertheless, was to claim 114 British and Commonwealth lives, and nearly 600 of the opposing Indonesian forces. It is also worth mentioning that much of the detail remained unknown to us at the time despite our intimate involvement in some aspects of the conflict. Like previous generations of servicemen, we concentrated on our small part in the war, leaving the 'big picture' to those in whom responsibility for the campaign as a whole was vested. Indeed, it was to be another thirty years before some aspects of the operations in which our helicopters had been involved were released from the Government's secret archives and provided another piece of the jigsaw of the whole picture.

The main reason for our ignorance of the situation here was because there was, and continued to be, a dearth of information on the subject in the UK press, which was then pre-occupied with the fierce British fighting around Aden and the Radfan in Southern Arabia, and the continuing and headline-grabbing escalation of the American struggle in Vietnam. The only times I recall this forgotten war capturing the news headlines was when the British Embassy in the Indonesian capital, Jakarta, was burnt to the ground in September 1963 by 'rioters', and again in 1966 when the announcement was made of the award of the Victoria Cross to a Gurkha soldier, Lance Corporal Rambahadur Limbu, for his heroism during a battle in Borneo the previous year.

While there were several incursions by Indonesia into Malaya and Singapore, much of the action of this campaign centred on the island of Borneo. At some 290,000 square miles (750,000 square kilometres), Borneo is the third largest island in the world, of which three-quarters is Indonesian. The remaining northern part, broadly comparable in size with the combined areas of England and Scotland, comprises the independent sovereign territory and British protectorate of Brunei, and the former British colonies of Sarawak and Sabah, the latter two sharing a border with Indonesian Borneo of almost 1,000 miles in length. The cause for the undeclared war was rooted in the opposition of Indonesia's President Sukarno to the proposed formation of the independent Federation of Malaysia. This would unite these three northern states into a single political union with Singapore and Malaya, thus thwarting his own ambitions for a regional federation of Malaya, the Philippines and a united Indonesia, to be known as Maphilindo.

An armed insurrection occurred in Brunei in late 1962, led by a local anti-colonialist Communist liberation party that played on local fears of being dominated by Malaya, favouring instead links with Indonesia with whom there were perceived closer cultural ties. This was encouraged and covertly supported by Indonesia. Following rapid intervention by British forces, aided by local tribesmen from surrounding Sarawak, the rebellion was quickly quashed. When the Federation of Malaysia eventually came into being in September 1963, albeit without Brunei, Sukarno then embarked on a course of open hostility, threatening to 'crush Malaysia'. The British Embassy in Jakarta was burnt down a couple of days after the Federation was formed.

The first action took place at Tebedu, close to the border with Indonesia and some 35 miles south of Kuching, where a police station was attacked and captured. More attacks followed, taking the form of raids across the border from Indonesia and targeting isolated villages and dwellings. In support of the new Malaysian Government, the British response was to deploy forces at strategic points throughout North Borneo from where they would attempt to patrol the 1,000-mile frontier and prevent incursions. In the almost total absence of roads, except close to the coast, river systems, aircraft and helicopters were the only means of communication. In the early phases of the campaign, the emphasis was one of restraint, with the enemy only being engaged after having ventured into Malaysian territory and 'hot pursuit' of them across the border was strictly forbidden. The SAS were mainly confined to vital intelligence gathering and reconnaissance in Indonesian territory. Frequently having to watch their quarry escape to safety across the border led to intense frustration on the part of the Army, and only later were these restrictions partially lifted to allow special forces and selected British and Commonwealth patrols to engage in cross-border operations within strictly prescribed limits. This initiative was authorised only at the highest level, code-named Operation Claret, and kept a close secret until the release of archived documents thirty years later. Neither I nor, to the best of my knowledge, any of my fellow pilots and crewmen had ever heard of Claret operations until those documents became available, despite the fact that many of us had participated in them.

This low-key approach was in marked contrast to the American overt and overwhelming use of fire-power, and the exceptionally large troop movements evident in the Vietnam War being fought barely 700 miles north-west of us. Another difference, and a key element in our eventual success, was the care taken with the hearts-and-minds campaign that had proved so telling in fostering trust between the local population and our armed forces during the earlier jungle campaign of the post-war Malayan Emergency. Our helicopters played a vital role in this hearts-and-minds initiative by enabling rapid access to medical help for the locals.

*   *   *

Meanwhile, having completed my intensive theatre training, I was now keen to start flying in Borneo. However, there was something of a hiatus in my progress, which delayed my deployment. HM The Queen had recently approved the award of a Standard to 110 Squadron. This took the form of a large ceremonial silk flag, or 'colours', on which were embroidered the squadron's crest and its battle honours. The squadron was due to receive its Standard the following month, and I was selected to be the Uncasing Officer at the formal parade at which the honour would be presented by the Commander-in-Chief Far East Command, Air Marshal (later Marshal of the Royal Air Force) Sir John Grandy. This duty entailed me parading with the furled Standard concealed inside its case and then, assisted by another officer, slowly withdrawing the case to reveal the Standard to the squadron. The Standard was then taken by Sir John and presented to the Squadron Standard Bearer to be paraded before the assembled ranks of squadron personnel. The award of this honour was an important milestone in the squadron's history and the events celebrating it went on for several days.

One of the squadron's past associations was with Hyderabad, one of India's semi-independent 'princely states', the squadron's formal title being 110 (Hyderabad) Squadron, with its unit badge sporting a 'tiger rampant'. The Nizam of Hyderabad at that time sent a congratulatory message and a generous donation towards a party. Several of our guests of honour were veterans of the Second World War, during which the squadron's Blenheim bombers had had the distinction of leading the first bombing raid of that conflict on 4 September 1939 against warships in the German port of Wilhelmshaven.

*   *   *

During my prolonged stay in Singapore, I made strenuous efforts to find ways of getting my wife out to me. I eventually settled on an assisted passage on a routine RAF transport flight from RAF Lyneham to RAF Changi, Singapore's main RAF transport station. For this privilege I had to pay the equivalent of a month-and-a-half's salary. Even then, no date could be guaranteed. I also had to apply to my Station Commander for permission to bring her out. In his temporary absence, his deputy reluctantly agreed.

At Seletar we shared our Whirlwind helicopters and squadron accommodation with our sister unit, 103 Squadron, and most of my fellow helicopter course members had been posted to one or other of these two squadrons on graduation. No. 103 Squadron also shared several of the Borneo detachments with my squadron. Shortly before my first detachment to Borneo the reality of the hazards soon to be faced was abruptly brought home to me. Both squadrons were shocked to hear that one of the 103 Squadron pilots, Flight Lieutenant Bert Fraser, had been shot down and killed just south of Kuching. His loss was particularly felt by the recent arrivals as Bert had been a member of our course all the way through helicopter training. He was shot down on his first detachment when he inadvertently flew across the border into Indonesia. There was much conjecture at the time as to why he had made this error, one theory being that his wrist-watch had stopped and he had simply mis-timed his run from his departure point and had over-flown his destination at Stass. All of the Whirlwinds' aircraft clocks had been removed from their instrument panels as being 'valuable and attractive items' and therefore at risk of being stolen from the unsecured cockpits. Consequently, we had no back-up for this essential navigational tool. Despite the shooting down occurring only a few hundred yards across the border, no rescue attempt was attempted. The area was known to be thick with Indonesian forces equipped with artillery and mortars, and a call was made for ground-attack support from the

Hunter fighter detachment at Kuching so that a ground or helicopter rescue could be mounted. Meanwhile, Whirlwind helicopters from both squadrons patrolled up and down the border listening for possible transmissions from Bert's emergency locator beacon in order to gain an accurate location for the crash site to assist any rescue attempt. There were no transmissions either from Bert or from his Army passenger. Equally disconcerting, however, was that no air cover was forthcoming. It had been decided at the highest levels that any overt action of that nature could have been construed as provocative and was therefore forbidden.

Against a backdrop of celebration for the presentation of our squadron Standard and sadness for our lost friend and colleague, I made final preparations for my first detachment to Borneo.

CHAPTER FIVE

FIRST ACQUAINTANCE
WITH BORNEO

Collected from the Officers' Mess at the crack of dawn with the other squadron pilots due their turn on detachment in Borneo, I was taken to RAF Changi, the RAF's main transport base located at the north-eastern edge of the island. There we boarded an Armstrong Whitworth Argosy, a twin-boomed transport aircraft nicknamed the 'Whistling Tit' in reference to its smooth round nose tipped with a nipple-shaped radar aerial, and the loud whistle emitted by its four Rolls-Royce Dart turbo-prop engines. I rapidly grew to dislike this aircraft when used in the combined passenger and freight role. There were no seats as such in its large hold. Instead there were two continuous fabric 'benches', each running the whole length of the fuselage sides, and on which the unfortunate passengers sat side-by-side in rows facing inwards. The support for these sagging seats was a metal bar located just under one's thigh and which contrived to ensure dead legs after a couple of hours of flight. Frequently freight would be piled from floor to roof along the whole of the central cargo area, and so close that it pressed against the passengers' knees. For some inexplicable reason, we RAF passengers were required to travel in our khaki bush jackets and long trousers, unlike the Army, who wore their jungle-green combat clothing. Anyone wishing to use the lavatory on the aircraft was obliged to walk on top of the knees of all the passengers between him and his destination. After several pairs of Army boots had left their mark on your previously immaculate khaki dress uniform, the effect was less than smart. Ration boxes for in-flight meals had to be passed from hand to hand down the whole length of the aircraft and rubbish collected by the same route, often with dripping empty fruit-juice containers adding to the stains on our uniforms.

Arriving at Kuching, the capital of Sarawak, those of us destined for onward travel were taken to the Malaysian Airways facility on the civilian part of the airfield where we boarded an ancient, twin-engined Douglas DC-3, known in the RAF as the Dakota. Despite the age of the aircraft, this flight was a very pleasant change after the discomfort of the cramped Argosy. Petite air hostesses served exquisite chicken sandwiches, along with tea and coffee, as we

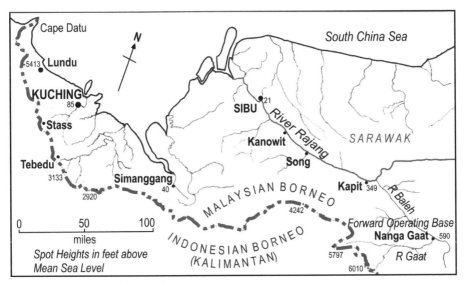

Map 2. Western Sarawak, North Borneo.

rumbled and bounced our way towards our destination just an hour's flying time away at Sibu.

At Sibu airport I was conducted to a small bungalow near the main street. This was the accommodation for the RAF officers who were attached to the staff of the Forward Air Transport Operations Centre, invariably abbreviated to FATOC. All requirements for air support, from troop movements by helicopter to the air-dropping of supplies to forward bases, were fed through FATOC, where priorities were established and the tasks allocated to the appropriate flying units. Apart from the infrequent occasions when we stayed with them in Sibu, usually because of a delayed flight returning to Singapore, they were unseen figures but ones who had direct control of all our day-to-day flying operations. For us, the FATOC bungalow was normally just a place to change from our khaki bush jackets into jungle green flying suits before taking over from the pilot who was being replaced. On the squadron we were paired up with an opposite number with whom we alternated detachments. My opposite number was Flying Officer Dave Collinson, another new arrival on 110 Squadron but an experienced Borneo pilot who, while on another Whirlwind squadron in Borneo, had recently been awarded the Distinguished Flying Cross for some daring and skilful flying while rescuing two members of an SAS patrol. We met once a month only for the time it took to complete the handover ritual before he boarded the DC-3 to start his journey back to Singapore. This handover included receiving our shared personal weapon, a Stirling sub-machine-gun with ammunition, and taking charge of the Whirlwind Dave had just flown in from Nanga Gaat, the forward operating base situated a further 115 miles away in the very heart of the jungle. As this was my first detachment, Dave had been accompanied by another pilot, Pilot Officer George Kelson, whose job it would be to show me, once only, the way to Nanga Gaat.

I had my first uninterrupted airborne view of Borneo as we clattered our way down the mighty River Rajang, at 350 miles in length the longest river in Malaysia. We soon left behind the modern buildings, skimming above the maze of *bashas*, the ubiquitous native huts built on stilts and clad with woven palm leaves, and on along the river margins and the swampy surrounding areas. As we progressed further along the wide muddy-brown river, the populated areas rapidly thinned out, leaving only the occasional riverside longhouse (the natives' communal dwellings) to punctuate our journey. My eyes were everywhere as I tried to take in as much as possible of what was an amazing new experience – the primitive canoes jostling with riverboats, the cheerful friendly waves of the natives as they fished or washed in the river's murky waters, the unexpected and incongruous sight of a colonial-style red-roofed, white-painted clapperboard schoolhouse or church suddenly appearing around a bend in the river as we passed small towns. Cloaking all this was the dank earthy smell of the river and the characteristic cloying sweet smell of decaying vegetation. Compared with what was to come, the navigation from Sibu to Nanga Gaat was simple – follow the River Rajang for 85 miles to the junction with one of its tributaries, the River Baleh, then follow this tributary upstream for a further 30 miles to another junction with the River Gaat. Here, on a small area of cleared jungle at the confluence of these two rivers was Nanga Gaat, my home for the next month and on many subsequent occasions.

*   *   *

Nanga Gaat was the most remote forward operating base in the whole of Borneo, and one we shared with an infantry company of whichever Army battalion was currently in residence. At this time, it was a company of the 1st Battalion, the King's Own Scottish Borderers occupying a defensive position on the upper slopes from where they commanded a view along all three branches of the river junction. Our helicopter detachment comprised four Whirlwinds, four pilots, four crewmen and a complement of ground-crew occupying the lower slopes of the river's banks. My first impression as the camp came into view was of a bustling small shanty village with several *bashas* scattered randomly about. Alongside these were our helicopter landing pads, terraced up the river bank and dug into the slope to provide a level surface. Prominent, and apart from the *bashas*, stood a substantial and smart wooden bungalow, which I initially took to be our accommodation. However, I was quickly disabused of this by George, who told me it belonged to Lam Ting, son-in-law to the Paramount Chief of the Ibans, the splendidly named Temenggong Jugah anak Barieng.

As soon as George had slipped the Whirlwind into the tight slot between fuel barrels on the landing pad with its nose nestling into the slope of the bank, the ground-crew busied themselves off-loading the freight and refuelling the helicopter. These ground-crew were separate from those we had on the squadron in Singapore and were posted to Borneo for a full unaccompanied tour of thirteen months. In the months that followed, I came to realise what a dedicated and well-motivated bunch of airmen they were. Nothing was too much trouble for them where maintenance of our helicopters was concerned, often working through the night by the light of hand-held torches to ensure that all four would be serviceable for the next day's tasking.

Once in the communal officers' *basha*, I was shown to my bed, one of five ranged along the woven palm leaf walls of the small room and so recently occupied by the pilot I was replacing, before setting about preparing a map for the next day's sortie on which I was to accompany George. I borrowed his map and started transcribing details of all the current helicopter landing sites onto my map. I was amused, but also somewhat disconcerted, to note the over-stamped warnings 'DETAIL UNRELIABLE', 'PLANIMETRIC DETAIL UNRELIABLE', 'POSITION APPROXIMATE'. What detail? There was precious little detail on the map, planimetric or whatever, to be unreliable. The section of maps of a scale of 1:250,000 covering most of our area of operations was largely blank, over-printed with a reference grid but, apart from the few well-defined major rivers, containing little more than tentative faint blue dotted lines where it was thought a river might be. Even the border was marked with an uncertain dotted line. Some indications of spot heights and contours were shown on the Indonesian side of the border. Apparently the Dutch had been far more assiduous in surveying their former colonial territory than we British had on our side.

At first sight, the prospect of ranging far and wide on operational missions with absolutely no navigation aids other than an almost blank sheet of paper and a wristwatch seemed somewhat daunting. George's map showed a series of lines to what seemed like focal points from which other lines radiated out to various locations along the border. The RAF helicopter pilots had adopted and expanded a system used by the Royal Navy when operating their Wessex helicopters from Nanga Gaat prior to our takeover from them. Over the course of the previous three years of confrontation, the Army had constructed numerous helicopter landing sites along the 1,000-mile length of the border with the Indonesian part of Borneo, to support and re-supply their patrols. Rather than flying in a direct line from the troop pick-up point at an Army location, the border landing sites had been grouped into regions, each with its own 'hub' or checkpoint. The helicopter would be flown direct from the Army base to the nearest appropriate hub, before taking up a final track towards the specific destination landing site. Each of these main hubs was identified by a name, and here the Navy had paid a touching tribute to their wives and girlfriends by naming several of these after them – Jackie, Sheila, Diana and so on.

The purpose in sticking as much as possible to 'standard' routes was two-fold – reporting by radio as each of these points was passed considerably increased the chances of being found by our colleagues if we ever had the misfortune to suffer a forced landing in the jungle and, secondly, these routes became increasingly familiar to the pilots using them. In many cases, probably only the final leg to a new helicopter landing site would be flown over unfamiliar terrain and, if the site could not be found, further attempts could be made after returning to one of these familiar hubs or checkpoints. I duly drew in all the routes shown on George's map, each marked with a compass heading and time, and annotated all the checkpoints, noting as I did so that most were on blank parts of the map. At the end of my efforts I was rewarded with a pristine map, about six feet long by a couple of feet wide, which I arranged concertina-like to allow access to any part of our area with a minimum of re-arrangement. With my map complete, I turned my attention to my large Bergen back-pack, checking its contents and taking advice from my fellow pilots on what was considered vital to carry with me on every flight. These Bergens contained our jungle survival kit, spare magazines of 9 mm ammunition for our Stirling sub-machine-guns and sufficient rations to last for several days. Although we were frequently fed by the Army as we passed through their company positions, we had to be capable of total independence should we find ourselves stranded with them at some forward location.

That evening, I eagerly waited to hear what our tasking would be for the following day. Our detached FATOC officer, Flight Lieutenant Bob Wood, received the tasking signals from Sibu and passed them to our detachment commander, Flight Lieutenant Tony Edwards, for allocation to one of his crews of pilot and crewman.

'I'll be taking you on a troop-lift out of Long Jawi to Blue 5246 on the border,' announced George, perusing my map. 'We'll lift off as soon as the early morning mist has lifted, then fly to Long Jawi, Blue 51. This reporting point "Felicity" is a distinctive gap in the Hose Mountains and is the highest point on that leg, then we drop down to Long Jawi by the river.' His finger then traced the route from Long Jawi southwards to the border, identifying the landing site at a height of about 3,000 feet. I pointed to the hub closest to Blue 5246 to which we would fly first before turning slightly left to put the landing site on our nose.

'What's this place?' I asked.

'Oh, that's just a dead tree,' replied George in his lazy Canadian drawl.

'A dead what?' I exclaimed incredulously, 'We'll be flying mile after mile over jungle and I'll be looking for a dead tree?'

'You'll see,' was his enigmatic reply.

*   *   *

Next to our *basha* was a long, timber-clad building that housed the cook-house and the various messes. The kitchen was presided over by our cook, Ah Ling, a tall, thin, emaciated-looking Chinaman, who appeared to speak neither English nor the local Iban dialect, and was reportedly given to occasional episodes of running amok with a meat cleaver, especially when one of our pet monkeys strayed into his kitchen to steal food. Our evening meal, as on so many occasions in the future, comprised tough pork followed by tinned peaches. Back in our *basha*, I wrote a letter to Marian, telling her of all my new experiences to date. Some of the other pilots were also writing to their wives back in Singapore. There were no other means of communicating with home, except in the direst of emergencies when the Army signals network would be used. Pilots and crewmen returning to Singapore would be entrusted with these precious missives to deliver or post in Singapore, and crews arriving from Singapore were met with eager anticipation of letters from home.

On completion of these duties I was taken to our local pub. This was another *basha*, complete with bar and with a sign outside declaring it to be *The Anchor Inn* – there were no prizes for guessing which service had instigated that facility. Here, ground-crew and air-crew mixed freely, frequently joined by officers and Senior Non-Commissioned Officers from our Army neighbours. This proved an excellent venue for building up and maintaining the strong rapport and trust that developed between us. Operational successes were celebrated appropriately, while the inevitable mistakes and misunderstandings were debriefed in a constructive and friendly atmosphere. The usual inter-service rivalries also found a healthy outlet here with various competitive activities, usually involving the consumption of alcohol. A strict dress code was enforced – only a long-sleeved shirt, a native sarong, flip-flops, and a wristwatch were permitted. Any additional clothing that came to light would cost the offender drinks all round.

Returning to our *basha* for the night, we reviewed the next morning's flying programme, then listened to the BBC's World Service on Bob's radio. We had the luxury of electricity throughout the camp during the day and evening, provided by a powerful, but noisy, generator. At 22.00 hours precisely, the lights flashed a couple of times in warning and then went off for the night, the generator suddenly conspicuous by the absence of its steady roar, as the night noises of the jungle re-asserted themselves.

I dozed fitfully that night, bathed in sweat in the oppressive humid air, scarcely different from daytime but now made even more claustrophobic by the necessary mosquito netting festooning each of our beds. Along with the smells of the jungle there was a pervasive sour, vinegary smell of a mattress and pillow that had absorbed too much sweat for far too long. There was no air-conditioning, no fan, nor could any breeze be called upon to ventilate the *basha*. I listened to the unfamiliar noises of the jungle but became far more aware of my immediate neighbours' grunts and snores. Things fell out of the woven palm leaves that clad the building, mosquitoes whined their busy way, seeking to find a chink in the netting, unknown creatures roamed freely in the undergrowth some 4 feet beneath the split bamboo flooring, snapping twigs, snuffling and grunting as they rooted around. Closer to my ear, some wood-boring insect was busy on its night-time mission. In the morning, I was surprised to find a neat round hole nearly half an inch across drilled deep into one of the *basha*'s supporting uprights and accompanied by an impressive pile of fresh wood dust on the floor immediately below the hole, mute testimony to the insect's nocturnal industry. With holes being drilled that fast, I had concerns for the integrity of the structure of our *basha*, particularly when many similar examples were pointed out to me. However, nothing fell down and any seriously affected timber was quickly replaced by the local Iban workforce who had originally constructed the building.

Being close to the Equator, the region's dawns and dusks were very short-lived and occurred with little variation throughout the year. I had been surprised the previous evening when, shortly after 6.00 pm, night had fallen within the space of just a few brief minutes. I was similarly aware of the short twilight period of dawn at about 6.00 am. In keeping with military tradition, the Army 'stood-to' at dawn and dusk, on full alert and manning all the defensive positions around our jungle perimeter. They recognised from long experience that these periods were the most favourable and likely for any surprise attack by the enemy. We 'stood-to' as well – as far as the Army were concerned, when on the ground we RAF chaps were simply soldiers, capable and responsible for defending ourselves and adding to their fire-power if required.

*   *   *

Despite some tiredness from my disturbed night's sleep, I looked forward to an exciting new day, finally getting to grips with a job for which I had spent the past eight months preparing.

CHAPTER SIX

MY FIRST BORNEO 'OP'

The following morning, we watched as the mist rose slowly out of the trees to form low cloud. Soon after, the cloud burnt off and it was time for us to go.

With me flying the helicopter, my guide and mentor for the day, George Kelson, sitting alongside me in the left-hand seat, and our crewman, Sergeant Brian Leighton in the cabin, I lifted off from the helicopter landing pad at Nanga Gaat. Turning eastward along the river and climbing in anticipation of the high ground ahead, I set course under George's directions for our initial destination, Long Jawi. This first flight to position the helicopter at Long Jawi to start the day's troop lift was a routine affair to my two fellow crew members but, for me, little in the previous day's flight from Sibu to Nanga Gaat had prepared me for the view that now greeted me – a vast, unrelieved wilderness of uniform green tree canopies. My first thought was, how on earth do you navigate over such terrain? Once away from the river, there appeared to be no features on which to base any assessment of position or progress. Voicing my concern to George, he assured me that by maintaining accurate headings and speeds we would eventually arrive at our correct destination.

The flight to Long Jawi took just over forty minutes and, as we approached the half-way point, the rocky outcrop of the 6,800-foot high Hose Mountains came into view, crossing our track ahead.

'Aim for the gap,' instructed George, 'then you can report at "Felicity" on the radio.' The radios we used for long distance communications were known technically as High Frequency Single Side-Band, or more commonly as HF SSB. These worked by bouncing the signal off the ionosphere and, with sufficient power, could theoretically bounce the signal right around the world. Unfortunately, this temperamental piece of equipment was almost useless for contacting our base when even a relatively short distance away. On a good day we could talk to Kuching and Sibu in Borneo, and to Singapore almost 700 miles distant, and sometimes we could listen in to the Americans having a hard time in Vietnam, but the chances of talking to anywhere or anyone nearby who could be of immediate assistance to us were fairly remote.

Passing 'Felicity' at over 3,000 feet, we started the long descent towards Long Jawi, once again over the expanse of green 'cabbage-tops', which the jungle resembled, featureless apart from the ridges and valleys stretching as

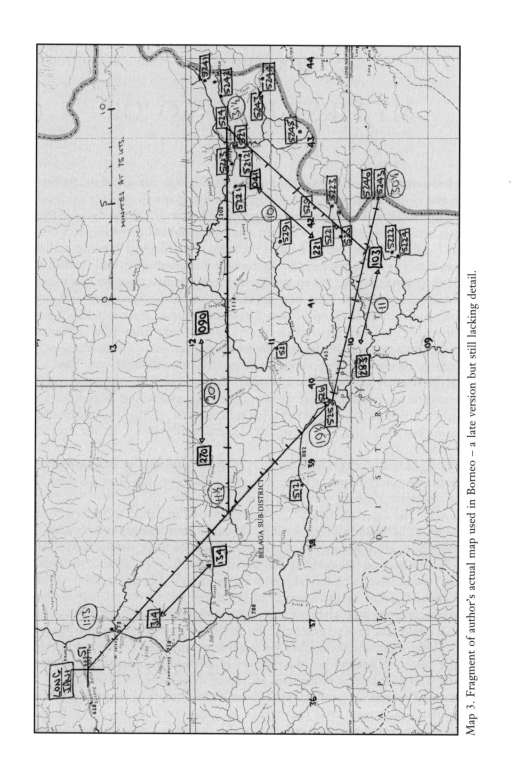

Map 3. Fragment of author's actual map used in Borneo – a late version but still lacking detail.

far as the eye could see. Picking up the river that ran by Long Jawi, I soon located the village with its large longhouse.

As we approached the village, George instructed me to land on one of the three prepared helicopter pads, where our passengers and freight awaited us. We were planned to carry out two lifts to the border and back, and George and I calculated what payload we could take on each one. On landing, Brian had immediately jumped out with a set of bathroom scales to start weighing the equipment and rations to be moved, and even weighing the individual soldiers themselves. It later became one of the abiding memories of my time in Borneo – watching groups of macho soldiers, armed to the teeth, waiting patiently in line to be weighed on a set of dainty bathroom scales by our crewman in order to juggle the combination of weights to match what we could carry. The scales also served to help convince the local Army commanders that weight and volume were two very different quantities. Having been used to packing 3-ton lorries to the roofs, they would peer suspiciously into the half-empty cabin of the Whirlwind, pleading to add just one more soldier or another small, but very heavy, box of ammunition. On the outbound leg of our first round trip of ninety minutes, we would be carrying four soldiers and a minimum of equipment. Brian, our crewman, would remain behind to allow the maximum number of troops to be carried – a normal practice in our area of operations where transit distances to and from the border from our forward operating bases were significantly greater than in most other areas.

* * *

Now, at long last, it was time to depart on my first truly operational flight, the carrying of fighting troops up onto the Indonesian border near to where intelligence reports had indicated the presence of enemy forces. Added to the potential hazards of operating a single-engined helicopter over such inhospitable and remote terrain was now the risk of coming under enemy fire as we operated on the border. It was with a frisson of excitement that I now lifted the helicopter to the hover in preparation for departure on this significant flight for me.

The need for careful control of the helicopter's weight became readily apparent on the departure from Long Jawi. We had to turn to face downslope towards the river, making use of the slight height advantage to accelerate in a shallow dive to reach climbing speed. Long Jawi had a high ridge across our intended track immediately to the south and, at George's suggestion, I circled a couple of times to gain sufficient height to cross it. Again, the featureless jungle stretched ahead.

'Check the time and count the valleys that we cross,' advised George as I carefully held the required heading and speed. The time to the next checkpoint ticked away. Suddenly, there it was – *the* 'dead tree' that had so puzzled me during the previous evening's briefings. It stood stark and white against its neighbours, probably the victim of a lightning strike. In the vast acreage of the jungle, it was obviously not the only dead tree around, but it was certainly the only one exactly at 134°, nineteen-and-a-half minutes flying time and twenty-three valleys away from Long Jawi. With a small alteration in heading, we were now pointing straight towards our destination on the border ridge. Before leaving Nanga Gaat, I had been shown a register of landing sites held in the detachment's Operations *basha*. This was an old school exercise book in which all the entries were hand-written. Not only would pilots visiting a new landing site enter their estimates of the map co-ordinates and a brief description of the type of landing site, they would often also include a sketch of the area, maybe a simple skyline view of the border ridge-line on which the new site would be clearly marked. By copying this sketch onto your knee-pad or map, it could be compared with the actual view as the ridge was approached. I now checked the sketch I had made of Blue 5246, scanning the ridge in the distance for a match. The border ridge stretched almost the whole length of Borneo, hardly discernable in parts of the eastern and western extremities, but rising to over 4,000 feet in the central regions where we were now operating.

Blue 5246 was a 'fly-through' landing site about 3,000 feet above sea level, built on a sharp, narrow ridge and showing up as a clean notch in the trees against the skyline. As we approached the border I dropped down to tree-top level to present a more difficult target to anyone on or near the border who fancied taking a shot at us. This also skylined the landing site, allowing a quick check for any obstructions. George then took over, pulling the heavily-laden Whirlwind slightly higher than the ridge and commencing a shallow descent towards the gap in the trees where we could now see an armed soldier standing by the rudimentary levelled pad. With insufficient power to establish a hover over the pad before landing, the descending approach had to be flown carefully and accurately so that we arrived exactly over the spot at zero speed and zero height. Even a small error at this stage could result in us either falling into the trees short of the landing pad, or dropping onto the pad from a significant height with probable resulting damage. Regularly used landing pads were sometimes surfaced with the logs of the trees felled when making the clearing. One of the more unusual hazards in landing on these pads was that they could deteriorate markedly over a period of time from rotting or insect infestation; the weakened log could easily fail or spring apart entrap-ping the helicopter's wheel, much to the embarrassment of the pilot.

With our wheels safely on the landing pad, George switched on the green light in the cabin, which also sounded a klaxon, indicating to the four soldiers seated there that it was safe to start unloading. They heaved out the ration packs and heavy boxes of ammunition before jumping out themselves. As the last one left, he reached upward to the cockpit and gave me the standard signal of a tap on the ankle to tell me that the cabin was now empty. This fly-through landing site was too small to allow a turn to fly out the way we had approached. Instead, we took off and flew straight ahead over the border, diving to gain speed before climbing back over the border for our return to Long Jawi. Landing back there I saw that Brian was ready with the upturned barrels of fuel and the small petrol-driven pump running ready for an immediate refuel. He had also weighed off our next load of freight and soldiers. Within minutes we were airborne again for a return visit to Blue 5246. Just under five hours later we were back at Nanga Gaat – mission accomplished. I had received my single familiarisation flight for our area and, from now on, would be in charge of my own helicopter.

Long flights were to become the routine for the majority of our flights in this part of Borneo – fly to a company position, ferry troops, equipment and rations to and fro, then return to our base at Nanga Gaat. The limited capacity of the Whirlwind operating at these heights and temperatures, and the lengthy distances between company positions, meant that numerous repeat flights had to be made, even when all four aircraft from Nanga Gaat were utilised on the same task. One advantage of this, however, was that routes to and from the most frequently used landing sites became familiar. While the jungle canopy still presented an uninterrupted vista of uniform green cabbage-tops, the subtle undulations, valleys, the occasional rocky outcrop, and even well-placed dead trees, gradually assumed a recognisable and reassuring pattern.

The run-up to Christmas was a particularly busy period for me with many more long flights and the challenge of a whole range of widely different landing sites. As Christmas Eve dawned, I received an early Christmas present. Bob Wood handed me a signal that read simply, 'WIFE OF LEEMING ARRIVING CHANGI 252100HDEC65.' In plain English, Marian would be arriving at Changi very late on Christmas Day. I was overjoyed. There were already arrangements in place for her to be met should she arrive during my absence, and a fellow squadron pilot, Flight Lieutenant Paul Deakin and his wife, Val, had offered to accommodate her until my return. It was only when Paul joined me in Borneo several days later that I learnt of Marian's ordeal on arrival. My squadron had got the date wrong; she had actually landed at Changi on Christmas Eve and no-one had been there to meet her. Remembering accounts in my letters home of the local taxi system and armed with the Deakin's address on a civilian estate on the opposite side of the island, she presented herself on their doorstep at midnight and joined the party that they were holding.

By the time I returned to Singapore nearly a fortnight later, Marian had found somewhere for us to live and had obtained a teaching post at the RAF Seletar Secondary School. I was most impressed.

CHAPTER SEVEN

JUNGLE SURVIVAL

My reunion with Marian after our enforced separation of over three months was short-lived. After a couple of days, I was off again. This time it was for a ten-day exercise in the jungles of the Malayan mainland, operating with a Scottish Army unit preparing for imminent deployment to Borneo. We tried sleeping in the cabins of our helicopters, parked overnight in a jungle clearing, but the claustrophobic heat and humidity saw most of us sleeping on the ground underneath the fuselages and taking our chances with the local wildlife. A regime of strict silence and no lights was enforced by the Army who anticipated a night-time attack from the 'enemy' – a Company of Gurkhas – so it was essential to take a careful note of your surroundings before the total blackness of night descended. Feeling the need to relieve myself in the middle of the night, I made my way gingerly towards a small bush that I had remembered was close to the starboard wheel. I was somewhat surprised in mid-stream when I sensed that the bush was moving. I was positively startled when the bush hissed, 'Sir! You're pissing in my left ear!'

Muttering a muted apology to the 'bush', I groped my way back beneath my aircraft, hoping that the guard would have changed before dawn.

Returning to Singapore, I hardly had a chance to say hello to Marian before I was off yet again; this time it was to attend a course on jungle survival. Because of my involvement with the presentation of a Standard to my squadron, I had missed attending what was normally considered to be an essential precursor to a deployment to Borneo – the RAF School of Jungle Survival course. Having now spent over six weeks living in the jungle, I felt that I was already fairly well acquainted with these surroundings but the course still had much to offer. It was designed to teach such esoteric skills as recognising and catching snakes and dealing with leeches and ticks, as well as the more obvious requirements such as navigation and the building of shelters. The course was conducted at RAF Changi, the RAF's main transport base located at the eastern edge of the island. The Survival School occupied a series of huts and *bashas* on a remote part of the airfield adjacent to the Straits of Singapore.

Here we were quickly introduced to the school's resident population of live snakes, examples of the types that we were likely to encounter in the jungle. One particularly memorable specimen was a large python that the instructor, Flight Lieutenant Jim Eyre, assured us was very tame and encouraged us to handle it. Heaving it out of its cage in the classroom, he bent a U-shape into its long body before draping it around my neck. I staggered under the unexpected weight as it arced its head slowly round until it was staring into my face from only a few inches away, its forked tongue flicking rapidly in and out as it sized me up as a potential addition to that day's lunch menu. Fortunately, I was totally comfortable with snakes and didn't mind its curiosity. However, soon bored at what it saw, it proceeded to slither along one arm, subtly coiling itself around my limb as it did so. Suddenly, the scaly coils started to tighten, exerting a very firm pressure that rapidly became painful. The coils continued to tighten further and I shouted out for help. Jim tried unsuccessfully to loosen the coils and called for more help from the assembled students. An almighty wrestling match ensued before the python was eventually unwound from my arm and restored to its cage.

'Sorry about that,' said Jim, 'Actually, we've only had him a few days. The previous one was very tame but it died on us a couple of weeks ago and we've been waiting for a replacement.' I spent the rest of that day's lessons nursing a lumpy aching arm.

Jim later redeemed himself with a graphic demonstration of how a leech latches onto its prey. We watched with sadistic pleasure as he placed a big black juicy bull leech on his forearm, allowing it to establish its sucker base on his skin before stretching out its fat body into a long thread, its questing head slowly weaving from side to side seeking out the warmest spot on Jim's arm. With a flinch and grunt from Jim, the leech buried its tiny invisible teeth into his arm, simultaneously injecting the anti-coagulant that would ensure the blood would flow freely without clotting. In fascinated horror, we continued to watch as the leech grew rapidly fatter before our eyes. Eventually Jim had had enough and placed a drop of iodine on the monstrous black worm. Instantly it screwed itself into a ball and dropped off, leaving Jim's arm still streaming with blood. Like superannuated Boy Scouts, we all made a mental note to be prepared for our future jungle ramblings, swapping woggle and jack-knife for a bottle of iodine and a packet of cigarettes. The latter were also effective in leech removal, the application of the lighted tip to the little monsters' bodies evincing an equally prompt response from them. Unfortunately, practice didn't always match the theory and there were several nasty cigarette burns at first as shaking, panicking hands sought to place the glowing cigarette tip accurately near exposed skin.

We were taught how to despatch live chickens, discovering in the process the origin of the phrase 'dashing around like a headless chicken', as the odd course student thought that decapitation with a machete would be quicker than the recommended breaking of the neck, and also how to avoid the self-inflicted 'machete bite' from an indiscriminately wielded weapon. After shelter-building and fire-making lessons, we moved on to a practical exercise in jungle navigation where our first task was to traverse a mangrove swamp near the centre of the island. This area was chest-deep in stagnant, malodorous water which obscured the twisted tangle of mangrove roots under our feet, making progress painfully slow and causing many trips and duckings in the foul, weed-covered mess. Adding to our discomfort were the frequent hard bites as leeches invisibly latched onto our underwater parts and mosquitoes danced in a whining haze about our heads. A few hours after starting, and not a moment too soon, we staggered out of the tangle of vegetation onto the grassy area of a rifle range, from where we were returned to Changi in the back of a well-ventilated 3-ton lorry. Having been forewarned about the probable state of our clothing after this exercise, I had taken the precaution of putting protective coverings on my car seat for the journey home. What I was not prepared for, however, was the reception when I arrived there. Marian flatly refused to allow me into our house, insisting on hosing me down in the driveway before permitting entry. Stripping off for a proper shower brought further unwelcome surprises; several blood-bloated leeches had been trapped in my gaitered trouser-legs, while my body was streaked with blood from the many puncture wounds where the leeches had recently fed. The foetid smell of the swamp persisted on my skin long after several lengthy showers.

*   *   *

The following week we were taken to begin a four-day stay in the jungle on mainland Malaya, during which time our classroom learning would be put to the test. We would have to navigate a route through the rain forest and sleep in various types of shelter, constructed ourselves from available materials. Together with me and three pilots from RAF Tengah, our group included two Malay firemen, part of a team who could be called upon to attend aircraft crashes in the jungle. Progress through the jungle was in single-file following, where possible, the slightly clearer routes of tracks and game trails. In this formation, the lead man hacked his way through the vegetation, while someone further back in the column would shout directions to maintain an approximate compass course. Another team member would count and log the number of paces taken, another would be in charge of the team's weapon, an ancient heavy .38 Smith and Wesson revolver issued to frighten terrorists or threatening wildlife, while yet another team member would be in charge of the snake stick. This vital piece of equipment comprised a stick of about 4 feet long with a loop of thin rope at one end forming a noose that could be tightened quickly by pulling on the remaining length of rope. The method of use was to place the open loop over the head of an obliging snake, pulling the noose tight before quickly winding the tail of the rope spirally around the stick to trap the snake's body. What one then did with the snake was a matter of some conjecture. At the most basic level, a snake represented food to supplement our meagre rations but the instructors at the survival school were always keen to add to their specimens at Changi. We were therefore under strict instructions not to kill or eat any snakes until they had been identified by the staff.

We didn't have long to wait to try out our new toy. We had been surprised at how gloomy the ground-level region of the jungle could be. Very little direct sunlight penetrated the trees' thick canopies, which were often in several distinct layers and extended upwards of some 200 feet above the jungle floor. Occasionally a shaft of pure sunlight would pierce the gloom, illuminating the forest floor as if by a spotlight. We had been hacking our way through the jungle for a couple of hours when we came upon one such brilliant spot of light in a small clearing by a stream and there, coiled up fast asleep in the centre, was a beautiful snake. Its markings were of alternating gold and black rings, probably identifying it as a member of the highly poisonous krait family. Pausing on the edge of the clearing, we summoned the snake-stick carrier to the front of the file. With scarcely a moment's thought he crept silently and slowly towards the sleeping snake as the rest of us watched with baited breath. Then, gently stroking its head with the rope loop, he slipped the noose deftly over the snake's head as it snapped itself erect, ready to strike. The snake wriggled and squirmed, held by its head in the noose, while our team member wound the rope around its body, binding it to the stick in the approved manner. We were all very excited by the fact that this simple piece of kit had worked so well and also with this possible addition to our very limited issued rations.

Recognising that this might fall into the 'unusual' category, we called for our instructors to come and see it. The snake was becoming rather lively at this point, and one of the team stunned it with a blow from the flat of his machete blade. Unfortunately, the blow seemed to have been too hard and appeared to have killed it. On the arrival of our instructors, the limp snake was untied, taken from the stick and passed from hand to hand for closer inspection. At one point one of our Malay firemen held it by its tail and teased his colleague with it, whereupon the semi-stunned snake suddenly reared up and struck at him, narrowly missing his face. In shock, the fireman dropped the snake at our feet, only for it to be hacked into many pieces by his frightened colleague. The instructors were not amused. This had been a prime specimen, but they did reluctantly allow us to keep it for that evening's meal.

On that first night in the jungle we were required to build a simple team shelter to accommodate all six of us. This took the form of a platform some 3 feet above the ground, constructed from jungle timber and covered in ferns and bracken to cushion it. Rather like a four-poster bed, the corner uprights supported a roof of several timber cross-members covered in ferns. Lying side-by-side, the six of us dozed fitfully after our arduous exertions of the day but were soon disturbed by irritated comments.

'Get off my foot!' said one voice.

'Keep to your own bit,' protested another.

After these exchanges became more frequent and irritable, someone switched on a torch and shone it down towards our feet. Many pairs of tiny bright eyes shone back at us. Rats! And very big rats too, scurrying around our feet and over our legs. As one, we tried to retract our feet from their attentions, wriggling and squirming in our confined space to get clear. Suddenly, with a groan and a crack, our shaky structure collapsed sideways, sandwiching us all between the base and the roof. We were now totally at the mercy of the rats who, after only the briefest of pauses, carried on foraging amongst us, even bolder now and running up and down our pinioned arms. After the initial panic, we took stock of our uncomfortable situation. The torch had been dropped and the only lighting was an eerie bluish-green phosphorescence emanating from the rotting vegetation around us. One of the team eventually managed to struggle free from the wreckage of our shelter and, one by one, the rest of us were extricated. The remainder of that night was spent sitting around a small fire, smoking to keep the mosquitoes away and trying to frighten each other as we listened to the wall of noise of a jungle very much alive in the darkness.

The following day found us hacking our way through even more dense foliage, scrambling up interminable small hills masquerading as mountains, to reach a rendezvous point where our instructors were waiting. Not only was clearing a path through the jungle extremely tiring, hampering progress to a slow walk and requiring frequent changes of the machete wielder, but even the vegetation conspired to hold us back. One particularly pernicious vine, known appropriately as 'wait-a-while', had long, whip-like slender tendrils equipped with very sharp backward-facing barbs that bit viciously into our skin, lashed our faces and became embedded in our clothing and makeshift packs as we brushed past. Such was the strength of these thin tendrils that it was impossible to break free simply by pulling, and each one had to be cut off. Our stock of iodine for combating leeches had long since been exhausted or lost and we had rapidly tired of burning ourselves with cigarette ends to make the creatures release their fierce bite. Any attempt simply to pull them off would have left their tiny triple-jaws still embedded in the skin and would quickly have led to infection. After the delays caused by dealing with the first few serious bites, we soon realised that you could be left out of sight of the party while wrestling with an iodine bottle or cigarette, so we ignored them. We chose instead to empty our trouser bottoms periodically at a natural break and stamp vindictively on their bloated black bodies, watching as our own bright red blood spattered the jungle floor.

We spent the second night in pairs, which seemed a more practical and companionable arrangement for shelter building. For the final night, however, we were required to space ourselves some 25–30 yards apart and make single-man shelters. With visibility through the jungle foliage rarely exceeding 20 yards or so, this meant that you were totally cut off from your nearest neighbour. The foliage also provided an effective sound barrier from other team members, even though it failed totally to deaden the noises of animals and insects. I had elected to construct a para-hammock for my shelter. This was a section of parachute strung between two trees about 5 feet above the ground, with additional parachute panels forming a small pitched cover to deflect the worst of the inevitable nightly tropical downpour. Having made myself fairly comfortable, I eventually dozed off, only to be awoken by a tremendous cacophony of noise directly underneath me. A foraging party of wild boar had discovered the remains of my rations, stowed carelessly underneath my shelter, and were now noisily snuffling and grunting their way through them, pausing only to squeal loudly in anger or pain as they fought amongst themselves over the scant morsels. I was terrified. My first desperate wish was that I had tied my hammock much higher up the tree trunks, despite the difficulty that would have presented getting into and out of it. Instead, I tried to levitate myself, arching my back as high as I could, imagining that any moment a sharp tusk would come ripping up through the thin nylon of the hammock. My second wish was that I had won the draw to hang onto the team's pistol for the night. A shot from that would surely have sent them running. These small, fierce animals deserved to be feared; they were one of the few species to attack on sight, seemingly fearless of humans and capable of inflicting fatal injuries very easily. An encounter with a pack would be almost certain death, and here they were, snapping at me from only inches away. My waking nightmare was eventually over as they finished all of my rations and moved on in search of new sport. In the dim light of dawn, it looked as if my kit had been ripped apart by a chainsaw.

Re-assembling as a team for the final trek to the finish point, I asked if anyone else had received any nocturnal visitors. No one had heard a thing, other than the now familiar backdrop of jungle noises. With a new-found healthy respect for wild boar, I clambered aboard the 3-ton lorry for the long, hot ride home.

Two days later, I was on my way back to Borneo to commence my second detachment.

CHAPTER EIGHT

SNAPSHOTS OF JUNGLE OPERATIONS

Returning to Borneo, I was soon immersed in the busy routine of troop lifts and re-supplies. Before leaving my base in Singapore I had read the current intelligence summary covering any notable activities and developments in the conflict with Indonesia during the previous few weeks. This secret briefing also detailed all the information known about the rapidly changing dispositions and strengths of the Indonesian forces ranged against us just over the border. One of the disturbing aspects was the forecast massing of Indonesian troops at particular points where, at times, they could outnumber the British forces by more than ten to one. I realised from these reports just how vital accurate intelligence was in ensuring that our smaller numbers were deployed accurately to best effect and the role of our helicopters in ensuring that this was done as quickly and efficiently as possible to counter the threat. These forces often included hundreds of disaffected Chinese Communists, the Clandestine Communist Organisation (known locally as CCOs), who had been trained and armed by Indonesia. One such build-up was forecast during my next detachment and I eagerly anticipated a lot of flying. I was not to be disappointed.

On 6 February 1966, all four of our helicopters were tasked to move more than fifty troops to the border. We took off as early as we could once the mist had risen well clear of the jungle canopy, flying in formation to Long Jawi, where we dropped off our crewmen and loaded up for the first lift to one of the border landing sites. Staggering our take-offs to avoid all of us arriving at the single landing site at the same time, we set off in long line-astern. Things soon started to go wrong as, one by one, the other three Whirlwinds dropped out because of various technical malfunctions and returned to Nanga Gaat, leaving me on my own. Shortly after, the engine fuel computer on my Whirlwind failed, forcing me to assume manual control of the engine. Aware of the importance of inserting the reinforcements, I continued, flying lift after lift, landing after landing, with no breaks – just a corned-beef sandwich and the occasional swig of 'jungle juice' to sustain me. The latter was a highly diluted, almost tasteless, drink made up from powders in our rations and rendered even less palatable by its tepid warmth. By now we could all emulate our helicopter instructors, flying with the cyclic stick clamped between our knees and controlling the height by gentle pressures on the collective lever with our left thigh. Now, however, we were doing it at near tree-top height while we munched our way through our rations. I devised all manner of methods to maintain concentration on these lonely flights – trying to knock off the odd few seconds from each lift or flying extremely accurately to use the minimum amount of fuel for each round trip. Eventually the job was completed and I landed back at Nanga Gaat seven-and-a-half hours later.

'Well done, Geoff!' was the greeting from the detachment commander. 'We would have been seriously embarrassed if you hadn't completed the lift. The Army were getting really worried that they wouldn't have enough men on the border by nightfall but they're OK now.' He added that the local Army commander had signalled his appreciation for my persistence.

I was too late on that occasion to participate in the usual evening five-a-side volley-ball matches. These were fiercely contested games between air-crew and ground-crew and took place in the hour or so before nightfall once all the aircraft had returned and had been prepared for the following day's tasking. The exercise was punishing and exhausting in that heat and humidity, but relief was at hand from an unlikely source. One of our pilots, Sergeant Fred Ayris, had discovered a copy of *The Field Officer's Handbook* dating from the First World War and in it was the design for a Field Hot Water System. The construction of this had become Fred's detachment project and, with various lengths of piping, fuel drums, ammunition casings and other unlikely plumbing materials obtained from the Army and other sources, the construction of a shower unit took place in a purpose-built *basha*. Fuel to heat the water was taken from the unusable waste at the bottom of every 45-gallon drum of the aviation paraffin that powered our helicopters' jet engines. While the thought of a hot shower might seem somewhat perverse in such high temperatures, the reality was truly and wonderfully invigorating.

Our accommodation *basha* was improved progressively during our month-long stays there. One major contribution to our comfort was afforded by lining the inside of the roof spaces with parachutes that had been used to drop supplies to us and which we had deemed 'damaged beyond economical repair'. These protected us, particularly when asleep beneath them, from the numerous crawling bugs and, frequently, from the cat-sized rats that disconcertingly scrabbled and fought amongst themselves just above our heads. These noisy encounters would sometimes result in two or more of the vermin losing their footholds and plunging into the safety net of our parachute ceiling. There, the fight would continue, with the bulging parachute indicating their exact location. The rodent combatants were encouraged to move on by our enthusiastic wielding of chunks of wood to bat them into another part of the roof lining.

Living in a remote area of a tropical rain-forest, it was inevitable that we came into very close contact with a wide range of wild animals, birds and insects as well as our domestic rats. Closest to us on a regular basis were the pets kept at Nanga Gaat. Here we had three macaque monkeys – Charlie, a fully grown male, Min, a female, and finally Little Min, who could be held in the palm of the hand. Between them, they provided hours of entertainment, ranging from amusement when watching Charlie sitting on a colleague's shoulder and doing unmentionable things to the poor chap's ear, or posting the contents of someone's wallet through the split-bamboo floor into the no-man's land underneath the *bashas*, to intense annoyance when it was your own property receiving Charlie's mischievous attentions. Another pet was Harry the Hornbill. He, we thought, was a magnificent specimen, with a splendid, huge yellow beak. It was rumoured that the squadron had been offered a significant sum of money for him by a British zoo but this had been steadfastly resisted. Harry repaid our loyalty shortly afterwards by falling off his perch – dead!

Nanga Gaat had previously been occupied by 848 Naval Air Commando Squadron with a flight of Wessex helicopters. Included in the handover to the RAF was a store of tinned rations. Unfortunately, frequent flooding of the store had resulted in the loss of all identifying labels but the Navy had assured us that the various supplies were grouped appropriately into tinned meats, potatoes, fruit and so on. However, it quickly became apparent that the vast majority of these tins contained only peaches in syrup and, as the supply organisation recognised only the number of tins without regard to their contents, we were stuck with a seemingly endless supply of the wretched fruit. It was during a breakfast of peaches with cornflakes, peaches with toast, and peaches with fried bacon, that I had my first encounter with a very large snake. Sitting around the table, I and my four colleagues became aware of a strange noise on the roof of the *basha*, followed by an ominous rumbling immediately above our heads. As one, we leapt to the opening that served as a window in the wall, just in time to see a large shape drop past. Rushing outside, we came across not only the largest snake I had ever seen, but larger than any I could have imagined. While the snake lay there, hardly moving and apparently stunned, we took the opportunity to examine it closely. It was a python, probably a reticulated python, one of the longest snakes in the world, and measuring well over 20 feet long. The Iban workers were very excited with this magnificent specimen. As well as probably providing a substantial amount of meat for their longhouse, the capture of a major predator on their livestock and a hazard for their children was very welcome.

A closer encounter with a snake came while several of us were returning to our *basha* in pitch darkness after an evening at the *Anchor Inn*. Walking in single file along the planks connecting the two locations, the front man stopped abruptly as his torchlight picked out the shape of a large lizard as it scurried across his path. At the same moment I trod on what I first thought was a small log of wood. My foot, clad only in a flip-flop, rolled on the object, throwing me off-balance and back into the arms of a fellow pilot, Flying Officer George McCracken. As he too fell backwards, he uttered the single shout, 'Snake!' and promptly dropped me across the 'log'. In a split second I realised with horror that I was now lying across a snake whose frantic writhing and wriggling felt in the small of my back conveyed only too clearly that it was as surprised and unhappy at the encounter as I was. Keeping my arms tight to my chest, I yelled for light so that I could work out which was the dangerous end of the snake. Unfortunately both ends were hidden in the long grass on either side of the narrow plank path and gave no clue as to which was which. I took a deep breath and rolled as fast as I could to my left. A good choice! The angry, startled reptile slithered off quickly to my right and out of sight.

The only occasion on which we actually felt threatened by the wildlife was during a rapid rise in the levels of the rivers following heavy rain around their headwaters. As the storms continued, we watched with some concern as the two rivers rose rapidly until they were some 40 feet above normal levels. Also the waters had become very fast, turbulent and muddy, and carried evidence of the havoc they had created upstream – tree trunks, branches and even complete uprooted trees rushed past us in the maelstrom, followed by destroyed *bashas* from the Army position just upstream of us. Disturbed from their riverbank homes, the various rats, snakes, lizards and frogs retreated from the advancing tide. As the water's edge became progressively closer, we could see the seething mass also getting closer and threatening to over-run us. We sat across their line of advance, Stirling sub-machine-guns at the ready, ready to shoot any dangerous reptiles that got too close. However, apart from popping off a few giant rats, the rest were saved by the flood level eventually peaking just a few feet short of our accommodation.

We occasionally came even closer to some of the species – we ate them. I had already shared a meal of snake while on the jungle survival course and now monkey was on the menu. I soon learnt to be rather wary before accepting any invitation for 'breakfast' with the Gurkha units with whom we worked. This meal, probably taken around mid-morning, often comprised curried monkey and rice.

*　*　*

Tasking from the Army continued to be heavy, which meant that we flew most days when weather and helicopter serviceability permitted. While most flights were carefully planned and co-ordinated by FATOC, sometimes a more pressing requirement would arise. During one flight involving troop lifts from Long Jawi to a border landing site, I was diverted to undertake a casualty evacuation flight to carry an injured soldier from another remote border site to hospital in Sibu. Quick evacuation of the sick or wounded was essential, not only for the morale of those suffering, but also because of the drain on the mobility and fighting ability of a patrol. Also, even apparently slight wounds could rapidly fester in the jungle's virulent environment. The patrol's position was in an area unfamiliar to me, so I needed to re-fold my large-scale map of the area to work out a suitable heading and time to get me close to the pick-up point. My initial estimate of the required heading from my starting point on the border took me close in and parallel to the border. Accordingly, I was flying just above tree-top height while struggling with my 6-foot long tightly-folded map, flying the helicopter with my knees. Suddenly, the draught through the two open cockpit windows caught the map, which billowed up, wrapping itself around my face and leaving an end flapping out of each window. Temporarily blinded and very conscious of my proximity to the tree-tops, I grabbed the controls and snatched at the offending map with my free hand, only for it to tear in two and disappear out of the cockpit windows.

I was now in a dilemma. I had lost my map and was in unfamiliar territory near to the border. In my flying suit pocket I had a small-scale map covering the whole of Sarawak. This was an emergency map and its overprint was in latitude and longitude, rather than the grid reference of my lost map. Neither map had shown any detail, but at least the grid reference passed to me for the pick-up location would have allowed me to put a spot on the map and measure a reasonably accurate course and distance to it. My crewman could offer no additional help, carrying only the same small-scale map as I had. I decided to stick to my original estimate of position. If I could find it, I knew that I could locate Sibu by flying northwards until I intercepted a major river before following it to the town. More by luck than judgement I found the general area of the clearing and was relieved to see a flare fired from the waiting patrol to indicate their precise location. After loading the casualty aboard, the onward flight to Sibu was straightforward and he was duly delivered safely to the hospital there.

*   *   *

One essential feature of our intense flying operations was the attention paid to servicing our helicopters. While most of the routine servicing was carried out by our own ground-crew at Nanga Gaat, our long hours of absence frequently made it necessary for the aircrew to complete some of it. Least popular was the vital task of keeping the complex rotor system adequately lubricated, for which task we would be equipped with a grease-gun and supply of grease. At the appointed number of aircraft flying hours we would shut down the helicopter and climb onto the scorching fuselage to carry out this very messy task. Occasionally, however, it was necessary to break off from tasking and return to Nanga Gaat for more specialised running repairs. Perhaps the most common of these was replacement of the tips to our 26-foot long rotor blades. These were easily damaged by the frequent strikes against the foliage of the trees and undergrowth when flying into the tightest of jungle clearings.

The dented or punctured blade tips gave rise to a distinctive whistle and 'chuffing' noise like a steam engine at full speed, alerting our ground-crew to our imminent arrival. The riverbank into which our landing pads were cut now served a useful function, the slope on some being such that the tips of our parked helicopter's drooping rotor blades came within a couple of feet above the grassy vegetation in front of the nose. As we manoeuvred our helicopter onto the small pad, one ground-crew member would position himself, complete with a spare set of tips, a hand-drill and rivet-gun, on the slope ahead of the arriving aircraft. Sitting cross-legged on the slope and looking down through the disk of the whirling blades and into the cockpit, he would marshal the pilot precisely into position with the blades inches from him and, with the engine still winding down, would then swing each blade in turn onto his lap where he would deftly drill out the rivets of the damaged caps and replace them with new ones. Meanwhile, his colleagues would be topping up the helicopter from drums of fuel stacked to within a foot or so of the aircraft sides, while the Army would commence loading the supplies and ammunition required for the next sortie. All-in-all, a very slick operation, and one that would not disgrace a Formula One pit-stop.

*   *   *

On receipt of the nightly signal for the following day's tasking, it was our detachment commander's responsibility to allocate crews and aircraft to meet the requirements. On most days all four helicopters and crews would be involved, sometimes all together in support of a major troop movement, but more commonly either singly or in pairs to meet a variety of tasks across the whole of our large geographical area of responsibility. The forecast flying time and the degree of difficulty and interest for each task varied enormously. The worst that could happen was to be left off the flying programme, either through sickness, or because of an unserviceable helicopter. The contrast between the excitement of operational flying and the boredom of a long day spent alone on mundane domestic tasks was very marked. It was not uncommon, therefore, for there to be quite lively bidding for the more interesting or longer sorties. Flying logbooks would be brandished in heated argument of one's case while the detachment commander attempted to maintain order and allocate the jobs fairly. Most sought after were those rare flights involving the insertion or recovery of the special forces. Special forces is the generic term to describe those elite military units which, normally operating covertly in small teams behind enemy lines, carry out specialist missions such as reconnaissance, surveillance and sabotage. In Borneo, these forces included the British SAS, locally recruited and SAS-trained Malaysian Cross-Border Scouts, specially selected Army units, and elements of the para-military Malaysian Police Special Branch. In early 1965, these groups were reinforced by the addition of SAS units from Australia and New Zealand.

To the best of my knowledge, our own SAS rarely, if ever, used our helicopters to fly backwards and forwards across the border, preferring instead to be dropped near to the border and left to make their own way on foot in order to retain maximum secrecy for their movements. This was in an era before the names of these elite troop formations became known to the British media and public, and their deeds the subject of books, films and open discussion. At that time, we ourselves knew little about their tactics, other than that they appeared to operate independently and undertook the most exciting and demanding missions. Our involvement with the special forces often included flights across the border into Indonesian territory and invariably to unprepared landing sites. These flights were probably part of Operation Claret and classified as Top Secret at the time, to avoid any charges of illicit offensive action being levelled against the British Government.

So secret were these operations to take the fight to the enemy rather than simply blocking their incursions along the border, that most, if not all of us, were totally unaware of the name of the operation, its aims or the strictly imposed limitations and requirements. All we knew was that for flights in close proximity to the border we were supposed to be in 'full precautions' mode. This included requirements for full helicopter armament and armour, two pilots and additional crew-members, all of which incurred an unacceptable weight penalty. However, with the fuel required for the long flights to and from the border in our area, the helicopter would have been grossly overweight before even a single soldier climbed aboard and we could rarely comply with these restrictions. The only occasion I can recall this procedure being used at Nanga Gaat was during part of a follow-up operation after Mike Ramshaw had come under fire just south of our base. The result was that we flew solo on nearly all of these cross-border missions with no protection other than a flak jacket and our Stirling sub-machine-gun strapped into the empty cockpit seat alongside us.

*   *   *

Unlike our normal regular troop lifts, Army cross-border patrols had to be completed in a single lift, at least to our side of the border. Any repeated returns to the same location on the wrong side of the border would quickly have attracted unwelcome enemy attention and could have proved highly dangerous. These operations therefore usually required some careful forward planning. For a typical cross-border pick-up, the first lift would be to take a few drums of fuel and a crewman to be dropped off at an area just short of the border. This might be a previously used landing site or a small natural clearing in the jungle. The much lighter helicopter would then continue across the border to pick up the patrol. Locating the patrol was usually by means of a SARBE beacon. This type of beacon, originally designed to assist in the location and rescue of aircrew who had abandoned their aircraft, transmitted a radio signal on the international distress frequency and could be received and homed to by suitably equipped aircraft. By modifying these beacons to transmit on a different range of frequencies, they could now be used to locate patrols on the ground without the need for visual or radio signals, which would probably be detected by the enemy. As long as the helicopter could be navigated to within a short distance of the pick-up point, a successful signal detection could usually be achieved. If no signal was received, we had little option but to return to our side of the border and try again later. What we couldn't do was carry out any sort of formal search pattern, including climbing higher to improve the detection range of the beacon. Such activity would soon have alerted the enemy both to our presence and to that of the patrol we were seeking.

On one occasion, I had dropped my crewman off on a gravel bank at the confluence of two small streams. Before jumping out, he had booted out two 45-gallon drums of fuel and a hand-operated fuel pump for our later use. Leaving him to prepare the fuel for my return, I climbed vertically above the clearing and took bearings on several prominent features to fix my position visually before setting off across the border to the pick-up area. I had already selected the homing function on my radio and now listened intently for the tell-tale 'bleep' that would indicate a signal. With nothing heard, I wound the volume control to maximum and watched the needle of the homing indicator, which would show from which direction the signal came. Still nothing. I was now some 8 miles across the border, flying just a few feet above the tree-tops, with my watch now indicating that I should have reached the correct location.

This was always a tense moment. Would the patrol be there? Was the beacon equipment working correctly? Had I selected the correct frequency for the homing? How long dare I search before I turned back for the border? The unremitting uniformity of the jungle canopy beneath me offered no clues. Suddenly, I was deafened by an ear-splitting screech in my earphones and a full deflection to the right of the needle on my homing indicator. I had arrived. With my left hand scrabbling at the radio panel above my head to turn down the volume, I threw the Whirlwind into a tight turn to the right to follow the indication of the homing needle. Almost immediately I spotted the patrol in a tight clearing beneath me, one of the troopers standing with his arms raised in a V-shape to confirm the patrol's presence and to indicate to me the suggested safest approach path towards them. Getting into the small clearing was fairly tight, but getting out again was more problematical. With the patrol safely on board, I lifted to the hover and applied full power to climb vertically and painfully slowly out of the confined area. Because of the extra power required due to the additional weight of the troops, the surrounding air was being sucked towards my rotors before being blasted through them to generate the required lift. With the air came the thin fronds of the surrounding branches, which were also sucked into the rotors creating the characteristic 'chittering' noise and causing a wild vortex of twigs and leaves around me. Eventually I was above the jungle canopy and racing back to the border.

Once safely across to our side, I started to match up the previously noted features to get my bearings to where I had left my crewman and fuel, but I was becoming concerned that there were far more little streams and gravel banks than I had previously observed. I was also looking out all the time for the reassuring sight of a flare, which I hoped my crewman would fire when he heard me in his vicinity. Getting very short of fuel and needing to land within the next few minutes, I was not doing too well in locating him and was starting to get seriously concerned. While still airborne I tried to radio my predicament to my base but without success. If I couldn't find my crewman he was likely to be in for a lonely night with just two drums of fuel for company. However, he also had with him his trusty Bergen, the rucksack containing sufficient rations and equipment to survive for several days in the jungle, as well as his own emergency SARBE beacon attached to his life-jacket, which he could trigger when he realised that I would not be returning.

My situation was different. I had a tired and hungry special forces patrol on board but, without fuel, we would also be stranded in the jungle. Our best bet would be if their radio expert could contact their base and alert them to initiate a search. Just as all these thoughts were crowding through my mind, I spotted the elusive gravel bank and my crewman and quickly landed alongside him. Not realising the problems I had experienced trying to find him, he merely apologisied for the lack of a flare because the cardboard casings of all the cartridges had become damp and swollen in the humid conditions and could not be loaded into the Verey signal pistol.

*   *   *

Another flight in support of a special forces patrol was an altogether more bizarre affair. The usual terse tasking signal gave me the time of the rendezvous, the number of troops to be picked up and their approximate location. The operation proceeded along much the same lines as earlier ones. Fuel was pre-positioned with my crewman for the return flight and, learning from my previous experience, I ensured that he was provided with dry signal cartridges. Crossing the border, I was pleasantly surprised to get an early reassuring 'bleep' in my headset, followed shortly after by a clear homing indication. Things were going well – I had the patrol somewhere dead ahead and merely had to maintain an accurate speed so that the timing of my run towards them would give me the best chance of finding them quickly even if I later lost the signal. Just as the homing signal indicated that I was practically overhead, I was even more surprised at finding myself over a sizable clearing with a lone, darkly-clothed figure standing there. The approach to land was quick and straightforward, and I landed the Whirlwind some 20 feet away from him. I gave a 'thumbs-up' signal to indicate that it was safe to approach my helicopter but there was no response and none of the usual sudden flurry of activity from boarding troops. An element of doubt began to enter my mind. The figure ahead of me made no move but just stood motionless and expressionless with his automatic weapon cradled in his arm and pointing at the ground in front of me. We stared at each other for what seemed like a very long time as I tried to puzzle out what was going on. The SARBE signal ceased but I still saw no movement from the figure in front of me.

Suddenly, he made a small gesture and more dark-uniformed figures crept slowly from the surrounding foliage and crouched on the ground on either side of me. My heart hit my boots and my guts turned to water as I surmised that I must have flown into an ambush. These did not look like the usual British or Gurkha troops. As well as wearing unfamiliar kit, they appeared swarthier and stockier than those with whom we were accustomed to working. My mind was in a whirl. Had the patrol been captured or killed and the SARBE beacon triggered by the Indonesians? What were they going to do with me? I dismissed the idea of pulling in all the power my Whirlwind could give in the hope of climbing quickly away; even the likely rate of climb for the unladen helicopter would not get me out of the area before I could be shot. Could I surreptitiously reach my Stirling sub-machine-gun and make a fight of it? With these thoughts chasing around my mind, I watched the figure in front of me. He now appeared to be listening for something above the noise of my aircraft, glancing frequently towards the figures on either side as if expecting some sort of signal. Without warning, he suddenly waved his free arm in an upward sweep, indicating that I should take off. However, thinking that I would rather be shot sitting where I was with my helicopter on the ground than making sport for them by being put up like a game bird, I stayed where I was. A few more seconds passed, then the signal was repeated, this time with more urgency. Clenching my teeth, I pulled the Whirlwind's collective lever up high to apply maximum power. As I started to climb I waited with baited breath for the bullets to come ripping through the thin cockpit sides and unprotected cockpit. Nothing! As I started to accelerate away from the clearing, I risked a backward glance. The clearing was deserted. Shaking with the reaction of my encounter, I flew flat out across the border and quickly located my crewman and fuel supply.

Later, back at Nanga Gaat, I related the incident to my colleagues. They were as mystified by the event as I had been. The only suggestion that might have made sense was that I had been used as a decoy by the special forces patrol who were, perhaps, trying to lure any pursuers into breaking cover once they had heard the sound of my departing helicopter and assumed that their quarry was on board.

Needless to say, operating in this covert role, no explanation or confirmation of this theory was ever forthcoming.

CHAPTER NINE

SINGAPORE ATTITUDES

Reporting back to my squadron after my return from Borneo and a two day stand-down, I received a most unwelcome surprise. I was summoned into my Squadron Commander's office with my hat on. This was the traditional attire for receiving a dressing-down or other formal interview. I was puzzled but not worried. After all, I had hardly been around long enough to be in any sort of trouble. The Squadron Commander wasted no time in pleasantries, informing me that I had been guilty of serious and blatant indiscipline. I almost laughed, thinking that this must be a prelude to some obscure set-up or joke. It was no joke. I stood to attention in front of his desk as he went on to cite several of the sorties I had flown during my recent Borneo detachment. Had I not deliberately flouted, not once but on three separate occasions, the specific regulation that limited our daily flying to six-and-a-half hours? My defence that I had only been doing my duty in completing the Army tasking after faults had reduced the number of our available helicopters was ignored.

'The RAF is not at war,' he said. 'As far as you are concerned, this is just an exercise.' I could hardly believe my ears.

'Has anyone told the Indonesians, Sir?' was my injudicious response. 'It's a bloody strange exercise when our colleagues are getting shot down and killed!' He was furious at my 'insolence' and dismissed me with the warning that he would be keeping a very close eye on me. I saluted and left his office feeling extremely angry, humiliated and very confused.

I sought out Flight Lieutenant Tony Edwards, who had been my detachment commander in Borneo during the time of my alleged indiscipline and described my disturbing interview. It was Tony who had been the first to congratulate me on getting the job done when the Army in our sector of the jungle had needed to reinforce their patrols on the border as a matter of operational urgency. He had also passed on the local Army commander's personal thanks for what he had described as a job well done. Tony was not surprised by my interview. He said that he had previously mentioned my contribution to the detachment's recent efforts and had then realised that the Squadron Commander did not view my performance in the same light. He warned me that things were very different back at Seletar and advised that I should just keep a low profile. In his opinion, I had done exactly the correct thing in Borneo.

* * *

A new Station Commander had taken charge of Seletar during my almost continuous absence on detachments following my own arrival and, a couple of days later, I was invited for a routine interview with him for what would be his first opportunity to welcome me formally to his station. After the initial pleasantries, the interview suddenly took an unexpected and unpleasant turn. Finding out that I had my wife out with me, he demanded to know who had given me permission to bring her to Singapore, adding that, had he be in post at the time, he most certainly would never have approved. He also disclaimed any responsibility for her, declaring that, if any civilian emergency evacuation or protection became necessary, I should not seek any help from the RAF, as would have been the case had I been over twenty-five years of age. He was aghast when told that Marian was working. Officers' wives did not work! He only relented slightly when I pointed out that she was teaching at the RAF Secondary School on his station. He questioned where I was living, declaring that he would have the accommodation inspected to ensure that it was suitable for an officer. At this, I lost my temper, saying that as he had already declared that he had neither interest nor responsibility for my wife's welfare, where she lived was none of his concern. I told him that we were on an estate where several officers from nearby RAF Tengah lived and that Tengah, in marked contrast to his attitude, already had her registered by the local RAF Warden as a service dependant and had assured me that she would be well looked after during my absences. I left his office with his threat to make me live in the Officers' Mess ringing in my ears and reflecting that, as far as my future career was concerned, in a very short time I seemed to have succeeded in alienating the two senior officers with the most direct influence on it.

*   *   *

These were the first of several incidents that I experienced at Seletar, which suggested to me that, unlike every other RAF station on which I had served, there was a lack of the full co-operation and general ethos of support for the operational flying units the latter might reasonably be entitled to expect. If my own experience was anything to go by, this antipathy towards aircrew, particularly towards those who spent so much time away on detachments, was evident throughout most of the sections on the station. I quickly came to the conclusion that Seletar was not a station at war, or even on a war footing, an opinion reinforced by many small incidents.

One night as Station Duty Officer, I was alerted by the RAF Police to suspicious noises coming from the Bomb Dump, a large secure compound on a remote, seaward part of the station. I ordered the Station Guard Force to meet me at the entrance to the compound and then grabbed a lift in the Police Land Rover. While *en route* to the incident, I extricated the issued box of ammunition from its many layers of sticky tape and loaded my .38 Smith and

Wesson revolver, mindful of the fact that, earlier in their campaign, the Indonesians had attempted an armed night amphibious landing on the beach at RAF Changi, a few miles further along the coast. Along with the Station Guard Force, the RAF Police had brought two dogs and their handlers who awaited my arrival at the gate to the area. I was somewhat disconcerted to discover that no inducements would make these dogs go through the gate. Usually bristling and ferocious in the presence of strangers, these particularly large Alsations were looking disturbingly cowed. Over the years the Bomb Dump had attracted rumours of supernatural activities within its barbed-wired perimeter. It was rumoured that this location, notorious as Area 9X, had been used as an execution ground by the Japanese during the Second World War and seemed to be possessed of a strange and sinister aura. Brandishing my pistol and displaying a bravado that I certainly did not feel, I led the armed guards into the area to carry out a lengthy check of the perimeter wire bordering the Straits of Malacca. Finding nothing untoward, I stood the guard down, unloaded my pistol and returned the rounds to their original box. I thought nothing further of the incident, other than to describe it in my report but there was much consternation in the armoury when I tried to return the unsealed box of ammunition at the end of my duty the following morning. Subsequently I was told to write an explanation detailing the circumstances of the 'unauthorised' loading of a service weapon. I refused. Failure to have loaded my weapon as a precaution in those circumstances would have been considered a dereliction of duty if I had been in Borneo. Fortunately, by the time I had returned from my next detachment, the matter had blown over.

I also fell foul of the Station Commander over my uniform. Unlike Army and Navy officers, we were not permitted to wear the practical beret as head-dress during exercises and detachments, being required, instead, to wear our formal Service Dress caps for which there was no approved alternative at that time. These were expensive items that had to be replaced at personal cost. Like most of my colleagues, I had a 'detachment hat', one that had seen better days but was more than adequate for wearing on exercises in the jungle, or being stuffed down the back of the hydraulic piping in the Whirlwind's cabin, a spartan area devoid of any places to stow an officer's accoutrements.

Returning one afternoon from an exercise with the Army in Malaya, I walked into the crew-room where the Station Commander was talking to my Squadron Commander. Catching sight of me, the Station Commander came over to me and asked what I thought I was wearing on my head. Dismissing my explanation, he ordered me to throw my hat in the bin. 'NOW!' I did so reluctantly, only to recover it as soon as he had left the room. Admittedly the cap had acquired a slightly green patina, having been everywhere with me since my arrival in the Far East. Also, I had grown very attached to it.

Arriving back from yet another exercise a few weeks later, I caught sight of the Station Commander's car parked outside the Squadron HQ. I quickly whipped my old cap off and held it behind my back as I entered the crew-room. The Station Commander glanced up from the map he was perusing but, instead of then ignoring me, he continued to stare intently at me. The crew-room went deadly quiet. I caught sight of one of my colleagues behind the Station Commander gesticulating discretely at his forehead, but couldn't understand what he was trying to convey; after all, my offending hat was safely tucked out of sight. I became increasingly uncomfortable under this relentless scrutiny and instinctively my hand went to my head. I was puzzled to find something still across my forehead before it suddenly dawned on me: the stitching of my hat-band had finally rotted through, leaving the band still around the top of my head like an Indian brave, but without the feather. Quickly muttering something about a 'sweat-band', I removed myself from the scrutiny and left the room as quickly as possible. I finally realised that I would have to ditch my precious relic and replace it with my current smart hat, digging deep into my pocket to buy another new one.

Financial matters were never far in the background. As an officer still aged under twenty-five and ineligible for either marriage allowance or the generous Local Overseas Allowance mentioned earlier, my pay was less than half that of my older colleagues of the same rank. The problem was compounded by the Ministry of Defence's attitude to detachments. One of the less welcome letters invariably awaiting my return to Singapore would be one from my bank manager in which he would regretfully inform me that 'as you have been rationed and accommodated by the RAF for the thirty-one days from ... to ..., we have been instructed to deduct the sum of £7.10s from your pay for this month'. Fantastic! Not only were we living in hot, leaking, palm-clad *bashas*, or sleeping in the cabins of our aircraft and fed on an indifferent diet of pork and tinned peaches, we were actually expected to pay for it. In short, unlike the RAF personnel based permanently at Seletar, we were being charged nearly 15 per cent of our monthly pay for the privilege of fighting an undeclared 'war'.

Despite the repeated wrench of leaving Marian behind and the financial penalty suffered while on detachment, it was almost a relief to return to Borneo. Like many of my colleagues at that time, I felt continually at odds with the attitudes of Seletar and its permanent occupants. In Borneo our activities were demanding, focused and appreciated.

* * *

Off-base, Marian and I lived on a modern estate of bungalows towards the western end of Singapore. Our bungalow was next door to Paul and Val Deakin with whom she had stayed on first arriving alone in Singpore.

Directly across the road lived Mike and Rita Ramshaw, the only other under-twenty-five married couple on the squadron. Not only did we live alongside each other, but our wives were all engaged as teachers at the RAF Seletar Secondary School and we three men all served on overlapping detachments at Nanga Gaat. This was a most fortuitous arrangement and one that provided considerable mutual support for our wives and reassurance for us during our frequent lengthy absences. While we were away in Borneo, our wives would share meals and transport for the long journey to and from school. This drive to Seletar was an exciting part of the day, negotiating near-suicidal taxi drivers as they furiously overtook and undertook, braking fiercely and skidding on the slick road surfaces after heavy rain, or squeezing past grossly over-loaded and overflowing ancient lorries along the dual carriage-way of the Yio Chu Kang Road. I had an old Australian-made Holden that I had inherited, along with a pile of parking and traffic offence tickets, from a homeward-bound squadron pilot. This three-speed, bench-seat car was built like a tank and proved a reliable defence against the taxis. Marian took to the driving challenge like a duck to water, demonstrating a flair and nerve never seen before and not seen again until driving in a crowded London many years later.

The combination of my absences and school routines conspired to keep us apart for much of our time during this Far East posting. My days off following my return from detachments or exercises almost inevitably coincided with the school week, while school holidays always seemed to occur during my detachments to Borneo. Despite this, we managed to explore much of the island of Singapore, fascinated by the marked contrasts in such a small area between the sophisticated and cosmopolitan city lying cheek by jowl with native *kampongs* – small farming villages just beside some of the main roads. My initial impressions on arrival that Singapore was a place that rarely slept was confirmed by the large number of street stalls, known as *amahs'* markets after the name for the live-in domestic helps and nannies, and the ubiquitous on-street cafes or *macan* stalls from which arose the most tempting aromas of cooking food. We soon overcame our western reservations and enjoyed some extremely tasty local dishes, cooked and eaten by the busy roadside.

We were all pleasantly surprised by the attitudes of local traders and shop-keepers to their businesses. Even casual browsers would be invited into the open-fronted shops and plied with an ice-cold beer or soft drink despite protesting a lack of interest in buying. These enterprising characters, mostly Chinese, would declare knowingly that 'One day you buy', and, of course, we did. I returned home after yet another Christmas spent in Borneo to find Marian puzzling over the delivery of a large box containing a Noritake dinner service. I assured her that I had made no such purchase of this famous Japanese chinaware, but the mystery was solved when our local grocer politely asked if we were pleased with our present. He explained that it was their custom to reward your customers rather than the western one of you rewarding the tradesman. Also, over that Christmas period, our landlord, Mr Chew Chin Ho, had entertained Marian and Val Deakin and several others of his tenants at a lavish party. We remarked that this seemed an admirable way of conducting business and one well worthy of emulating back home.

One of the biggest drawbacks to being in the Far East was the difficulty in communicating with family and friends in the UK. Telephones were rare and calls were exorbitantly expensive, letters took weeks to arrive and any British newspapers were already several days old by the time they were received in the Officers' Mess. When in Borneo, communications were even more dire. The sense of isolation from home was made more acute by the almost total absence of news in the British press of what was going on out there. Only rarely did some event, such as the award of the Victoria Cross to a Gurkha soldier referred to earlier, make headlines back home, prompting questions from anxious relatives about our safety. Neither was there any reporting of casualties nor repatriation of the bodies of those killed in Borneo. The fallen were quietly returned to Singapore in an Argosy for a military funeral at Kranji War Cemetery.

CHAPTER TEN

'BONZO' AND NANGA GAAT

It is, perhaps, difficult to describe the circumstances of the native peoples of Borneo without sounding patronising. It should therefore be said at the outset that all who came into contact with them, who enjoyed their hospitality or, in the case of the Army, had them fighting alongside them as scouts and trackers, had the highest regard and affection for these fearless, hardy people. We marvelled at their loyalty to the British, based on long memories of a shared enemy during the Second World War. Many of the longhouse elders displayed evidence of their wartime exploits. They had had a finger joint tattooed for each Japanese soldier's head that they had taken – the hands of some of the elders were so heavily tattooed that they looked as if they were wearing lace gloves. The leathery, shrunken heads of these unfortunate Japanese soldiers were still often displayed around the walls or in the rafters of the longhouses, frequently alongside a portrait of our Queen.

During the war these old men had seen something of the wider world beyond the immediate jungle environment of their longhouse but it was still surprising to see the speed with which the younger members accepted and embraced modern technology. Machinery and equipment which, only a few years before, had been beyond their experience or imaginations, was now commonplace to them. Former head-hunters, still wearing their scant native dress, turned out to cheer like schoolboys as RAF Hawker Hunter jets carried out regular, near-supersonic low level passes to 'show the flag'. They would help collect parachutes and errant supplies they had watched being dropped from Argosy and Hastings transport aircraft. Their native craft, often scarcely more than dug-out canoes, now raced along the waterways, driven by powerful outboard motors fuelled from our waste paraffin. At Nanga Gaat, a temperamental military generator powered electric lighting and our base radios, and was accepted as a useful tool by the natives for penetrating the early and sudden onset of jungle nightfall.

A keenly anticipated part of our entertainment at our jungle forward operating bases was provided by films distributed by the Services Kinema Corporation, the SKC. These films would be projected onto a sheet stretched between two trees, accompanied by the busy night-time jungle noises and giant fruit bats flitting amongst the tree-tops. We sat in the open, swatting away the vicious mosquitoes, oblivious to the occasional downpours, while the younger inhabitants of the local longhouse would creep out of the shadows and sit at our feet. Quite what they made of the epics and their locations unfolding in front of them – cowboy films, murder mysteries, love stories, and war dramas – was impossible to imagine, but their wonder and delighted 'Oohs' and 'Aahs' at close-ups of the lovely young Julie Christie spoke volumes.

Even nearer to home for them, of course, was the presence of our helicopters in their midst, parked alongside their longhouses or bustling busily to and fro in support of the Army. As mentioned earlier, a key part of the strategy in achieving a victory in the conflict with Indonesia was the hearts-and-minds campaign, the winning and maintenance of confidence and support of the local population to counter their inherent ethnic and cultural affinity with Indonesia and suspicion of Malaysia. Our helicopters played a vital role in this, chiefly in moving sick or injured natives from the depths of the jungle to one of the distant hospitals at the main centres of population such as Sibu or Kuching. Our local Army medics would treat all manner of medical emergencies but those requiring specialist intervention were referred to us for expedient evacuation. The Army's success in this role and our prompt assistance with helicopter lifts inevitably engendered considerable trust on the part of the natives, as well as high expectations. Usually there was a happy outcome to these interventions. Sick family members would be entrusted to our care as they were loaded on board the helicopter and, several days or even weeks later, a fit and well patient would hop excitedly from another passing helicopter, full of stories of new experiences beyond the horizons of their known world.

*   *   *

Sadly, not all these sorties had happy endings. One day, while refuelling on completion of an Army task at a forward base, I was presented with a tiny newly-born baby in something like a shoebox. Its mother was prevented from travelling because of the needs of her other children but she appeared almost relieved at any chance for treatment of her sick baby and trustingly surrendered the tiny infant to me. As I had completed the Army task flying solo, I strapped the shoebox in the cockpit left-hand seat alongside me and took off for Sibu. On arrival, an Army driver took me and my tiny passenger to the hospital, where the baby was handed over with the minimum of formalities. Several days later I again found myself in Sibu, and called at the hospital to enquire of the baby's condition. I was dismayed to hear that it had died shortly after admission and that the hospital doctor would like me to take the baby back to its mother. I set off for the return flight, the baby in the same shoebox, but now with a lid taped onto it and strapped into the seat alongside me. I was dreading handing the tiny body back but, when I met the headman at the longhouse, he took the baby away without fuss or question.

The natives in our part of Borneo belonged to the Iban tribe, also known as Sea Dyaks, a branch of the main Dyak population. Fortunately for us, all of the natives were friendly. Rivers were the main highways for communication and trade, and generally they lived alongside them, either in villages or, further inland, in longhouses sited on or close to the river banks. The longhouse, as its name implies, was sometimes nearly 150 feet or more in length, elevated on poles some 20–30 feet above ground level, and employing the same methods of construction as used for our *bashas*. The larger longhouses provided accommodation for as many as fifty families. The floor area beneath it was given over to their animals, principally goats, pigs and chickens. Access to the domestic accommodation was usually by a notched log inclined at a steep angle. This deterred most of their animals and other unwelcome guests as well as proving a tricky obstacle for us to negotiate in our slippery jungle boots. Nevertheless, during our visits, we frequently shared our sleeping area with chickens, or even noisily snuffling piglets. Inside, the longhouse was divided along its whole length by a woven partition. The open front half comprised the communal area, which was the centre for all social activities and longhouse business. The rear half of the longhouse was further divided into family cubicles, essentially private areas for sleeping and storage for personal possessions – very small and basic.

One notable longhouse visit in June 1966 was made by my pilot colleague, Mike Ramshaw. Delayed by bad weather, he was returning late in the day in his Whirlwind from a long task when he encountered even worse weather just a few miles upstream from Nanga Gaat. Finding continued progress impossible because of near-zero visibility in torrential rain and hemmed in by the narrowness of the river valley, he made a precautionary landing on a gravel bank in the middle of the river. While sitting in the cockpit, hoping that the rain would ease before the imminent and rapid onset of darkness, a native Iban passing on the bank gesticulated to Mike that the river would shortly rise and would engulf the helicopter. Seemingly with no alternative landing place in the immediate vicinity, Mike was in a predicament. He decided that he would disembark his passengers, three Gurkhas and a Malay-speaking Army medic, allowing them to wade ashore into the care of the Iban. He would then wait until he was forced by the rising water to takeoff and, alone, attempt the dangerous night flight along the river back to base. About an hour later the critical moment came and Mike lifted into a low hover, sweeping his helicopter's landing light from side to side, trying to discern the over-hanging tree branches on either side of the narrow river as he inched slowly forward into the darkness. Suddenly he became aware of flickering flames a short distance ahead together with a group of natives on the bank trying to attract his attention. Sensing that he had little to lose, he followed their directions and was amazed to find a helicopter pad. Now well clear of the flooding river, he landed his Whirlwind, overcome with relief at this apparent miracle. It transpired that the first Iban that Mike had seen had come from a nearby longhouse, Rumah Ugoh, and it was there that Mike's passengers had been taken. The Malay-speaking medic had managed to describe Mike's predicament to the Ibans who, remembering an area used by Navy helicopters a few years earlier, had assembled a working party and had hacked at the overgrown site to make it usable once more. The impromptu lighting had been from a fire started with a recent and prized copy of the *Playboy* magazine, reluctantly donated by the Army medic. Mike and his passengers were treated as guests by the longhouse headman and spent an interesting night there before flying safely to Nanga Gaat the following morning.

This event coincided with arrangements being made for a visit two months later to Singapore and Borneo by the BBC Television *Blue Peter* team. Back at Seletar, our redoubtable Officer Commanding Helicopter Wing, Wing Commander John Dowling, brought Mike's experience to the team's attention. This resulted in the longhouse becoming the focal point for their Borneo story, which was nicely rounded off when they were flown there, with Mike, in a Bristol Belvedere, known to the natives as the 'flying longhouse' because of its long fuselage and twin rotors. Presentations were made to the headman of a squadron plaque and a signed and framed Certificate of Commendation from the Air Commander, Far East Air Force, expressing gratitude for their efforts in saving an RAF helicopter. A great time was enjoyed by all, although Valerie Singleton, the main presenter, reportedly had to ward off the amorous and determined approaches of an elderly Iban warrior. She was probably the first white woman he had ever set eyes upon. Unfortunately, all the film, photographs and sound recordings of this visit were lost many years later in a fire at BBC Television Centre.

As this incident shows, communicating with the Ibans was generally fairly straightforward. Sign language proved remarkably universal, aided by their quick intelligence and eagerness to please, while regular workers soon picked up a smattering of English. Our attempts to learn their Iban language was aided by the discovery, in our officers' *basha*, of a carton containing numerous journals of the Sarawak Museum. These had been written by Tom Harrisson, a colourful, eccentric anthropologist and highly decorated Army officer who had been parachuted into Sarawak behind enemy lines to lead the natives in guerrilla warfare against the Japanese. (It was because of his encouragement that headhunting was revived during the war, having been virtually eradicated a century before.) He had been curator of the Sarawak Museum since 1947 and his writings, as well as containing a wealth of information on the jungle flora and fauna, and the customs and practices of the Ibans, included an English-Iban dictionary. Spoken Iban is practically without accent; Iban words spoken phonetically from the dictionary would invariably be understood. Coincidentally, the longhouse headman had been the chief tracker for the British during the Japanese occupation and had almost certainly worked in that capacity for Tom Harrisson.

*   *   *

One Iban who was very fluent in English was a remarkable young nine-year-old boy called Bunsu, invariably and affectionately known as Bonzo. Bonzo appeared one day with a working party of Ibans from the local longhouse just along the river. Apparently his father had been injured in a hunting accident and it was now Bonzo's intention to find work to supplement his family's income. Unfortunately, he had had to discontinue his education at a mission-ary school where he had excelled in English. Bonzo soon made himself useful helping to interpret between us and the native workers, as well as carrying out domestic tasks such as our personal laundry and tidying our accommodation. One day I asked him if he would like to try and teach us some Iban and he agreed with enthusiasm. He arrived the next day with a supply of chalk and a small blackboard around which he carefully arranged a few chairs, quickly assuming the role of schoolmaster, imitating what he had witnessed at his missionary school. Rain was sheeting down, preventing any immediate pros-pect of flying, so four of us sat down to be schoolboys for the morning. It soon became apparent that we had grossly underestimated Bonzo's grasp of the English language. He set us little tests, getting us to repeat after him until our inflections satisfied him. At one point I asked him the meaning of a particular Iban word.

'Ah, Mr Leeming, unfortunately you do not have a word in English which means exactly the same, but it is most like . . .' and then proceeded to reel off a string of very plausible synonyms. Under his expert and pedantic tutelage, we proceeded rapidly beyond the usual 'Hello', 'Good Morning', 'Yes', 'No' and 'Thank you', and were soon able to communicate fairly well with the locals. This proved particularly useful when I force-landed in a river in spate several months later and was able to enlist the aid of a nearby longhouse to save the helicopter from being washed away.

During one of my detachments, Bonzo was not his usual, cheerful self. He appeared listless and even pale under his dark skin, while complaining of abdominal pains. We referred him to the Army medic, who diagnosed pos-sible appendicitis and recommended immediate evacuation to the hospital at Sibu. Despite our busy Army tasking, a helicopter was provided to fly Bonzo there – and I was to fly it. We had no spare crewman for this task, so I strapped Bonzo into the vacant cockpit seat alongside me. As we lifted off and headed down the river towards Sibu, his obvious amazement at his new vantage point high above his surroundings appeared to make him temporarily forget his discomfort and pain. I then dropped down to low level, weaving the aircraft around the bends in the river, Bonzo royally returning the waves of the natives as we flew past. I began explaining how I was controlling the helicopter and, bit by bit, allowed him to take control. He was too small to reach the yaw pedals and could barely see over the instrument panel ahead of him but, within a short time, he was confidently copying what he saw me doing, with me gently riding the controls for safety. Flying like this, the journey seemed to pass very quickly and we were soon shutting down at the small airport at Sibu. I secured the aircraft and led Bonzo out of the airport terminal exit. As I waited to cross the road outside, I suddenly became aware that he was no longer with me. I quickly looked round and saw him pressed against a wall, a look of sheer terror on his young face. I rushed back to him, fearful that his suspected appendicitis had taken a sudden turn for the worse. His response to my anxious questioning at first puzzled me. He pointed along the road and managed to stammer out,

'What is it Mr Leeming? What is it doing?' Only after his pointing finger followed a passing Land Rover did I realise that he meant the vehicles on the road. Despite all the other wonders of modern technology that he had seen, and now even flown, the little chap was terrified by his first sight of vehicles moving along a town street.

* * *

Bonzo's appendicitis happily proved to be a false alarm, and he was soon back with us, as enthusiastic and cheerful as ever. Sadly, I never had the opportunity to take him flying again.

CHAPTER ELEVEN

TAKING AN EARLY BATH

'Shit! My bloody engine's failed!' I exclaimed while instinctively squeezing the radio transmit button hard. An emergency klaxon was sounding in the cockpit, my engine was slowly running down and we were now descending towards the jungle canopy below – fast!

* * *

Tuesday, 18 October 1966. It was Marian's birthday and I hoped that she had followed my instructions to find the present and card I had hidden before leaving home for this detachment. The day had started well for me. I had left the airport at Labuan earlier that day for what promised to be an interesting and fairly leisurely, lengthy flight. A couple of months earlier we had left our forward operating base at Nanga Gaat and the detachment was now established at the airport at Labuan, an island just off the north shore of Brunei in northern Borneo and part of Malaysia. This redeployment was in response to recent political upheavals in Indonesia that would ultimately lead to peace. However, new pilots were still being posted to the squadron as others returned home at the end of their two-and-a-half year tours and it fell to the more experienced pilots amongst us to guide these recent arrivals around our operating area. I was taking a new pilot, Flight Lieutenant Elwyn Bell, on a tour of the forward operating bases and landing sites. For some reason we did not have a crewman to accompany us but, as we were not expecting any tasking during this long flight, this did not seem important at the time. We flew south from Labuan on a round-trip that took in Long Pasia, Long Semado, Ba Kelalan and Bario. The latter contained an airstrip that had been built in 1945 during the Second World War by a small group of British special forces, Z Force, with the assistance of the local Kelabit tribesmen. Set high on the Plains of Bah, Bario had become the headquarters for surveillance and sabotage attacks against the occupying Japanese, as well as for training the local natives in effective resistance against them. Tom Harrisson, the Curator of the Sarawak Museum and compiler of our useful English-Iban Dictionary mentioned earlier, had been a key member of that Force. The area around Bario was markedly different from our previous operating areas. It was pleasantly sited on a high plateau but its major drawback was its proximity and easy access to the border, making it an important but difficult location to defend.

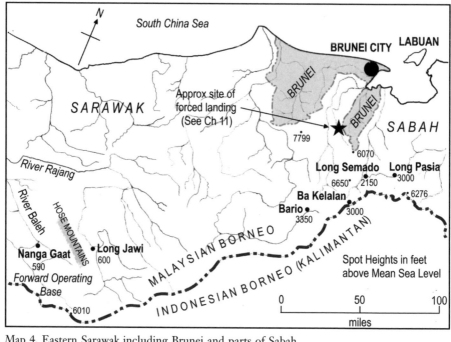

Map 4. Eastern Sarawak including Brunei and parts of Sabah.

Landing at the airstrip at Bario, I was immediately presented with a dilemma. I was approached by a young Chinese man, a trained Air Traffic Control assistant, who had been visiting his family. In tow he had an elderly-looking native woman who, he said, was seriously ill and who had missed one of the few flights out of Bario to a hospital appointment in Brunei. The question was, could I take her to Brunei City? With no crewman to man the cabin and an important familiarisation flight to complete in order to qualify my colleague to fly solo in this area within the next few days, the answer should have been 'No'. However, the young man was very persistent, explaining that the woman was in a stable condition and could walk unaided. He even offered to accompany her to act as interpreter. Against my better judgement, I reluctantly agreed. I explained that I needed the other pilot in the cockpit with me to complete his important familiarisation and that the young man would need to accompany the woman in the unattended cabin. This arrangement was far from ideal, but I was impressed and reassured by the young man's intelligence and quick grasp of my detailed briefing to him. With him supplied with a spare intercom headset and with both him and the woman securely strapped into the cabin, we again set off, this time northwards towards Brunei while reconnoitring another couple of regular landing sites on the way.

*   *   *

The loud klaxon and sudden lurch of the helicopter startled us. We glanced at each other in disbelief as I made my unorthodox radio call. Following the emergency drill for this situation, I quickly selected manual control of the engine and opened the throttle in an attempt to stop the engine winding down. This had little effect, other than to slow the rate of decay very slightly. I continued to open the throttle until I was demanding full power but there was no response except for the temperature in its jet-pipe to rise rapidly to over twice its safe maximum value. The engine had lost all its oil pressure and was quickly failing, leaving us descending to meet the jungle canopy beneath. Apart from being hit by enemy fire, this was every jungle helicopter pilot's worst nightmare. The chances of surviving a crash into the tops of the 200- to 300-foot trees were negligible. On first contact with the top branches the rotors would be destroyed and the fuselage would then plummet in almost free-fall through the jungle canopy and hundreds of feet onto the undergrowth beneath. This had been the unhappy fate of another Whirlwind and its crew some months earlier. There had been no survivors.

Gathering my wits, I resorted to the more conventional phraseology of 'Mayday! Mayday! Mayday! Mission 539 has engine failure 30 miles south of Brunei. Carrying out forced landing.' Realising that any ground station capable of receiving this long-range radio transmission would be too far away to provide any immediate assistance, I kept my finger firmly pressed on the radio's 'transmit' button, giving a running commentary as I fought to re-gain some power from the ailing engine and searched desperately for somewhere to carry out a forced landing. Instead of being at our customary height just above the tree-tops, I had, most fortuitously, recently climbed a few hundred feet higher in order to increase our visual horizon and point out a particular feature to Elwyn. This gave me a few vital extra seconds before we would hit the trees. There was a slight valley off to our left where a stream or river could be running and, steering towards it, I was rewarded with occasional glints of water along the line of the valley. Landing in water was an infinitely more preferable option than an encounter with jungle trees.

The Whirlwind was still descending rapidly and it was touch and go as to whether I could reach the almost hidden river. As impact with the trees seemed inevitable, the full extent of the river appeared across our track and I was able to haul the aircraft round in a hard turn to my right, pulling the nose high into the air to reduce speed in preparation for what I thought would be a sudden and very wet arrival. Just when we were about to hit the surface, a shallow bank of gravel appeared in the middle of the river and I threw the Whirlwind onto it. With a final terrifying screech of tortured metal, the engine finally stopped, leaving an eerie silence broken only by the gentle swishing of the slowing rotor blades and the tinkling sound from the rapidly cooling engine. Miraculously we were safely down. We re-checked our maps, trying to pinpoint our exact position in the network of rivers tentatively marked there, before I transmitted this position on the long-range High Frequency radio as well as confirming that we were all safe. There was no reply.

We were now sat on an isolated bank in the centre of a fast-flowing, muddy-brown river. I climbed out and recovered my two passengers from the cabin. The young man seemed to have taken it all in his stride and was chattering away excitedly but the old woman was in a state of near collapse. I hauled my emergency Bergen rucksack out of the cabin and searched through it for my supplies of tea and clean water. There were numerous bits of wood and branches on our little island and we soon had a small fire going on which we set the water to boil. While Elwyn tended this, I took my SARBE distress beacon from my life-jacket and pulled the operating toggle, which switched it on, and allowed its coiled aerial to extend fully. Reassured by a faint audible 'bleep', I propped the beacon against a stone and went to attend to my passengers. The tea, when it came, was like nectar and it also had an immediate and restorative effect on the sick woman who began chatting animatedly with her fellow passenger. We sat in the heat of the afternoon and considered what our best course of action should be. I had made a long transmission on the radio during our brief descent and had managed to send a fairly accurate position once we had landed. Assuming that some or all of these radio transmissions had been received, we might reasonably expect rescue aircraft already to be planning their search for us. This search would now be greatly aided by the transmissions from my emergency beacon. We occupied ourselves by gathering as much driftwood as possible to make a signal fire. If we weren't located before nightfall, this would also serve to help keep the voracious mosquitoes away.

Our sudden arrival had evidently not gone unnoticed as a small group of natives had gathered on one of the banks and started calling to us. Soon, a canoe was found and two of them joined us on our island. Sitting around our makeshift camp-fire and drinking tea, it was gratifying to find that Bonzo's lessons on the Iban language and aided by Tom Harrisson's dictionary had not been in vain and, although of a different tribe and dialect, many of the basic words seemed to be similar. Our exchanges were also much aided by the young Chinese man acting as interpreter. They examined my helicopter with great interest, touching and stroking it. Only when I opened the engine cowling to reveal the still-smouldering and tinkling jet engine did they recoil in fear and surprise at its heat. They made to return and offered to row us across to the bank some 30 or so yards away but I declined, explaining that we were waiting for another helicopter to come for us. Right on cue, a Scottish Aviation Twin Pioneer came into view, flying directly towards us at about 1,000 feet. These aircraft and their smaller single-engine counterpart, the

Pioneer, belonged to 209 Squadron, based alongside us at RAF Seletar. They serviced all small, otherwise inaccessible, landing strips scattered throughout Borneo and shared with us many of the dangers and problems of poor or non-existent navigational and communications facilities. We stood and watched its approach, waving casually in the certainty that the distress beacon and our fire had made his task of locating us an easy one. We were somewhat puzzled therefore when it droned directly overhead and disappeared from sight. I went over to my emergency beacon to check that the aerial was still pointing vertically upwards and then picked it up to check the audible 'bleep', confirmation that the beacon was still operating correctly. As I was holding the beacon I heard the sound of another aircraft nearby. I quickly replaced the beacon on the ground and grabbed a signal rocket I had been carrying in my Bergen. The sound grew louder but the aircraft was still obscured by the tall trees on the river bank.

Suddenly, there it was, the Twin Pioneer again, still at about 1,000 feet, but now flying almost towards us from a different direction. It seemed apparent that my distress message had been received and that a search for us was definitely underway. Surely it would now only be a matter of a few minutes before we were spotted. Just to make absolutely sure I fired the signal rocket. This was a powerful rocket and, with a loud bang, a hiss and trail of white smoke, its brilliant red flare arrowed its way towards the approaching aircraft. So close did it come to the slow-flying aircraft that I thought for a moment that there would be a direct hit. Instead, however, the flare continued harmlessly above and beyond the Twin Pioneer, which then appeared to fly through the remaining arc of smoke without any deviation or sign that the flare had been seen. In the instinctive manner of all survivors, Elwyn and I jumped up and down, waving our arms and shouting pointlessly at the aircraft, willing it to see us and make some sign in response as it flew over us and continued into the distance.

Nothing! I was now at a total loss to explain why we had not been located. If all of my message had been received, the final part of my continuous transmission would have told my searchers that I was aiming to ditch in a river; a small but smoky fire was burning at the scene alongside my disabled helicopter and, most puzzling of all, my emergency locator beacon was working. Or was it? I picked it up and put it to my ear and once again heard the 'bleep' of the homing signal being sent. As I went to place the beacon back on the ground slightly further away from the helicopter, I noticed that our small gravel island had become noticeably smaller and the flow of the river alongside us significantly more rapid and turbulent. So focused had we all been on scouring the sky above us that none of us had noticed how precarious our situation was rapidly becoming. Before long the water reached the aircraft, putting out our fire, dispersing our stock of firewood, and starting to lap around our feet. This could only mean that flood-water from heavy rain further upstream had reached us. How high the river would rise was anyone's guess but, from earlier experiences at Nanga Gaat, I knew that increases of over 40 feet within an hour or so were not unusual. My passengers retreated to the aircraft cabin while I signalled to the natives still watching us from the riverbank.

Soon they returned and, through my passenger as interpreter, I explained that I needed very long ropes with which I could try to secure the helicopter to trees on the river bank. As with Mike Ramshaw's earlier incident near Nanga Gaat, the response of the natives was immediate and, in short order, long ropes woven from vines were mustered on the riverbank before being ferried out to us in canoes. With the help of the natives, Elwyn and I managed to lash one undercarriage leg to a distant tree. I debated where to place my distress beacon and decided that the best location would probably be on top of the aircraft. As I held the beacon, checking yet again that it was still working, I paused, listening to the distant drone of another searching aircraft. Suddenly the air above seemed full of the noise of aircraft. Almost immediately one of our squadron's Whirlwinds flashed overhead, turning hard to keep us in view, while another Twin Pioneer appeared from yet another direction. The gravel bank was now totally submerged and, with us standing knee-deep in river water, there was now nowhere for the helicopter to land. I climbed back into the cockpit and selected the distress frequency on my VHF radio. All the searching aircraft would be listening out on this frequency, the same as being used by my own beacon. Now that I had another aircraft in line of sight with me, I should be able to talk to the pilot. Absent from the radio, however, was the expected 'bleep' from my own beacon's signal.

I soon found myself talking to a fellow helicopter pilot from our detachment, Flying Officer George McCracken, explaining that I had two unexpected passengers to be evacuated and requesting long steel spikes, ropes and sledge-hammers to make my helicopter even more secure. George's crewman lowered a rescue strop on his winch cable and the native woman and the Chinese young man were winched aboard in turn before being whisked off to hospital. George had relayed my requests to Labuan and, soon after, another of our helicopters appeared carrying the necessary equipment. By now we were waist-deep in water and struggled to hammer the long spikes into the gravel on either side of each main undercarriage leg before frequently ducking beneath the water to lash them together to secure the helicopter. Not only would it have to withstand probable total immersion, but also the force of the rapidly flowing water. By the time we had finished we were having great difficulty keeping a foothold against pressure of the torrent. Finally, gathering as much of our equipment as possible, we were winched aboard the Whirlwind for our return to Labuan.

At Labuan we were quickly checked over by the Medical Officer, who gave us the unwelcome news that we had been paddling around in what was possibly the most virulent river known in the region for the Leptospirosis infection. He had been engaged in private research into the disease and had acquired samples from that particular river in the course of his study. Without treatment, this rat-borne infection, also known as Weil's Disease, could easily prove fatal for westerners who had not developed the natives' natural immunity. The medical intervention came in the form of twice-daily administration of massive doses of penicillin delivered by a hypodermic needle that looked like the medical equivalent of a bicycle pump and left an egg-sized lump on our backsides, which took hours to be absorbed.

Questions were asked as to why I had not left my emergency beacon transmitting. Searching aircraft had reported only very intermittent signals that had been frustratingly short and of insufficient duration for accurate bearings to be taken. A detailed technical examination of my beacon revealed a badly worn connecting cable between the beacon and its battery. With the beacon held in my hand it had worked; when placed on the ground it had ceased working. Hence the puzzling and apparently erratic behaviour of the aircraft when searching for us.

The following day George McCracken and I flew back to the site of the incident, but only the helicopter's rotor head and part of the tail rotor were now visible above the racing brown flood. With nothing to be done, we left the Whirlwind to its watery fate. Returning a few days later, we found the Whirlwind sitting high and dry on the original gravel island. We landed alongside and surveyed the damage, most of it from trees that had been uprooted and flushed along the raging river until coming up against the obstruction of my helicopter. Various branches had penetrated the thin fuselage skin and the cabin was filled with a 2-foot thick layer of evil-smelling silt. The rotor blades, still surprisingly attached, were twisted out of shape. All in all it was a sorry sight. We salvaged whatever loose items were still in the aircraft, including my precious Bergen rucksack, took some photographs and returned to Labuan.

On the basis of our photographs and informal survey, and its inaccessible and flood-prone location, my Whirlwind, XP393, was written off – scrapped. The Medical Officer, concerned perhaps that my heavily contaminated Bergen might spread the disease, condemned it and all its contents to be burnt. Up in smoke went all my unaccountable 'treasures', the product of a couple of years of careful acquisition – a hammock for stringing up inside the aircraft for a night-stop, spare maps, camouflaged clothing and a waterproof poncho cape scrounged from the Army, along with spare food sealed in ration packs. I was mortified. The loss of an aircraft could often bring aircrew into direct conflict with their Supply Officer counterparts when it came to writing off equipment on personal loan to individual officers. Where no satisfactory explanation could be given for a lost item, then the officer responsible would be charged for its replacement. Supply Officers were a naturally suspicious breed and not without some justification. On too many occasions an accident was seen as an opportunity for balancing the books, and what was or was not on board could become the subject of prolonged wrangling. Investigators into the cause of many an aircraft loss might reasonably have cited gross overloading as a primary cause if the weight of all the equipment mysteriously claimed to have been aboard the doomed aircraft had been taken into account. Fortunately, at Labuan we had a very pragmatic and sympathetic young Supply Officer, Flying Officer Colin Cummings, and all was quickly sorted out at a stroke of his authoritative signature.

Against the odds, however, my Whirlwind was later recovered as an underslung load, dangling precariously on a long strop beneath a Belvedere helicopter. Following progress in peace negotiations, helicopter tasking had reduced significantly and advantage had been taken of this to undertake the difficult and time-consuming recovery. The Whirlwind was taken back to Singapore, re-built and flown for a further ten years.

CHAPTER TWELVE

CHANGING TIMES

Since mid-1966 our flying activities had taken place against a background of peace negotiations with Indonesia. Indonesia was in political turmoil, with popular demonstrations, political assassinations and increasing tensions between the Army and the President over the latter's support for the Communists. A failed Communist coup was followed by an Army counter-coup. While this initially left Sukarno as President, the true power was gradually assumed by General Suharto who eventually succeeded the deposed Sukarno to the presidency early the following year. Suharto had outlawed the Indonesian Communist Party, the PKI, purged the government of its members and sympathisers and, in August 1966, in defiance of Sukarno's wishes, Suharto formally declared an end to Indonesia's policy of *Konfrontasi*, or Confrontation.

Following these developments in the local news media and through our own intelligence briefings, we imagined that this would result in an immediate cessation in our activities. In fact it was to be several more months after the peace declaration before our involvement ceased. In the meantime, ground operations were increasingly being managed by the Malaysian Army for whom we provided similar helicopter support for troop movements and re-supply missions as previously given to the British Army. This meant some re-deployment of our helicopters. In September we had moved out of our jungle home at Nanga Gaat to Labuan. As well as being a sizable civil airport, Labuan was also a fully functioning RAF station, complete with a Group Captain Station Commander. We occupied crumbling bungalow-style accommodation nearby that had been the former property of the Shell oil company. We now had a room each, but these could become stiflingly hot as they lacked much in the way of ventilation. The buildings had been designed for air conditioning but, with an eye to saving a few pounds on the maintenance of this equipment, the distant bureaucrats in the Ministry of Defence had had it removed on the RAF taking possession of the properties earlier in the campaign. Our working accommodation at the airport had been equally neglected. We now had lockers in which to store our flying equipment but these were located in large tents on the airfield perimeter and were stood on duck-boards to try to keep their bases clear of the frequent swirls of water that followed the heavy daily down-pour. Our kit was invariably damp and mouldy.

On the positive side, the move placed us in a different area of operations and we now made daily flights to other forward operating bases from where we lifted troops and supplies to an equally remote border area over similarly inhospitable jungle to that with which we had become familiar when flying from Nanga Gaat. As well as supporting the Malaysian troops, many of our flights were to place British Army survey teams on high peaks in the area from where they could carry out their triangulation and observation tasks in order to improve the standard of mapping in the area. The maps we used had slowly improved over a period of time, a fact that owed much to the Singapore-based 81 Squadron flying English Electric Canberras in the photo-reconnaissance role. While still lacking much in detail, the later maps did at least show the accurate disposition of the main topographical features as a photo-like monochrome green mosaic onto which we could transcribe our own information.

*   *   *

On my return to Singapore from this detachment I suffered a life-changing event – I fell out of a Whirlwind and broke my back! At least, that is what I discovered much later. I was carrying out a ground-run on one of our heli-copters at Seletar following a change of engine, a procedure that called for the aircraft to be tethered securely to the ground in order to allow full power to be applied to the rotors while fine adjustments were carried out by my ground-crew. All went well up to the point when a torrential downpour hit us, making further checks impossible for the time being. While the ground-crew scurried off to seek shelter in a distant hut, I quickly shut the engine down and prepared to sit out the storm in the cockpit. After some time I began to get cold and shivery and a steady stream of water from a leaking cockpit roof was directing itself down the back of my neck. As there was no sign of any let-up in the downpour, I decided that I would be better off inside the cabin so I started to climb out. The pilot's exit from the cockpit of the Whirlwind was at best an ungainly procedure that involved sticking the right leg out of the sliding cockpit window while grasping hand-holds around the window and heaving oneself around onto the sill so that the right leg could scrabble for a foot-hold in a kick-in panel on the aircraft's smooth side.

I reached this awkward state in the proceedings and was in the process of lifting my left leg over the sill when my right foot slipped out of its foot-hold. I immediately fell backwards, saved from falling all the way to the ground by my left leg becoming trapped under my recently-vacated seat. I was now hanging inverted on the side of the aircraft, trapped by my left leg and choking from the constant flow of rainwater up my nose. Something needed to be done – and quickly. By curling my fit young body I found that I could just reach the cockpit window sill and aimed somehow to pull myself upwards and back into the cockpit. At that moment my seat decided to pivot upwards, releasing my left leg and sending me plummeting the remaining 8 feet to the ground in an almost horizontal foetal position.

When I eventually came round, I found myself lying alone alongside my helicopter with the rain still lashing down on my face. My head hurt and I gingerly felt around for evidence of any injury. My 'bone-dome' flying helmet was shattered like a broken egg-shell and there was blood on my hand from a cut on my head. Apart from my arms, I couldn't move. I had lain there for what seemed an age, shivering with cold and drifting towards unconsciousness again, before my ground-crew eventually returned and found me. I was immediately taken to the Station Sick Quarters where, after a cursory examination, the Medical Officer declared cheerfully that my head wound was superficial and there were no bones broken. 'Just a bit of severe bruising, dear boy. Heat treatment and massage will soon sort you out.' With that, I was consigned to the tender mercies of one of the nurses who gave me the prescribed treatment before allowing me to drive home. On arrival there I just couldn't get out of my car, and only after much lengthy and painful manoeuvring with Marian's assistance was I able to get into the house. I laid on the floor, almost motionless, for over a week when, quite suddenly, all the pain ceased and I was able to resume flying on the squadron. I was not to know until much later how serious my injury had been.

*   *   *

A new Squadron Commander had recently arrived to take command of 110 Squadron. He was a large, uncommunicative and saturnine squadron leader who, as well as earning the nickname 'Prince of Darkness', was also known as 'Humph' from his monosyllabic response to any greeting or salute. He lost no time in making his views on junior officers abundantly clear, dismissing us all contemptuously as 'junior crud'. What had brought about this cynical and unwarranted view of at least half his squadron pilots was never discovered but it soon became a source of resentment amongst us. Particularly niggling was his refusal to endorse the recommendations of external examiners of our individual flying abilities. Each year every squadron pilot submitted himself to detailed checks on his flying performance under a wide range of conditions and lengthy exercises, as well as searching oral questioning. These periodic checks were conducted by independent helicopter instructors from the Helicopter Wing Headquarters, presided over by an experienced wing commander. On completion of these checks a written report would be submitted to the appropriate Squadron Commander, detailing the standard achieved and making a recommendation for the award of a flying category. These ranged from 'Below Average' to 'Exceptional', with most of the squadron being assessed as a good, sound 'Average'. There was no slur attached to this assessment but, like most professional pilots, we had aspirations to improve and worked hard to do so. It was particularly galling, therefore, as one became ever more skilled and experienced on active operations, to have the examiner's recommendation for 'Above Average' to be consistently rejected by one's own Squadron Commander on the grounds that we were 'insufficiently experienced'. This was later to be my own experience.

* * *

In early January 1967, I returned to Labuan for the last time and, experienced or not, I unexpectedly found myself the Detachment Commander after the originally nominated senior squadron pilot was recalled to Singapore at very short notice. I had recently been promoted to Flight Lieutenant and was now in charge of three other helicopter pilots, four crewmen, an assortment of ground-crew and four operational Whirlwind helicopters. However, I was still almost a year short of the magical age of twenty-five when I would automatically become 'married' in the eyes of the RAF and, despite my sudden temporary elevation to this position of responsibility, I was still being paid less than half of what my older subordinates on detachment were receiving, as well as significantly less than my Senior Non-Commissioned Officers.

Command responsibilities at a young age were not considered remarkable at the time. Indeed, it is only with the benefit of hindsight that one realises the extremely low level of helicopter experience within the operational squadrons. From the Squadron Commanders and executives down to the most junior officers, the majority were on their first helicopter tour, with many of the youngest also being on their very first squadron, a situation examined in Roger Annett's book *Borneo Boys* (Pen & Sword, 2012).

As part of further redeployments brought about by the Indonesian political situation, my task on this detachment was to organise the transfer of my four aircraft and their crews to Kuching some 450 miles to the south-west. While the ground-crew and all our helicopter tools and spare parts would be flown there by an RAF Argosy transport aircraft, we would have the pleasure of a five-hour flight along most of the beautiful northern coast of Borneo. Getting airborne, I called the Whirlwinds into close formation on me before we thundered low over the Station Headquarters in a farewell salute. Moments later came a call from Air Traffic Control saying that the Station Commander had a message for the formation leader. Fearing that I had overdone the flypast, I waited in some trepidation for his call. I was pleasantly relieved when he congratulated us on our spirited formation flying and wished us *Bon voyage!* for our journey.

Three refuelling stops later, we all landed safely at Kuching ready to start work in yet another area of Borneo previously unknown to me. Our squadron already maintained a permanent detachment there but, as we tended to specialise mainly in just one area, few of us from my group of pilots had actually operated from here and only knew it as a transit location *en route* to Nanga Gaat or Labuan. Like Labuan, Kuching served the dual function of both civil airport and RAF station. Kuching, the capital and most populous city of Sarawak, was a revelation to us former jungle-dwellers, boasting a bustling market with numerous bars and eating places, attractions that had been denied us at other locations. At Nanga Gaat there had been absolutely nowhere to go except the occasional visit to a nearby longhouse. At Labuan we had taken few opportunities to visit the town, but now we spent evenings in the noisy market consuming the local speciality, large cooked cockles, brought to our outdoor tables in buckets and eaten in huge quantities. The price paid for these excursions was painfully raw thumbs the following morning, the result of prising open so many tight cockle shells while anaesthetised by the local Tiger beer.

One evening found a group of us starting the long walk to the RAF camp along the main road from the city when we were overtaken by a sudden burst of heavy rain. We were most grateful, therefore, when an RAF Land Rover drew up alongside and the driver called to us offering a lift. We piled in, three of us across the front seat, the remainder in the back. In time-honoured fashion, the occupant of the centre seat took charge of the gear-lever, changing at the call of the driver. All went well until the combined emanations from our steamy clothes conspired to obscure the view through the windscreen.

'Give the windscreen a quick wipe, will you?' called our driver, 'You should find something on the shelf in front of you.' The pilot alongside me reached forward, screwed up a rag and obliged. Turning the 'rag' over, he suddenly exclaimed, 'Hey, this is a flag! Isn't this the Station Commander's?' I took the flag and examined it in the dim light from the instrument panel, recognising it immediately from its shape as an Air Commodore's pennant.

'Oh, that's mine,' said our driver, the Air Commander for Borneo. Some chauffeur. What a pleasant change it was to be dealt with in such a friendly manner by a senior officer, in marked contrast to my experiences back in Singapore at RAF Seletar.

* * *

Our new base at Kuching introduced us to more unfamiliar territory and new helicopter landing sites. With the inclusion of this area, I had now operated throughout the whole of Sarawak. The flying, however, proved something of a disappointment after the demands of Nanga Gaat. This area had been the location for regular and hard-fought engagements with the Indonesians and had been the scene of the shooting down of one of our colleagues the previous year, but now it was relatively quiet. Along with the peace with Indonesia had come a large reduction in Army tasking and a political decision to transfer most of the remaining helicopter work to a squadron of the Royal Malaysian Air Force, the 'Tunku's Tigers', Tunku being a reference to the princely title of the Malaysian Prime Minister, Tunku Abdul Rahman. While it was perhaps unfair to accuse them of 'cherry-picking' the best jobs, it sometimes appeared the case that we flew most frequently when the weather was bad or when there was an unpleasant job to be undertaken. One of my last jobs there qualified on both counts.

I was sent to Lundu, a large village north of Kuching, to support a Malaysian Army unit in pursuit of some remnants of a group of Communist guerrillas. They had been detected in the area and were now trying to make good their escape across the border west of Lundu. It was a miserable wet day, with solid cloud down to a couple of thousand feet. While most of this part of Sarawak was much flatter terrain than that to which we had become accustomed in our previous locations, this particular part of the border was defined by an isolated 4,000-foot ridge running up towards the north-west tip of Borneo. My first task was to ferry the troops to the base of the ridge before lifting them in smaller groups to put them on the ground just below the cloud-base. The first group, lightly equipped, wanted to be placed as high as possible to initiate the hot pursuit, leaving their supporting party to follow up at a slower pace. As I approached the cloud-base I took a careful bearing on a distant feature on the low ground before the 'red mist' of anger and frustration came down – I was determined that these guerrillas would not find easy sanctuary in the cloud.

Concentrating hard, I established a hover against the steep tree-covered slope and then, carefully increasing engine power, I started to climb steadily sideways and upwards, my eyes glued to the tree-tops as they passed slowly beneath me. Higher and higher I climbed – 2,000 feet ... 3,000 feet. The cloud was thickening, making my progress more difficult. Just as I realised that I couldn't get much higher, my crewman told me that the patrol leader was satisfied with this position and wanted to be put down as soon as possible. My crewman guided me into a low hover over a small rocky spur and the patrol jumped down into the undergrowth. With them clear, I pulled away from the slope onto my safe heading in preparation for my descent below cloud, aware as I moved away of the muffled crackle of small-arms fire very nearby. With the remaining members of the patrol only wishing to be inserted just below the cloud-base and well below their colleagues, we quickly completed the remainder of the troop lift and returned to Kuching.

The following three days saw continuous torrential rain, which ruled out any chances of flying. Despite the Malaysian helicopter crews poaching the best jobs, we were nevertheless on friendly terms with them and, during the enforced grounding, indulged ourselves in good-natured banter over the intercom system, the 'squawk box', which linked the various units on the station, taunting each other with childish ditties. One of ours included a refrain, sung to the tune of the *Camptown Races*:

The Tunku's Tigers piss us off,
Doo-dah! Doo-dah!
The Tunku's Tigers piss us off,
Doo-dah! Doo-dah day!
Don't want to fly by night
Don't want to fly by day
The Tunku's Tigers piss us off
Doo-dah! Doo-dah day!

Retribution was swift when the following day dawned hot and clear. The main helicopter task for the day was the recovery of the bodies of six Communist guerrillas from the ridge where I had dropped the Malaysian Army troops four days earlier. Apparently, I had landed the troops almost directly on top of the fleeing guerrillas whom they had instantly engaged and killed. The Tunku's Tigers suddenly found that their helicopters all required an urgent and lengthy 'technical inspection' before they could be flown. Would I carry out the task for them?

Half an hour later I was on my way with my crewman to the spur where the bodies awaited collection. On arrival we were somewhat disconcerted to find the corpses lying scattered around, uncovered, under a haze of flies and obviously decomposing quickly under the influence of three days of rain and hot sun. My crewman remonstrated with the Malaysian troops in attendance but apparently there were no body-bags available in which to seal the remains. Reluctantly he supervised loading three of the bloated corpses on board. Fortunately for him the Whirlwind was now too heavy to include him on this first lift, so I quickly took-off and started my long descent towards Lundu. The stench flooding up from the cabin was appalling. Controlling the heli-copter with just one hand, I had my left hand firmly clamped over my mouth and nose, scarcely daring to breath. Even so, the all-pervasive smell made me retch uncontrollably all the way down. The reception committee of half-a-dozen soldiers at Lundu was only slightly better prepared. Masked soldiers unceremoniously heaved the bodies from my aircraft and threw them onto the ground. Then it was the long climb again up to the spur, flying the aircraft almost sideways in a vain attempt to ventilate the cabin. At the ridge, my crewman sat upwind and well apart from the remaining three corpses, his expression showing how little he relished the thought of sharing the cabin with them. The descent into Lundu was the same but now both of us were afflicted, eyes streaming and retching in unison.

With our macabre load delivered into the care of the Malaysian Army, we returned to Kuching. One glance in the cabin had our ground-crew running for the edge of the concrete dispersal to be violently sick. No one would touch the badly contaminated aircraft until a medical team had been summoned from the Station Sick Quarters and suitable protective clothing donned. Despite being thoroughly scrubbed out with disinfectant and the protective wooden floor covering being replaced, the cabin retained the malodorous evidence of this flight for many days to come. There were no pats on the back for me for this one – only a severe and justified dressing-down from my detachment commander for accepting the task before confirming that body bags would be available. I retreated to find the 'squawk box' to vent my feelings on the Tunku's Tigers.

*   *   *

A flying task in March 1967 a few days after was a much more pleasant occasion. Two of us were to fly a visiting Combined Services Entertainment party (successor to the wartime ENSA) led by my boyhood comedy hero, Harry Secombe, and including a singer, the lovely Anita Harris. While the Detachment Commander flew Harry Secombe, I flew in formation with him in another Whirlwind with Anita Harris in my cabin. Harry, a keen photographer, filmed us from the cabin door of his aircraft as we took them on a brief tour of the local jungle area. That evening the whole camp was treated to a memorable concert performance from the arch-Goon and his glamorous companions. They were all accommodated with us in the RAF Officers' Mess at Kuching where the ensuing spontaneous party went on until the early hours of the morning.

*   *   *

With the peace arrangements now secure there were further major changes. Almost overnight our helicopter detachment became redundant in Borneo and we were withdrawn to Singapore leaving the Tunku's Tigers to look after the Malaysian Army. Back in Seletar it was readily apparent that the two Whirlwind squadrons were now significantly overmanned, having double the normal peacetime complement of aircrew. In anticipation of rapid shrinkage, those of us who had been there the longest were earmarked for an early return home and were asked to express preferences for a future posting. As many of the UK-based helicopter posts had already been taken by pilots already returned from Singapore, few positions remained for those of us now returning. The only flying appointment offered to me was to re-train as a flying instructor on fixed-wing aircraft. I accepted this, disappointed at being unable to use my newly-developed helicopter skills in my preferred choice – search and rescue – and prepared for another uncomfortable lurch in the progress of my flying career, starting once more at the bottom of yet another ladder where my previous experience would be of negligible immediate and direct relevance.

*   *   *

I was given two week's notice of my posting back home; my 'married' colleagues were granted at least six weeks. This brought about another bruising encounter with administrative bureaucracy. When I protested that two weeks was insufficient to pack up my home, particularly as nearly half that time would be spent away on yet another exercise in Malaya, I was again reminded that I was technically a 'single' officer and could therefore be moved at a moment's notice. I persisted and was told that a small extension might be possible and instructed to report back on my return from the exercise. I was then informed that I had been granted a small delay; I now had a further two weeks before flying out. I reluctantly accepted this date until it was made clear to me that Marian would not be allowed to accompany me and that I would have to make my own arrangements to get her home. I was furious. Had my tour not been terminated almost a year before the due date, I would have reached the age of twenty-five and all would have been well. The situation was further complicated by the fact that Marian was now pregnant with our first child. I wrote pleading letters, demanding letters, made numerous increasingly angry telephone calls, refusing to leave Marian behind. Even after living frugally and just within our means for the whole of the tour, we had no savings amounting to the four month's pay it would have cost me to purchase a civilian airline fare home for her. With so many servicemen, both Army and RAF, now being returned home, there was not even the facility for me to pay for her on an RAF flight as had been the case when getting her out to Singapore at the start of my tour.

  I flatly refused to leave Marian behind and was warned that my continued refusal would probably result in a Court Martial for disobedience of a direct order. I still refused. Eventually, after a stand-off that wasted most of the extra two week's grace that I had been granted, the RAF relented and grudgingly allowed her a seat for the flight home with me, provided that she paid for any in-flight rations consumed. We finally departed after a further delay and arrived back in England in May 1967, feeling a mix of emotions – delight at being back with our families again, relief at feeling the freshness of the English countryside and seeing again the subtle greenery but, sadly, also a simmering resentment at the off-hand manner in which we had been treated by the RAF authorities in Singapore. Our stay in the Far East had been an amazing experience for both of us, but one that had been soured on several occasions by indifferent and crass management.

*   *   *

Ironically, my very last flight on the squadron had been the periodic renewal of my flying category. After a couple of days of intensive examination I was shown the annotation on the examination report, '*Recommended TC (Transport Command) B Cat – Above average.*' The endorsement that my Squadron Commander felt obliged to add read, '*Confirmed TC C Cat – Average, Insufficient experience in theatre.*'

*   *   *

It no longer mattered – this 'junior crud' was going home.

CHAPTER THIRTEEN

BACK TO BASICS

On 4 June 1967, following a short period of disembarkation leave on my return from Singapore, I reported to the School of Refresher Flying located at RAF Manby, near Louth in Lincolnshire, to begin a forty-hour intensive fixed-wing flying course. This course was designed primarily for those pilots who were returning to flying after spending a tour or so in non-flying ground appointments, but it also catered for pilots like me, who were making the change back from helicopters to fixed-wing flying.

Although the course was basically a re-run of my earlier flying training, the pace was so much quicker. Also, we were treated by instructors as responsible adults, a fact that probably owed much to the wide range of ranks of their students, covering the whole spectrum. I shared an instructor with an Air Commodore student. All the previously familiar exercises were covered but there was still a frisson of excitement flying one's first solo on a new type of aircraft. The aircraft I flew there was the Hunting Jet Provost TMk 4, which I found a worthy successor to its stablemate, the Piston Provost, flown during my earliest flying training. The course was a particularly popular one to undertake as the sole activity required of the student was to fly and where there were no extraneous duties to be carried out. For this reason it was especially popular with senior officers for whom the temporary relief from their responsibilities was most welcome. I was fortunate also in that I was again flying in home territory, a part of Lincolnshire that was equally familiar to me both from the air and on the ground.

With scarcely time to draw breath at the end of the refresher course, I crossed the country to RAF Little Rissington, near Burford in Oxfordshire, to start my five-month flying instructor course at the Central Flying School, the internationally renowned establishment responsible for the provision of flying instructors to all three British services. Each of the courses run there had a complement of around thirty-five students, destined to supply flying instructors to upwards of half-a-dozen busy flying schools. Marian joined me there, having stayed with her parents in Boston during my refresher course, and we set up temporary home in a lovely Cotswold-stone cottage close by the boundary of RAF Brize Norton. After the relaxed atmosphere at Manby, it was back to work with a vengeance. We now had to learn how to maintain a convincing and informative verbal commentary, or 'patter', while flying to exacting standards of accuracy for the various flying lessons. We also had to demonstrate a thorough knowledge of all the relevant related flying subjects such as aerodynamics, meteorology and navigation, and learn how to teach these in a classroom environment.

The flying, when it started, was a big disappointment to me. Students here were taught on one of four aircraft types – the Hunting Jet Provost, the Vickers Varsity, the Folland Gnat (at a detached site at nearby RAF Kemble), and the de Havilland Chipmunk. Without any choice in the matter I was allocated to the Jet Provost Squadron and was looking forward to continuing my recent acquaintance with this aircraft. Unfortunately, however, this was the Jet Provost T Mk 3, a very different animal from its more powerful successor flown at Manby. My first attempt at a take-off in the Jet Provost was an embarrassing disaster. Selecting full power and letting the brakes off, the little jet trundled forward with all the verve and alacrity of a loaded supermarket trolley. Halfway down the runway and still, seemingly, not much faster than walking speed, I glanced across at my instructor, enquiring, 'What's wrong? We're just not getting anywhere.' Sensing my concern, he agreed with my decision to abandon the take-off. We stopped safely on the runway – it wasn't a problem, as we had been going so slowly.

'OK,' he said. 'Obviously you've seen something wrong. What's the problem?' When I stated what seemed to be the obvious, he looked puzzled. 'What aircraft have you been flying?' he asked. When I replied that I had just completed a refresher course on the Jet Provost Mk 4, he uttered a sigh of resignation and told me to taxi round to the end of the runway for a further take-off. The flight, when we eventually became airborne, was equally unpromising. I fell out of aerobatic manoeuvres that I should have been able to perform with my eyes closed and, when it came to returning to the airfield for a landing, I got seriously low on the approach despite using full power. I did not like this aircraft one little bit. I had heard the derisive description of this under-powered jet as being a 'constant thrust, variable noise machine' and, after that brief introduction, I wholeheartedly agreed.

My next few flights followed a similar unsatisfactory pattern and earned less than glowing assessments from my instructor. Meeting my former captain from my tour on Valiants, Flight Lieutenant Tony Langmead, now an instructor on the Chipmunk Squadron, I asked him what my chances were of swapping to the Chipmunk. He made enquiries but, because most of the postings on successful completion of the course would be to University Air Squadrons, I could not be considered. I had neither a degree nor university education, qualifications then deemed almost a necessity for such a posting, whereby one would understand the academic environment and have appropriate credibility and empathy with the undergraduate students. I accepted my disappointment and continued on the wretched Jet Provost, only to be approached by Tony a few days later asking me if I were still interested as they had had a short-notice withdrawal from the Chipmunk course. I accepted with alacrity and sailed through the remainder of the course with few problems. The Chipmunk was a delightful aircraft to fly and one to which I formed a close attachment over the following years.

One late October day, well into the course, our first baby, Catherine Emma, was born at home. As only a midwife was in attendance, I managed to get the day off to help with proceedings. All went well and we gazed in awe at our new arrival as we were left alone later that evening. Fortunately, this was a Friday, which allowed time for my mother to arrive and provide reinforcements before I resumed my busy course the following Monday.

With the course graduation in sight and success almost a foregone conclusion at this late stage, we received our postings. Mine was to the four-man team of instructors at the Northumbrian Universities Air Squadron, based almost astride Hadrian's Wall at RAF Ouston, near Corbridge in Northumberland. As the instructor I was replacing was being posted a few weeks before I was due to arrive, I was asked to drive up to Ouston as soon as possible in order to take over all of his secondary duties. As well as inheriting his students, I would also become the Mess Secretary for the Officers' Mess and the Chief Ground Instructor, responsible for arranging all the students' academic lessons to supplement their flying ones. After a flurry of signatures and the briefest of handovers, I was on my way back to Little Rissington to complete my course.

The course Graduation Dinner at Little Rissington was a formal affair in the Officers' Mess where, as well as being wined and dined by our fellow officers, prizes were awarded for particularly good results in the various main aspects of the course. In addition to the Flying Trophy, the Aerobatic Trophy, the Ground-School Trophy and several others, the Central Flying School traditionally awarded a 'trophy' to the worst-performing student. This took the form of a top-hat that had somehow been 'liberated' many years before from the doorman of one of the prestigious London hotels. The unfortunate recipient had then to wear this hat while making a speech to the assembled company. In a humorous manner, our course 'dunce' poked fun at the establishment, letting it be known that we, the former students, thought that the Central Flying School's performance had also left much to be desired and deserved similar recognition. On cue, the doors of the dining room flew open and a low trailer was pushed in by members of the junior course. A giant top hat sat atop the trailer, which was positioned directly in front of the Commandant, the Station Commander and other senior officers from the station. From somewhere in the background the unmistakable strains of *The Stripper* rang out whereupon a scantily-clad young lady burst through the crown of the hat and proceeded with her exotic routine. This was greeted with enthusiastic cheers and whistles until the reaction of the top table was noted. A frosty, un-amused silence greeted the performance from that quarter but, like a true professional, the stripper carried on, working her way around the room apparently oblivious of it all. Her final act was to come up behind the Station Commander and drape her bra over his stony face. He was not amused. Following her departure was a stunned silence. It was apparent that a boundary had been crossed and that there would be repercussions.

The following day, the various squadrons got rid of our course members as quickly as possible and just before a Tannoy message ordering any member of Number 240 Course to report to Station Headquarters immediately. Unfortunately, although technically finished, two of us on the Chipmunk Squadron were slightly short of the total hours prescribed for the course. Our instructors acted quickly and we were soon airborne together in a Chipmunk, in foul weather, with orders to go anywhere, but not to return to Little Rissington until much later in the day, by which time the fuss should have died down.

We returned a few hours later, almost goggle-eyed after concentrating so hard while completing numerous 'blind' approaches to various airfields in poor visibility using only the aircraft's instruments.

CHAPTER 14

UNIVERSITY AIR SQUADRON

We arrived at Ouston, 15 miles west of Newcastle-upon-Tyne, on 1 January 1968, not realising that this was a public holiday in this part of the country, unlike the rest of England and Wales at that time. It was a bitterly cold day and we had major problems trying to get our married quarter heated. Having recently become 'officially' married in the eyes of the RAF on attaining the age of twenty-five, I had taken the opportunity to take over the empty quarter during my earlier visit, but had failed to arrange for any coal or coke supplies, assuming that I would be able to buy it on arrival. Friendly neighbours soon helped us out and we managed to keep our infant daughter warm as we huddled together in one room.

Flying started in earnest the following day when, after a brief introductory reconnaissance flight of my new operating area, I was let loose with my first student. The flight was a real eye-opener, especially when I found myself upside down in close formation with another Chipmunk. This had not been on the Central Flying School's training syllabus, although I had been un-officially led through some advanced formation manoeuvres earlier. Fortu-nately, my student, a senior member of the squadron, appeared to know what he was doing and produced a very acceptable performance. I soon came to realise that my new Squadron Commander, Squadron Leader Tony Back, was an inspirational leader who believed in setting his students challenging targets in their flying activities. While the approved syllabus for the University Air Squadrons was progressively revised and reduced, removing such demanding elements as night flying, all of these were quietly retained at Ouston.

University Air Squadrons were affiliated to many of the major universities with the dual aims of providing undergraduates with an introduction to a career in the RAF, whatever their subsequent chosen specialisation, and of exposing undergraduates going into civilian careers to the functions and running of the RAF. University cadetships had recently been introduced by the Ministry of Defence for all three Services under which scheme under-graduates, who had already been selected by their chosen Service, were granted probationary commissions as acting pilot officers or equivalents and were sponsored throughout their degree studies. Alongside them were those who had not committed to a career in the Services but who received exactly the same training. These undergraduates were granted the status of officer cadets but without the benefit of the generous financial sponsorship of their commissioned fellow students.

The instructors on the University Air Squadron worked an unorthodox week where Mondays and Tuesdays became our weekends, with Saturdays and Sundays being our busiest times when a minibus service brought our students in from the three academic institutes – Newcastle University, Durham University and Sunderland Technical College – from which our students were drawn. Additionally, Thursday evenings were devoted to ground-school in our Town Headquarters in Newcastle, while every Saturday evening the head-quarters were used for a social gathering at which all the instructors were expected to be present. The busy weekend and evening work was off-set to some extent by fairly light tasking during the rest of the week when only a trickle of students found their way out to the airfield. Also, we instructors had to fit in our secondary duties during this period.

My main one was as the Mess Secretary to the Officers' Mess at Ouston, in which capacity I was responsible for maintaining all the accounts, paying the various bills and presenting all the Mess members with their monthly bills for food and accommodation. My officer training had included many subjects totally unrelated to flying, but nothing on accountancy. I suddenly had to get to grips with double-entry book-keeping, ledgers, balance sheets, and profit-and-loss accounts. In those pre-decimal coinage and pre-computer days, and in the absence of even a basic mechanical calculator, this was a daunting task and one that was prone to error. Finding myself short by three-pence (less than one-and-a-half decimal pennies) at the year-end reconciliation of cash with cash-book, I put three-pence of my own money into the cash-box. I had spent hour after frustrating hour trying to trace the discrepancy but to no avail. I deposited all the books with a Newcastle firm of auditors for their annual review and report. Collecting them a couple of weeks later, I was congratulated on well-presented accounts.

'Oh, and I've found your missing three-pence – just a simple carry forward error on page 42, so you're now three-pence too much in your cash-box.' I took my three-pence out of the cash-box and thought no more about it. No more, that is, until I had a visit from a Command Accounts officer. When I explained what I had done he was horrified.

'You don't seem to realise how serious this is,' he said. 'You could be in very serious trouble.' I invited him to leave my office – immediately.

*   *   *

'When did you break your back?' asked the white-coated consultant standing with his back to me and closely scrutinising my X-rays on an illuminated wall panel. I was lying on an examination couch in Newcastle's Royal Victoria

Infirmary, stripped to a pair of shorts and surrounded by several curious medical students.

'I've never broken my back.' I protested after a moment of surprised hesitation. He turned, peering over his glasses at me.

'You are Geoffrey Leeming, are you not?' he asked, no doubt wondering if he had the correct patient lying there.

The episode had started the previous night when I had let my Beagle puppy out for a final sniff around before bed. I was suddenly rooted to the spot by a searing pain in my back. The only thing I could think of was that I must have been stabbed in the back. I stood there for what seemed ages, sweating with waves of nausea washing over me and on the verge of fainting. I scarcely dared to breath and was unable to turn or even put one foot in front of the other. Somehow I managed to shuffle slowly back indoors before Marian took me to the hospital.

When I confirmed my identity, the consultant regarded me with some puzzlement.

'You must know whether or not you have broken your back. You can't have done this amount of damage and not known about it.' He then started to quiz me, posing various possible scenarios that could have accounted for my injury – perhaps a road accident, or a bad fall?

'I fell out of a helicopter about a year ago,' I ventured. I then recounted my incident at RAF Seletar in Singapore when I had fallen from the cockpit of a Whirlwind helicopter sitting on the ground. I demonstrated as best I could my posture on hitting the ground.

'I suggest that when you fell out of your helicopter you crushed some of the vertebrae in your lower back. You're a very lucky young man that you weren't paralysed.' I didn't feel very lucky at that moment as thoughts of an immediate end to my flying career flashed across my mind.

A lengthy period followed during which I spent most of my time lying flat on my back on the floor, relieved only by regular sessions of traction and physiotherapy. Not surprisingly, the RAF medical services soon started to take an interest in my condition and I was summoned to attend a medical assessment at the nearest RAF hospital at Nocton Hall, near Lincoln. Travelling by train from Newcastle, I was met by an ambulance at Grantham station and conveyed to the hospital. The medical examination concluded that I was now down-graded to A4 G4 Z1. In simple terms, I was officially incapacitated – unfit to fly and unfit to carry out any duties on the ground. I could, however, be incapacitated in any geographical zone in the world!

I was then ordered to attend a full Medical Board at the RAF's Central Medical Establishment, just off London's Oxford Street, for confirmation of this category and an assessment of my future employment. This was a serious business and involved a medical examination every bit as thorough and searching as the one I had undergone on first applying to join the RAF. Although it was only my back causing my problems, I was directed in turn to the examination room of each specialist – eyes, ears, nose and throat, electrocardiogram, and so on, a procedure guaranteed to engender a degree of paranoia in even the fittest aircrew member, a feeling that somehow something else would inevitably be found wrong. I need not have worried on that score. All the tests were fine but, as for my back injury, a few brief minutes sufficed.

'Does it hurt when I do this?'

'Yes!'

'Does it hurt when I do that?'

'Yes!'

'OK, report back in three months.' And that was it.

Three months later I repeated the procedure – the whole procedure. My protests to the flight-sergeant at the desk organising the flow of patients to each clinic went unheeded. The same examinations – the same result. Three months later I returned for the same procedure but now, thoroughly confident that nothing else was wrong with me, I refused the flight-sergeant's invitation to go and have my ears tested yet again. Ten minutes later I was standing to attention in front of a group captain, the President of the Medical Board.

'This is my establishment,' he thundered, 'and I will not have its running messed about with by a junior officer!'

'And this is my body, Sir,' I riposted injudiciously, 'and I won't have it messed about with unnecessarily. There is clearly nothing wrong with me apart from my back injury and you are wasting my time and that of your establishment with all these pointless additional tests.'

'Get out of here!' was his considered response. I duly visited each of the clinics yet again, seething with anger. In the eye clinic, the ophthalmologist peered curiously at me.

'Haven't I seen you recently? Is there anything actually wrong with your eyes?' she asked. I explained my situation and she agreed it would be pointless to re-examine me. We got talking about the eye test itself and before long I was examining her eyes with the specialist equipment. On my next appointment I was greeted by the flight-sergeant. 'You've won, Sir! Orthopaedics, next floor down, Room Four, Sir.' Within thirty minutes I was outside and on my way back to Ouston.

The appointments for assessment of my progress and the physiotherapy continued for almost a year. At first, all I could do was lie flat on the floor and keep up to date with my Officers' Mess accounts but, as I gradually regained some mobility, my Squadron Commander was happy for me to recommence flying unofficially in the unit's Chipmunks. These flights were all dual and initially limited to gentle manoeuvres but I was gradually able to resume aerobatics without adverse effects. This turned out to be a deciding factor in the decision to restore my medical flying category. At yet another Medical Board, some doubt was expressed that my back would be able to withstand aerobatics. At that point I confessed my recent flying activity and, after a further brief deliberation, I was granted a limited flying category that enabled me to resume my job as a flying instructor on the squadron, albeit with the assistance of a steel-banded corset.

*   *   *

One of the highlights of the year was the annual summer camp. This was a four-week detachment for our four aircraft and instructors to an operational RAF airfield. Our students joined us for two-week periods, during which they could benefit from the intense and continuous instructional flying as well as visiting the various sections on the station and, if they were lucky, flying in a variety of the station's aircraft. By way of introduction, our squadron always put on a party in the Officers' Mess and invited a cross-section of the host station's key officers. This was an invaluable exercise that paid dividends in the contacts made for ensuring that each camp was as memorable as possible for our students. My first such camp was to RAF West Raynham, set in rural Norfolk near Walsingham and home to two squadrons of Hawker Hunter jet fighters. This was a heady atmosphere for our students, now in the company of real fighter pilots, some of whom were of similar ages to them. One of the resident Hunter squadrons – No. 54 – was away on detachment themselves and had generously allowed us the full use of their accommodation. Our students were suitably impressed by the numerous trophies and historical mementos displayed in the crewroom, as well as by the comprehensive briefing facilities at their disposal. We instructors flew as many as possible of the station personnel in our Chipmunks and I had the pleasure of flying the Senior Air Traffic Control Officer, a former Spitfire pilot during the Second World War. My little Chipmunk was soon being flown smoothly and competently by this veteran, a fact I later mentioned to my Squadron Commander.

'Send him solo then, if he would like it and you think he is up to it,' was his response. On a later occasion while flying with him I said nothing of this suggestion but carefully and discreetly checked out his flying skills. After a well-flown series of take-offs and landings I broached the subject with him.

'You've obviously not lost much of your previous skills. How would you like to go off on your own for a couple of circuits?' He was speechless, but the broad smile on his face signalled his acceptance of my offer. I climbed out, secured all my loose straps then strolled over to the Air Traffic Control tower from where I could monitor his progress and witness his final, perfect three-point landing.

Another satisfied customer was a new student of mine and one who benefited enormously from the continuity of instruction afforded by these summer
camps. I watched as he confidently taxied away from me to line up on the
runway and take off on his very first solo after only seven hours of instruction.
His moment of glory was almost marred when a formation of four Hunters
roared into the circuit and carried out a run-in and break. Suddenly the sky
seemed full of Hunters with my student's Chipmunk in the middle. Fortunately, he kept his head and carried out a very nice landing behind the last
Hunter. In the bar that evening he was treated to an apology from the
formation leader and plied with several celebratory beers.

During a low-level navigation exercise through the Norfolk Broads with
one of my advanced students, he suddenly called out that he had just spotted a
Lotus Europa, the latest sports car from that company's stable. He pointed
down to the car speeding around what appeared to be a disused airfield. I took
control and maintained formation on the car as it whizzed around the circuit,
holding the Chipmunk in a tight turn. Keeping the usual sharp look-out for
other aircraft, I spotted another light aircraft about 1,000 feet above, circling
slowly and also apparently watching the Europa being put through its paces. I
broke away and we resumed our navigation exercise, landing back at West
Raynham about half-an-hour later to find a message ordering me to contact
the Station Commander immediately. He wasted little time in coming to the
point. What had I been doing and where had I been during my flight? I
pointed out my route on my map and described the nature of the exercise.
He seemed satisfied with my explanation but then went on to say that he
had just received a complaint from Colin Chapman, the renowned designer
and founder of Lotus Cars, who had been in the aircraft orbiting the airfield
above me and had been trying to land. I left the Station Commander's office,
promising to write a letter of apology to Colin Chapman but, on impulse,
I decided to ring him. Within seconds I was talking to the great man. I
explained what I had been doing at the time, citing the cause of our loitering
above his airfield as a genuine interest in his new Europa design. He, in turn,
apologised to me for any trouble he might have got me into, explaining that
he had been in a hurry to land in order to make an urgent telephone call.
He sounded pleased at our interest in the Europa and invited us to fly over
and visit the factory. When I said that we had several engineering undergraduates on the camp with us he told me to bring as many as I could and gave
me the number of his factory manager to make the arrangements. He told me
that he too had been a member of a University Air Squadron in his student
days.

Several days later, our four Chipmunks arrived in close formation over
the Lotus airfield and Head Office at Hethel, about 10 miles south-west of
Norwich, and, after double-checking that we were not delaying any other

aircraft, we proceeded to give a couple of low fly-pasts. On landing we were received with great enthusiasm and escorted around the factory. Of particular interest was the screened-off area where Graham Hill's Formula One Lotus was being prepared for the next race of the Grand Prix season, prompting suitably searching technical questions from our engineering students. Some of us were even treated to a high-speed circuit of the airfield in Graham Hill's own Europa. As we prepared to leave, we were asked if we could repeat our low-flying formation for the benefit of the workforce who had temporarily downed-tools in anticipation and come out to watch our departure. We duly obliged, putting our four Chipmunks through a tight aerobatic routine just a few feet from the ground. A few weeks later we were pleasantly surprised to receive a copy of the Lotus Cars house magazine with the front page taken up with a photograph of our 'bomb-burst' over their factory.

Our four-Chipmunk aerobatic team had gained official RAF approval and, as the 'Northern Lights', we undertook engagements at local air displays and fetes. On one occasion we were to perform at Matfen Hall, a stately home just a few miles west of Ouston and then used as a Cheshire Home for the disabled. The actor, Richard Todd, had been booked to open the summer fete there and we were delighted to meet him when he flew into Ouston for the engagement. The event was blessed by a hot summer afternoon and, after the grand opening, I led the team through its aerobatic routine over the extensive grounds. I could see the home's residents assembled on the patio at the front of the building and, acting on a sudden impulse on completing our display, I called the team, 'Long line-astern – Go! Breaking left, follow me – Go!' These people deserved to see something directly in front of them without having to strain to peer above their heads into the bright sun. I rolled my Chipmunk almost onto its back and descended towards the field in front of the house, pulling out of the dive to weave my way through the scattered stands of trees, followed at regular intervals by my team mates. With a final low run across the front of the house we returned to our base. This was much easier flying for us than close formation, but the proximity of the aircraft made the display much more exciting for our audience. We were contacted later to thank us for our participation and were told of the enthusiasm with which our display had been received.

*   *   *

'Remember, the tail will come up a bit quicker and you will climb a little faster without me in the back. Off you go and enjoy your flight.' Another final word of advice from me to yet another student embarking on his first solo flight. Except that this was no ordinary student. This was the Station Commander of RAF Ballykelly in Northern Ireland being sent solo on his own airfield. Group Captain Mansell wore the aircrew brevet of Observer, marking him as a veteran navigator and bomb-aimer from the Second World War, and had never before piloted an aircraft himself. This was probably a unique occasion in RAF history.

The date of that year's camp at Ballykelly in July 1969 was notable for the first deployment of British troops during the Irish 'Troubles'. Towards the end of our camp, the airfield was suddenly alive with Wessex helicopters deployed from RAF Odiham in Hampshire to support the troop movements in the province. Among the pilots were several former colleagues from my Singapore and Borneo days, and I was soon refreshing my hovering and helicopter handling skills sitting alongside them. The first civilian fatality of that long and bloody campaign in Northern Ireland had occurred during our time at Ballykelly and there was a frisson of danger and even excitement in the air. It is difficult to remember that the British service personnel were not normally under any threat in those early days. On one visit to nearby Londonderry, a group of us even stopped to watch a small riot, during which a paint factory was burnt to the ground in a spectacular blaze. We had parked our distinctive Austin 1800 staff car, complete with RAF roundel, in a side street a short distance away without any qualms. In the local area we also visited several bars, some of which were later to become notorious as the scenes of some of the worst atrocities. When the troops were deployed on the streets just a few days later, they were greeted as protectors by both sides of the sectarian divide and plied with cups of tea while on patrol. History shows that this relatively happy state did not continue. Within weeks there was major rioting in the province and the casualty figures, both military and civilian, started their inexorable rise.

*   *   *

The following year found us visiting RAF Waddington, near Lincoln, and the home of three squadrons of the delta-winged Avro Vulcan bomber. Although the station proved hospitable, the airfield was a little too busy to accommodate Vulcans and several Chipmunks in the circuit simultaneously, especially with the latter being flown by inexperienced pilots. Instead, we made arrangements to use the small airfield at RAF Newton, just outside Nottingham, and soon our students were happily bouncing their way over its smooth grass surface. We flew our aircraft out from Waddington each morning and brought them back in the early evening. While the Vulcan operated off a single 9,000-foot runway, we could get away with using only a few hundred feet, a huge difference in performance that occasionally put us at odds with Air Traffic Control. Returning alone one evening, I was informed that the cross-wind was almost twice the limit for my Chipmunk. I requested the use of one of the disused runways lying directly into wind. This was refused because a Vulcan was parked at the far end of it – over 7,000 feet away. No amount of remonstrating with them over the radio could change their decision, so I positioned the aircraft to land across the 300-foot width of the main runway and had stopped before reaching the half-way point. Nothing was said on this occasion but, returning a few days later to very similar conditions, I manoeuvred to carry out the same landing procedure. The only difference was that this time I was leading a formation of four Chipmunks. My plan was thwarted by Air Traffic Control, who again also ruled out the use of any of the disused runways. Feeling that they needed to be educated on a Chipmunk's low-speed performance, I positioned my formation upwind of the airfield then, with my colleagues maintaining a perfect tight formation, I progressively reduced my speed until we were all flying backwards across the airfield, blown by the strong wind on our noses. As we came almost over the control tower, I increased my airspeed slightly until we were just hanging in the air, hovering motionless above it. Even this demonstration failed to change the controller's mind, so we carried out a spirited formation break over the airfield before tackling the tricky cross-wind landing.

* * *

Aerobatics featured strongly in our students' flying course, actively encouraged by my first Squadron Commander, who had been the RAF's display pilot on the Hawker Hunter fighter. Having failed to make any particularly favourable impressions on my own instructors during my training ('Leeming obviously enjoys aerobatics and throws the Vampire around with great enthusiasm but not necessarily with any high degree of accuracy!'), I was surprised to find that my skills in this art had much improved. So much so, in fact, that not only did two of my students win aerobatic competitions and go on to represent the squadron in the annual national events, but I was selected to be the Chipmunk solo display pilot for the northern area of the country. As with our formation displays, I performed at local airfield Open Days, Battle of Britain displays and other similar events. In June 1969 I was booked to appear at an Open Day at RAF Acklington, some 20 miles north-east of Ouston and the station where I had completed my basic flying training eight years earlier. We instructors each had our own Chipmunk, personalised with our names stencilled on the side and distinctive coloured propeller spinners, which we flew almost exclusively. On the Saturday afternoon of the display, I took off in good time for my display appearance. Suddenly all the electrical components in my aircraft failed, leaving me without radio contact with the display controller at Acklington. I quickly returned to Ouston, jumped into the Squadron Commander's Chipmunk and set off again.

I was still in good time and whiled away the remaining ten minutes before I was due to commence my run-in by going quickly through my opening routine. My start would be the 'falling leaf', a distinctive but rarely seen manoeuvre in which the aircraft appears to slide from side-to-side while descending rapidly. This is achieved by positioning the controls to induce a spin but, just as the aircraft responds, the controls are applied to induce a spin in the opposite direction, then repeating the procedure several times. My own Chipmunk had always behaved impeccably and predictably during this man-oeuvre but I wasn't so sure about my replacement aircraft. Several practice entries into the falling leaf manoeuvre reassured me and I duly ran in towards the crowd to start my display. From the spectators' point of view this was a graceful manoeuvre, but inside the cockpit it was a different situation as the airframe shuddered and rattled in protest as it flicked first from one side, then to the other. Suddenly, to my horror, the Chipmunk flicked onto its back and into a full spin. This was not a good situation to be in, just a few hundred feet above the ground and out of control. I immediately applied corrective controls and waited for them to take effect. Just as suddenly the spin stopped, leaving me just above the ground and pointing once again towards the crowd. With tense, shaking hands I eased the Chipmunk into a gentle climb, desper-ately attempting to claw back sufficient height in order to continue my display.

I had been asked to finish my display with a level fly-past so that the crowd could enter a competition to guess my height and speed. After landing, I duly made my way to the commentator's position to pass on these details, where I found an old friend and experienced flying instructor.

'Bloody hell, Geoff. That was fantastic!' he exclaimed between announce-ments. 'I've never seen that manoeuvre before. How did you manage to stop the spin right on target?'

'I didn't,' I confessed, showing him my still shaking hands. 'I was just bloody lucky!'

*   *   *

During my tour, I had worked to improve my instructor rating, first from 'B2-Probationary' to 'B1-Average' under the enthusiastic tutelage of the Chief Flying Instructor on the squadron, Flight Lieutenant Les Anderson. After his posting, I succeeded him as Chief Flying Instructor and re-doubled my efforts to prepare for examination for an upgrade to 'A2-Above average' at the hands of the Central Flying School. I flew my Chipmunk down to Little Rissington where I started off with the oral ground exam, which included giving spontaneous practice lessons and pre-flight briefings, and answering questions on a wide range of flying-related topics to 'test your depth of knowledge'. One of my first questions was, 'Describe "Frontolysis".' I was floored. Did my examiner want a description of hair removal, or perhaps an obscure electroplating process? As I was grappling with that and other eso-teric questions, a head popped round the door to announce that he had taken a telephone call from my Squadron Commander at Ouston announcing that my wife had just gone into labour with our second child. I was asked what I wanted to do. Twenty minutes later I was airborne, flat-out for the return flight to Ouston, pausing only for a quick *en route* refuelling stop at RAF Wittering, near Peterborough. Arriving home, I was in good time to assist the midwife with another home birth as Rebecca Jane made her entry into the world.

* * *

Having avoided what would almost certainly have been a humiliating failure at Little Rissington, I sought help from the nearest Chipmunk RAF flying school at RAF Church Fenton, near York. All RAF flying training schools had a 'Standards Squadron', which was tasked with periodic refresher instructional flying for all the staff of the school and for their preparation for instructor category upgrades. This is what I had missed on our remote University Air Squadron and I now surrendered myself to a week of mock examinations. This proved an invaluable experience and, arriving once again at the Central Flying School, I sailed through the ground and flying examinations without a hitch and gained my 'A2-Above average' instructor's rating. Several weeks later, I received a telephone call from a colleague with whom I had shared a room in the Officers' Mess for our final month of basic training at RAF South Cerney over ten years earlier. Flight Lieutenant Derek 'Taff' Lewis was now the *aide-de-camp* to the Commandant of the Central Flying School and was calling to invite me to attend a board for the selection of a new member of staff to join the Chipmunk Squadron there and instruct trainee instructors. I protested, pointing out that my A2 category was still very new and untried. He persisted, however, telling me that it was just to make up the number of candidates and that I would be doing him a big favour. I was still protesting when, a week later, Taff ushered me into the Commandant's office for an interview. This proceeded along friendly lines until he asked me how I felt about joining the Central Flying School in about a month's time. I was shocked.

'What about the other candidates?' I asked in panic.

'You're the one I want,' he replied. I was now very unhappy with the turn of events and, as before, protested my lack of experience and also the fact that I didn't see myself as fitting into the play-acting role frequently required of the staff instructors. I enjoyed teaching 'proper' students, and wanted to continue in that role. This did not please the Commandant who accused me of turning down a post at 'the top of the instructional tree'. He also hinted darkly that he wouldn't be surprised if my next tour was not a flying appointment.

A few months before the date for the end of my tour at Ouston, I was sent to the Junior Command and Staff School, known irreverently as the Jackass Course from its initials JC&SS. Here I learnt how to write Service Papers, analysing problems and proposing the best course of action, how to be a member of a Court Martial, how to command a parade, along with numerous other skills that no ambitious junior officer should be without. One part of the course we were all looking forward to was the rare opportunity to meet the officers who would decide our next postings. Up to now this had been a distant and anonymous procedure with no opportunity to discuss stated preferences or possibilities. We waited outside one of two doors, one marked 'Ground Postings', the other 'Flying Postings'. I sat outside the latter. The 'Ground Postings' door opened and a squadron leader called out my name.

'I'm waiting for the other one, Sir,' I replied.

'In here, Leeming. You're with me,' he replied. With sinking heart I seated myself opposite him as he perused my file. I asked why I was being sent to a ground posting when I could reasonably have expected to continue as a flying instructor, making the most of my recently gained qualification.

'You can't talk to an Air Commodore like that and expect to get away with it,' he replied. When pressed, he refused to confirm that the Commandant of the Central Flying School had exercised any influence whatsoever in my posting. After a minimum of preamble he informed me that I would be posted to the Ministry of Defence to be a sub-editor on the three-man production team of the RAF's *Manual of Flying*. My only consolation was that the post was located at RAF Manby, where I had completed a flying refresher course five years earlier.

My career was becoming distinctly fragmented as it took yet another lurch into unfamiliar and unwelcome territory, and I resigned myself to becoming the new boy once again.

CHAPTER FIFTEEN

HARDBACK WRITER

Early September 1971 found me in the editorial office of *Air Publication 3456*, *Royal Air Force Manual – Flying*, later to become known universally as simply *AP 3456*. This short title belied the manual's true size. It was planned to comprise ten hefty volumes covering such a wide range of aeronautically related topics – The Principles of Flight, Aircraft Performance, Air Navigation, Weapons Employment and so on – all brought together under the single title from previous individual titles. It also included a volume on Mathematics, Physics and Electronics, which, I was relieved to note, was not one of the five volumes for which I had responsibility. That particular onerous task went to my navigator colleague in the office, Flight Lieutenant 'Jock' Hughes. Some previous volumes, such as Air Navigation, were more or less complete in themselves and simply required a change of cover and title to be incorporated within the new manual, but most required extensive re-writing and editing, and the production of considerable amounts of new material. In charge of the two of us was a squadron leader, designated The Editor, who reported to our masters at the Ministry of Defence in London.

At first acquaintance this appeared a daunting task. The manual was very much in its embryonic stage and only small parts of it were already in use. By the time I was posted from the job three years later, all ten volumes of the manual had been issued and were then subject to the endless repetitive tasks of amendment and revision as continual developments and changes in techniques and equipment took place in the fast-moving world of aerospace.

Our method of working was first to define a topic and then to identify an expert who could be relied upon to produce the required material. We would then try to identify other experts in the field to provide peer reviews of the new work. Our job as editors was to tidy up the presentation of the scripts, a lot of which simply appeared as copies of lecture notes from various courses and, where necessary, adjust the level of content to suit our aircrew readers. Much of our success depended heavily upon our powers of persuasion. All of our contributors were busy officers and there was no payment, recognition or attribution for their work in print. On the occasions when we failed, we were obliged to write the particular chapters ourselves before submitting them for subsequent review. We soon learnt the diplomatic art of flattering egos.

All this was a world away from the flying environment for which I now pined, but some measure of relief from the routine daily drudgery of proof-reading, commissioning artwork and checking for split infinitives was at hand. Although technically a department of the Ministry of Defence, for convenience this editorial office was attached to the RAF College of Air Warfare at Manby. As well as the Jet Provost training jets of the School of Refresher Flying, Manby also had several twin piston-engined Vickers Varsities, the latter actually flew from a satellite airfield, RAF Strubby, a few miles away. Sharing Strubby with them was a squadron of twin-engined Hawker Siddeley Dominies, forerunner of the HS125 small executive passenger jet. These were for use by the General Duties Aerosystems Courses, the navigator's equivalent of the Empire Test Pilot's School, and by the Specialist Navigator Courses, which prepared experienced navigators for instructional duties.

I soon made myself known on all these units and, before long, was flying regularly with them. In order to avoid conflict with my 'day job', I frequently flew as co-pilot on Varsities for long night navigation exercises. As reward for undertaking these unpopular flights, I was often invited on training flights operating over weekends, flying into RAF Gatow, situated on the outskirts of the British sector of Berlin.

This was still the era of a divided Germany and crossing the border into that secretive eastern part always caused a frisson of excitement. We flew along tightly controlled corridors that had been established during the famous Berlin Airlift of 1948. From Gatow we often visited the centre of the city to sample its remarkable and distinctive night-life and to view the infamous Berlin Wall. On a couple of occasions, I took the opportunity to fly with the Army Air Corps on routine helicopter patrols along the whole length of the Berlin Wall, the border between East and West Berlin, enjoying a leisurely and unique bird's-eye view of the whole of the city.

I enjoyed a similar arrangement for long weekend flights with the Dominie squadron and I flew as co-pilot all over Europe from Gibraltar to Norway carrying students from the various courses.

In the immediate post-war era, the Empire Air Navigation School undertook a series of long-range pioneering flights using extensively modified Lancaster bombers to explore the problems of air navigation in the Polar Regions where normal magnetic compasses are useless. In 1952, the school moved from its base at RAF Shawbury in Shropshire to Manby, where the tradition of these high-latitude flights was continued, providing challenging conditions for advanced navigator training. In 1972, I was privileged to be invited to join one of these polar flights which, by this time, were being flown in Bristol Britannias, workhorses of the RAF's long-range transport fleet. The Britannias used for these flights had had all the passenger seating stripped out and replaced by a series of work-stations for the several two-man teams who would be working there. Each of the stations in this flying laboratory was equipped with one of a range of navigational devices ranging from the latest experimental inertial navigation systems, supplied by manufacturers seeking government contracts, right down to beautifully engraved antique bronze astrolabes, the origins of which dated back to 150 BC. Also at each position were detailed instructions for the setting-up of each piece of equipment and the method of taking readings.

We first flew out to the American Air Force Base at Thule in Greenland, where we took the opportunity to visit the American Ballistic Missile Early Warning System, one of the five radar stations, like Fylingdales in Yorkshire, built to give advance warning of a Soviet missile attack on the West. This proved to be an unnerving experience. We arrived by coach and entered the large secure reception area. As our names and identifications were being carefully checked against their manifest, we were startled by the loud sound of a klaxon and a series of flashing red lights. Simultaneously, massive steel doors slid closed, sealing off the tunnel to the underground Operations Centre. With a remarkable lack of concern, the young American officer supervising our arrival calmly announced that the signals heralded a warning of a missile attack and that we would not be allowed inside until the threat had been evaluated and, hopefully, declared a false alarm. Apparently, such events were far from rare and could be triggered by certain astronomical phenomena, or even by the flight of birds near to the sensitive antennae.

While waiting, we wandered around the reception area, looking at framed inscriptions, citations and photographs, all the time wondering if the world was about to end in four minutes' time.

'Hey Geoff, come and look at this.' called one of my colleagues from the back of a long alcove off the main reception area. Looking towards him I saw him examining several gleaming red fire tenders of an open-topped style reminiscent of an earlier era. As I walked towards him, a silver-helmeted statue came to life alongside me, raising his rifle to take aim at my colleague and inviting him to step back across a red line painted on the floor. My colleague either did not hear the warning or chose to ignore it whereupon the guard cocked his rifle, still pointing at my colleague.

'Step back across the red line, Sir, or I shoot.' he repeated. I couldn't believe what I was seeing and hearing. Here we were, isolated in a sealed-off reception area in a remote area in the Arctic Circle, expected visitors and wearing our full formal RAF uniforms, and now threatened with being shot. My outraged order to the guard to lower his weapon went unheeded and only when my colleague was completely back across the correct side of the red line did the guard snap back to attention, motionless and inscrutable. Confronting the American officer, I asked what the guard would have done if my colleague had not complied.

'He would have shot him, of course. Those are his orders,' was the chilling reply.

Later, we were admitted to the Operations Room where a simulation of a Soviet missile attack was run for our benefit. We watched, mesmerised, as the many pale green phosphorescent trails arced their way inexorably across the screens and display boards towards their targets in the UK and North America. This was how the end of the world would be recorded if we ever entered a nuclear conflict.

* * *

The following day we set off on our mission to fly over the North Pole, climbing out over the pristine whiteness of the Arctic ice-cap. For this transit of the North Pole I was teamed up with a Canadian Forces navigator for whom the equipment was almost as much of a mystery as it was to me. Nevertheless, with careful reading of the comprehensive instructions, much hilarity and several dummy runs, we managed to obtain the required readings. These were taken at regular intervals on a countdown over the intercom system, after which we moved on to the next station to start all over again with a new piece of kit and a new set of instructions. On our return to Manby, all the observations would be analysed and an assessment made of each piece of navigational equipment, noting in particular its accuracy and reliability as the North Pole was approached. In those days, long before the introduction of satellite navigation, it was sometimes disconcerting to realise the limitations of equipment in current use. We all peered out in curiosity as the average of the best equipment indicated we were exactly over the North Pole but the featureless expanse of ice gave no clue to the global significance of this position.

* * *

My tour was interrupted by yet another change of RAF stations when the decision was taken to close Manby and move the College of Air Warfare to the RAF College Cranwell in Lincolnshire, where it became the Department of Air Warfare. Rather than wait for a married quarter to become available for us at Cranwell, Marian and I decided we would buy a house at Boston, only 20 miles away. There, not only would be able to renew our acquaintance with the town of our shared childhood, but also we would be close to Marian's parents still living there. With the arrival of Elizabeth Anne at the beginning of the tour, we now had three daughters. By coincidence, Catherine, the eldest, attended the same primary school that both Marian and I had attended and was taught by the same teacher.

* * *

As part of my job I visited most of the RAF's flying stations in the United Kingdom and, at many of them, managed to fly in whatever aircraft were operated there. On one visit I fulfilled the dreams of every schoolboy by flying with the Red Arrows, the world-famous RAF aerobatic team. Flight Lieutenant Des Sheen, a fellow student all the way through flying training and my best man at our wedding, was now a member of the team. I had arranged a series of meetings at the Central Flying School at Little Rissington but managed to find time to visit Des at nearby RAF Kemble, the Red Arrows' operating base.

After a detailed briefing for a practice session from the team's leader, Squadron Leader Ian Dick, I climbed into the rear cockpit of the small Folland Gnat advanced jet trainer, trying to control my breathing after the exertions of strapping into an unfamiliar and tight cockpit. Soon we were airborne, surrounded by the rest of the nine-aircraft team, all painted in the distinctive and iconic red paint scheme and flying just a foot or so apart from each other. I was relieved that my body was well used to the high physical stresses of aerobatics and was therefore able to enjoy the flight to the full. Des was one of the 'Synchro Pair', two of the most experienced team members who, during the display practice, broke away from the main formation and performed spectacular high-speed manoeuvres that involved us flying directly at each other at closing speeds of about 800 miles per hour and just a few feet above the ground, before passing each other with seemingly only inches separating us. Only two years earlier the two aircraft being flown on these manoeuvres had collided, killing both pilots and their two passengers. On one particularly close cross-over during our practice there was a sharp 'crack!' on the canopy from the shock-wave of the other aircraft as it flashed past in a red blur, prompting Des to grunt, that that had been 'a good one'! After a finale 'bomb-burst' manoeuvre, which left the sky festooned with red, white and blue ribbons of coloured smoke, we landed for the de-brief. There was little time to relax, however, as we were soon back in the air repeating the display routine. I landed exhausted but elated by the experience. Later that day we flew another display practice, joining up with the French aerobatic team, the *Patrouille de France*, flying their nine Fouga Magister jet trainers to make up a spectacularly large and tight formation.

Less exciting, but nevertheless interesting, was a flight in a Handley Page Victor from RAF Marham. My navigator colleague had organised the visit but somehow the lines had become crossed. As the take-off for the training flight was scheduled for early morning, Jock and I arrived the previous evening to introduce ourselves. It had been raining heavily and both of us were wearing uniform raincoats as we made brief arrangements for the morning's flight with the staff crew who would be flying with us. As I became warmer I removed my raincoat whereupon there was a stunned silence. They had assumed I was a navigator like Jock and had allocated me the place of Radar Navigator on the crew. Seeing the pilot's wings on my uniform now gave them a problem – both pilot crew positions had been allocated but they were short of a navigator. I had often tried my hand at navigation when on the Valiant and had played around on the radar simulator during V-Force training, so I immediately volunteered my services as a navigator. I assured them that, if Jock could switch on all the kit correctly, I should be able to provide the required radar service without too much prompting. Somewhat reluctantly they agreed and, early the next morning I found myself flying for the first time officially as a navigator.

After several busy hours we returned to Marham – on time and without mishap.

*   *   *

While there was no official objection to personnel on ground tours flying as active crew-members in RAF aircraft, neither was there any encouragement. Despite tightening rules and regulations, which made such participation increasingly difficult, I was gratified to note that I had added four new aircraft types to my log book, amassing over 225 hours in the process during my three-year 'grounding'. As the end of my tour approached I agitated for a flying posting and was eventually relieved to hear that I had been posted to search and rescue helicopters at last – only nine years after my initial request.

CHAPTER SIXTEEN

SEARCH AND RESCUE – AT LAST!

In late September 1974, I joined a helicopter refresher course at RAF Tern Hill and, after a happy few hours being re-acquainted with the Whirlwind, I was soon on my way to RAF Valley to complete my formal training as a helicopter search and rescue pilot. The course there was similar to the one I had undertaken as part of my initial helicopter training nine years earlier. This time, however, the exercises were far more comprehensive and rigorous, as befitted preparation for the challenging role that was search and rescue. Five weeks later I arrived at RAF Lossiemouth, situated on the Moray Firth just north of Elgin, to begin my acceptance and familiarisation training on D Flight, 202 Squadron, whose area of responsibility covered a large, remote and mountainous part of northern Scotland and its outlying islands.

* * *

When I first joined the Flight, there had been much speculation as to who would replace the Flight Commander who was due for posting. Being the 'new boy' in search and rescue, I was unfamiliar with the possible contenders but followed with interest the various frank discussions on their comparative merits or otherwise. I was astonished, therefore, to be called into his office to be informed that I was to be the new Flight Commander. Despite disbelieving my earnest protestations that I had known nothing of this development before that call, all the members of the Flight quickly rallied round to make my assumption of the responsibility a painless exercise.

It was to be the start of the most challenging and fulfilling phase of my RAF career.

* * *

Later years have seen many major changes in the UK helicopter search and rescue services and, before relating my experiences of that tour, it may be helpful to describe something of the background to the RAF's organisation and participation in that role and at that particular time, and take a brief glimpse at the domestic routine of life on one of the flights.

The primary aim of the RAF search and rescue helicopters has always been the rescue of military aircrew and assistance to civilian aircraft in distress under the terms of international treaties. In practice, however, the vast majority of assistance was to civilians in trouble, be it climbers trapped or injured on our mountains, lost or missing persons in remote areas, or casualties in emergencies at sea. The helicopters were also used in the airborne ambulance role to transfer seriously ill or injured patients, particularly where

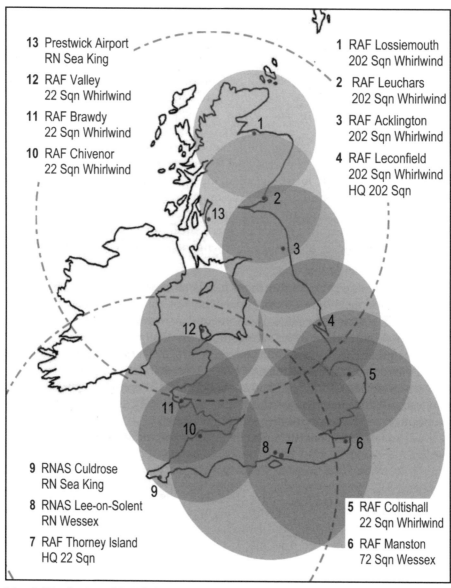

13 Prestwick Airport
RN Sea King

12 RAF Valley
22 Sqn Whirlwind

11 RAF Brawdy
22 Sqn Whirlwind

10 RAF Chivenor
22 Sqn Whirlwind

1 RAF Lossiemouth
202 Sqn Whirlwind

2 RAF Leuchars
202 Sqn Whirlwind

3 RAF Acklington
202 Sqn Whirlwind

4 RAF Leconfield
202 Sqn Whirlwind
HQ 202 Sqn

9 RNAS Culdrose
RN Sea King

8 RNAS Lee-on-Solent
RN Wessex

7 RAF Thorney Island
HQ 22 Sqn

5 RAF Coltishall
22 Sqn Whirlwind

6 RAF Manston
72 Sqn Wessex

Map 5. Distribution of SAR helicopters within the UK in late 1974.

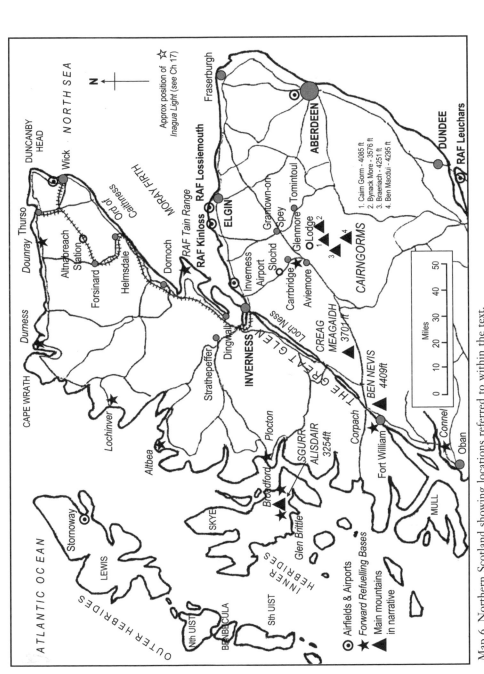

Map 6. Northern Scotland showing locations referred to within the text.

the distances or remoteness of the patient from a suitable hospital would have involved lengthy or difficult journeys.

To meet this task in late 1974, the RAF maintained eight helicopter flights from two squadrons dispersed around the UK coastline. In the north, 202 Squadron operated from Lossiemouth, Leuchars near St Andrews in Fife, Acklington near Alnwick in Northumberland, and Leconfield, near to Beverley in South Yorkshire, and also the Squadron Headquarters. South of a line approximately from the Humber to the Mersey, 22 Squadron maintained flights at Coltishall near Norwich, Chivenor near Braunton in Devon, Brawdy near St Davids in Pembrokeshire, Valley on Anglesey and Squadron Headquarters at Thorney Island. A single detached flight of 72 Squadron from Odiham provided cover from Manston in Kent. Each flight, commanded by a flight lieutenant, comprised four three-man crews of pilot, navigator and winchman, supported by the same number of four-man ground-crew teams. The two RAF squadrons were each commanded by a squadron leader. Search and rescue along the south coast was covered by the Royal Navy at RNAS Culdrose in Cornwall and Lee-on-Solent near Portsmouth, while a further Royal Navy unit operating from Prestwick made occassional contributions to the long-range helicopter cover on the west coast of Scotland.

Broadly coincident with this north/south divide were the two RAF Maritime Air Regions, each running a Rescue Co-ordination Centre responsible for the day-to-day operational tasking, or 'scrambling', of the search and rescue helicopters, and of the RAF mountain rescue teams with whom the helicopters frequently worked. All came under the command of an air marshal, the Air Officer Commanding 18 Group, whose other major asset was the Nimrod long-range maritime patrol force.

* * *

In 1974 both squadrons were equipped with the Westland Whirlwind Mk 10 helicopters, the same single-pilot operated type I had flown in Borneo. A piston-engined version of the Whirlwind had entered service with the RAF in the search and rescue role as early as 1956, but had been fitted with a jet engine in 1962. Apart from modifications to the airframe and rotor transmission to cope with the greater power output of the new engine, the helicopter had remained essentially unchanged since 1956. Compared with its successors in the role, the Whirlwind was a very basic and unsophisticated helicopter, lacking many of the features now considered essential for all-weather, day/night operations. It had no radar or visual imaging system to assist in the location of survivors or to navigate through mountainous areas at night. It had neither radio altimeter nor an auto-pilot or stabilisation system and even lacked any means of trimming the controls for hands-off flight. Despite its engine upgrade, it was still relatively under-powered and its maximum speed was only a modest 95 knots. Other serious limitations specifically in the search and rescue role were its short winch cable, measuring only 55 feet, and its desperately slow winching speed of barely one foot per second. Its radius of action, in other words how far the helicopter could fly before being forced to return for fuel, was only approximately 100 miles in still air. For the southern flights, this latter limitation was usually only of immediate concern when undertaking distant rescues at sea; for most land-based rescues there was usually a convenient civilian or military airfield nearby where refuelling could be carried out during the mission. In northern Scotland, however, the paucity of such facilities demanded other arrangements. This was achieved by locating dispersed fuel dumps at strategic coastal locations throughout the western Highlands, as well as near popular climbing areas such as the Cairngorms, Ben Nevis and the Cuillin Hills on the Isle of Skye. Here, some two dozen 45-gallon drums of aviation fuel would be stored in secure sheds constructed from redundant storage boxes for large jet engines, along with primitive hand-pumping equipment. Usually a local farmer or landowner would be charged with keeping an eye on the facility, while visiting the sites for re-stocking and monitoring fuel quality became a full-time job for a small, dedicated RAF team from Lossiemouth.

While easy to fly in good weather, the Whirlwind's lack of stabilisation or autopilot systems made it difficult and tiring to fly in poor visibility, especially for long periods at night or in cloud, where the pilot's utmost concentration was vital. Because of these perceived difficulties and the lack of effective illumination, no rescue capability was offered over the sea at night. Despite this, however, many successful night-time maritime missions were undertaken, with the crews exercising exceptional care and skill.

One essential feature of our role equipment was a small trolley on which was loaded a pile of optional rescue kit, which was too heavy to be carried on every flight. Instead, the trolley would be positioned by the door of the standby helicopter from where the crew would select items essential for each specific rescue mission. This might be a large, multi-seat inflatable dinghy for a long-range sea rescue, or one of the suitcase-sized 'portable' radios un-officially loaned to us by the police so that we could communicate with them when necessary. These police radios, patched into the Whirlwind's electrical system and used with temporarily attached aerials, were officially banned for use in our helicopters and technically illegal for us to operate. However, we had a close working relationship with the Chief Constables of our adjacent areas and they turned a blind eye to this minor matter. Later helicopters would have radios that covered all emergency service frequencies but, at this time, this was merely a dream.

* * *

Each of the eight search and rescue helicopter flights of 22 and 202 Squadrons normally maintained two Whirlwinds on standby, one to be used by the first standby crew, who had to be airborne in response to an emergency call within fifteen minutes by day or one hour by night, and a second one for use by the second standby crew, who had to be capable of responding within one hour during daylight hours only. If the first crew were scrambled, then the second crew would be called in to assume the status of first standby crew. In practice, these response times were invariably considerably shorter, with under five minutes by day and only fifteen minutes by night being regularly achieved. Because of the remoteness and isolation of much of our area of responsibility, there was an unwritten understanding at Lossiemouth that, whenever a crew was called out to the mountains or to a sea emergency during the night, a second crew would always come in to provide cover for their activities in case the first crew got into difficulties. All the other flights to the south of us had overlapping areas of responsibility and could therefore provide mutual cover, but the extensive areas to the north and west of Lossiemouth were our territory alone.

Another departure from the normal at Lossiemouth was that we usually held what we called the 'North Scottish spare', a backup Whirlwind to replace any of the two each at Lossiemouth and Leuchars that was likely to be unserviceable for an extended period. This was a situation I exploited to the full and, at busy times, it was not unusual for us to have all three helicopters airborne simultaneously on different rescue jobs, the third crew being drawn from those on stand-down or even on leave locally. Such was the dedication of the crews that there was never any difficulty in manning all three aircraft despite the additional demands it placed on crew duty times and rest periods. Indeed, such was the keenness to be involved that I sometimes had difficulty in persuading surplus volunteers to go back home and rest in preparation for later action should the demands of the situation look like extending over a lengthy period.

*   *   *

When taking my turn on shift, a typical routine for me would start at first morning light, at which time I would assume the role of second standby crew, on-call at home. Well before 1.00 pm, I would arrive at the Flight and, with the rest of my crew, be briefed on the current meteorological situation, the state of the helicopters and any other matters of relevance. I would already have changed into my flying kit, which included a single-piece waterproof immersion suit complete with attached rubber boots and with neoprene seals at the neck and wrists. Thus prepared, I and my crew would be ready to react immediately to any call once we had taken over standby from the previous crew on the stroke of one o'clock. If no emergency tasking was obviously imminent, we would plan, brief and fly an afternoon training flight, which would include exercises such as operating on the nearby cliffs, wet winching in the Moray Firth, which bordered the north side of the airfield, or carrying out a series of 'engine-off' landings with the engine disengaged from the rotors to replicate an actual engine failure. All these exercises would be recorded in our individual training records and would contribute towards the total number of mandatory exercises that had to be completed each month without fail. Next would come preparation for dinner. All of our meals were taken at the Flight's accommodation, with raw basic rations being provided by the messes but cooked by the crews with widely varying degrees of culinary success. The tasks of cooking and washing up were shared between air and ground-crew. If no night flying training was planned, the evening would be given up to personal administration, swotting up for visits by the flying examiners, known to us as the 'trappers', or relaxing with newspapers or the television. At Lossiemouth, a variety of locations had served for our sleeping accommodation, ranging from a misappropriated airman's married quarter adjacent to our hangar, to a Portacabin in the hangar, before bedrooms and changing rooms were finally built into a spare bay inside our hangar.

Assuming there had been no call-out during the night, my new day would start at 8.00 am with a thorough pre-flight inspection and engine runs on both Whirlwinds to allow the full length of their winch cables to be run out and inspected by my winchman. My navigator, in the meantime, would have updated the meteorological briefing and made his first calculations on our rescue capabilities in the light of the prevailing wind before preparing a cooked breakfast for us all. Again, any training flying required during the morning was carried out before briefing and handing over to the on-coming new crew. My crew would retire to their homes where we would again resume second standby duties until 1.00 pm the following day, when the whole cycle would be repeated. We normally worked for a continuous period of six days to this pattern before standing down for three days.

On some occasions this was a fairly routine sequence of events but on others I might be away from home on continuous duty for most of the six days. The job was very wearing on our wives, particularly for those of us with young children. They would never know for certain from one day to the next if, or when, we would be home during the shift periods and, even when on stand-down, we could disappear for days on end during particularly busy periods of emergency tasking as, for example, during the Scottish blizzards. Our social lives took quite a battering too, and it was sometimes the case when I would have to make my excuses and disappear during a supper engagement, exchanging the comfort of good company and food for a battle against the weather towards the mountains or out to sea in a draughty, dark cockpit scarcely half-an-hour later.

Despite all this, and also the fact that we were based on a busy, major RAF station, I thoroughly enjoyed the life on our small, self-contained unit that was permanently on a twenty-four hour operational standby for the saving of life. This would be the background for the next four years.

CHAPTER SEVENTEEN

A 'FAR-FETCHED AND UNREALSITIC' RESCUE?

One of the things that makes flying a search and rescue helicopter such a hugely satisfying job is the very wide variety of rescue missions undertaken. While missions can be broadly categorised into such general areas as land or mountain rescue, sea rescue, and medical evacuation, no two jobs in any of the categories are ever precisely the same. For the most part, tried and tested standard operating procedures are adopted to meet the situation presented, often requiring only minor adaptations to meet specific circumstances. Occasionally, however, these procedures are simply inadequate or impractical and the crew is then thrown on to its own resources to resolve the problem. This was especially true of operations in the ageing Whirlwind, where the extremely limited aircraft radio capability in our area of Scotland often meant that you were frequently out of contact and unable to seek additional help or advice. This, in itself, gave an 'edge' to the job and developed a high degree of self-reliance in my crews. The approach to a rescue was also often hampered by the limitations of the aircraft itself. Such was the case on 21 June 1975, when we were called to take an injured seaman off a cargo ship in thick sea fog.

This Saturday had dawned bright, sunny and calm but this early promise of good weather was rapidly changing. As we conducted the briefing for shift change-over from the previous crew soon after midday, a creeping wall of dense, cold sea mist rolled slowly across the airfield from the nearby coast, its grey tendrils insinuating themselves around the adjacent hangar and even obscuring our Whirlwind helicopter, sitting on the dispersal just outside the crew-room window. This sea fog, known locally as a *Haar*, was an unwelcome, but regular, feature of the north-east Scottish coast's summer weather. Perusal of the meteorological forecast for the region showed the fog was expected to cover large areas of the sea, extending from just inland from the coast to well beyond the distant oil platforms in the North Sea. With visibility on the airfield now down to just a few yards, there was no prospect of getting airborne for a training sortie, so Flight Lieutenant Dave Pells, my navigator, Master Air Electronics Operator Tony Goodyear, my winchman, and I settled down to a quiet shift hoping, perhaps, for a call to the Cairngorms and the possibility of some warm sun further inland.

Our various administrative activities were interrupted by the scramble bells ringing, heralding a call from the Rescue Co-ordination Centre. The Rescue Controller had received a call from HM Coastguard asking for an injured seaman to be lifted from a ship, the *Inagua Light*, engaged in oil rig support work and currently some 40 miles north-east of Fraserburgh. The vessel was making its way to put the injured seaman ashore at Aberdeen, but his condition was now giving cause for serious concern and urgent assistance had been requested. The Rescue Controller was aware of the meteorological situation and the vessel's crew had confirmed to the coastguard that they too were in thick fog. After a brief discussion with the Controller, I decided that we would get airborne to see what the precise conditions were and assess whether we could reach the ship.

Normally in very poor visibility or low cloud base, we would have carried out a take-off by sole reference to the Whirlwind's flight instruments but, once in the fog, or having climbed into clear air above it, we would have no means of descending below it to re-gain essential visual contact with the sea surface. It was essential, therefore, that I stayed in visual contact with the surface of the sea from immediately after take-off if we were to have any chance of finding the ship. Again, the Whirlwind's lack of modern equipment, in this case radar, was turning what should have been a fairly straightforward job into something of a challenge.

I took the precaution of taking on the absolute maximum fuel before setting off. This put the Whirlwind's weight up to its emergency overload limit but also imposed a maximum speed limit of 80 knots to reduce the additional stresses incurred on the rotor blades. I reasoned that we would need to fly much slower than our normal maximum of 95 knots in order to maintain good visual contact with the surface of the sea. This would also give us an extra twenty minutes or so of search time without too much of a penalty.

Unable now, because of our excessive weight, to carry out a vertical take-off, we lumbered airborne from a lengthy roll down the dimly discernible runway ten minutes later, at which point I was surprised at just how thick the fog was. However, by flying very low, a matter of a couple of feet above the calm sea, I was able to occupy a small gap where I could just make out sufficient of the surface ahead of me and to the side to provide me with some essential height reference to avoid flying into the sea. One of the Whirlwind's many shortcomings in the search and rescue role was the absence of a radar altimeter. This equipment bounces electronic echoes off the surface beneath the aircraft and gives the pilot a direct indication of his height above that surface to a precision of just a few inches. The standard barometric altimeter is all but useless in this situation, our present height above the sea being represented by an unreadable tiny fraction of the needle's width. We would have hit the sea before registering any change in indication. An added problem was that I was essentially flying the helicopter using its flight instruments to maintain straight and level flight, keeping an accurate speed and heading for Dave, my navigator, while glancing out frequently to avoid the sea. With the Whirlwind lacking even the most rudimentary stability or autopilot system to assist the pilot, flying it on instruments was demanding at the best of times. Now it required every ounce of my concentration – a few feet too high, and we would enter the dense fog and be forced to abort the mission, while a few feet too low would have us hitting the surface of the sea, with the inevitable disastrous consequences. Despite this, we settled into a steady interception course with the freighter, albeit still with a daunting one hour's flight time away at our optimum speed of 60 knots.

Because of our extreme low altitude we were not surprised to be unable to contact the vessel using our marine radio but communications with the coastguard were also proving less than satisfactory. For navigation in those pre-GPS days, we were using a now obsolete system called the Decca Navigator, which had been introduced into service towards the end of the Second World War. The navigator would take readings from four small gauges in the cockpit and then plot his position on a specially overprinted map. This system was accurate to within a few yards at fairly short ranges from the groups of aerials used in the system, but became progressively more inaccurate towards the extremes of reception. The system had been readily adopted for maritime use after the war and was particularly popular amongst fishing fleets. Its advantage lay in the fact that you could return precisely to a previous location by carefully manoeuvring until the Decca gauge indications exactly matched those corresponding to that position. However, it was not so good in fixing absolute positions in, say, latitude and longitude, and it was in this format that we were receiving intermittent reports of the *Inagua Light*'s progress, as well as the positions of other shipping in our proximity from the coastguard. Fortunately, there were very few other ships to navigate clear of; an encounter with a fishing boat suddenly appearing out of the fog would have made a very unwelcome addition to our day. To make matters worse, the fog then thickened appreciably. Even by reducing speed further, it was becoming almost impossible for me to see the sea surface adequately.

Just as I was on the point of turning back, my winchman, Tony, had the idea of lying prone on the floor of the cabin with his head stuck out of the open door and relaying to me the height of the wheels above the sea. One of the key elements in search and rescue helicopter operations is the mutual bond of trust and reliance that must exist between all of the crew members. The pilot is used to being unsighted when overhead a casualty, whether that be on land or over the sea, and is totally reliant on an accurate and informative commentary from the crew member in the cabin, usually the navigator, to position the aircraft with extreme accuracy where required, and also to ensure its clearance from obstructions, particularly around the tail rotor, as well as the safety of the winchman hanging below the helicopter. So it was not such an unusual situation for me to be in – I could concentrate on flying the aircraft very precisely while listening to the calm, measured tones of Tony instructing me to climb or descend a foot or so to maintain height just above the smooth surface of the sea.

*   *   *

Our situation was now well outside the realms of our standard operating procedures. We were extremely low over the sea, in thick fog, only intermittently in radio contact with the coastguard, and using a navigation system that could not guarantee getting us within visible range of our moving target. At any time, of course, I could have put the helicopter into a climb to get above the fog layer into bright sunshine and gone home. However, we agreed as a crew that, having come this far, we would press on a bit longer.

As we got nearer to the vessel, it soon became apparent that we had no communications with it whatsoever. Its crew could talk to the coastguard, and the coastguard could talk intermittently to us but, through some perversity or distortion of the radio transmission and reception, we could not talk directly to the *Inagua Light*. This posed another problem, as my plan had been to get the vessel to stop engines, get the crew on deck to listen for our approach and then guide us slowly towards it. On later reflection, the blanketing dense fog would probably have rendered our approach inaudible, but the lack of radio was not even going to give us the chance to try. We debated using the three-way link through the coastguard for the same approach, but reasoned that any delay, interruption or misunderstanding in the messages reaching us would probably result in an almighty CLANG! as we hit its side.

One well-tried navigational technique, used when trying to locate say, a small, or ill-defined feature on a coastline towards which you are flying, is to aim off deliberately by a small amount to one side. The idea here is that you do not fly directly to the feature but, when you hit the coastline you will know which way to turn along the coast to guarantee finding it. This was all very well, but we didn't have the luxury of a coastline or any similar line feature to utilise. However, if we could get the ship to increase its speed to the maximum when we got closer and get the crew to start dumping rubbish overboard to leave a well-marked wake in the calm water, we could then fly deliberately to pass the vessel on one side. Once sure of having passed it, we could then turn at right angles until we intercepted the wake. At this point I would then be able to turn to follow the wake until we came to the vessel. The coastguard passed this plan to the *Inagua Light* and Dave re-calculated our course so that we would pass the vessel on our starboard side by a safe margin.

.. HM The Queen reviews the Passing-Out Parade of No. 157 Course, RAF South Cerney. Author econd from left on front rank. (*Alpha Photo Press Ltd*)

!. De Havilland Vampire T11 (top) and Gloster Meteor T7 as used for advanced flying training at RAF Swinderby. (*Crown Copyright*)

3. Award of 'Wings'. Author seated front left, Des Sheen behind. Martin Todd seated front right, Tim Webb behind. (*Crown Copyright*)

4. Valiants of 90 Squadron engaged in air-to-air refuelling. (*Crown Copyright*)

No.55 BASIC HELICOPTER COURSE

PLT. OFF.	FG. OFF.	FLT. LT.	FG. OFF.	FLT. LT.
I.S. BALDIE.	G.H. LEEMING.	P.V. DEAKIN.	G.W. MOFFATT.	I. WINES.

PLT. OFF.	PLT. OFF.	PLT. OFF.	FG. OFF.	PLT. OFF.	PLT. OFF.	M. PLT.
N. MACGREGOR	D.J. CAREY.	N.R.W. HIBBERD.	J.H.B. WILKINSON.	F.M. RAMSHAW.	M. BETTS.	G.E. VENABLES.

FG. OFF.	FLT. LT.	FLT. LT.	FLT. LT.	FLT. LT.
D.R. COSBY.	A.C. COOPER.	R.H. CUNNINGHAM.	A.R. FRASER.	I. M. CHALMERS.

5. 'Rogues' Gallery', Tern Hill 1965. (*Crown Copyright*)

6. Nanga Gaat, Borneo from the air. (*The Author*)

7. Whirlwinds of 110 Squadron operating at Nanga Gaat with a rare visitor, a Belvedere of 66 Squadron. (*Crown Copyright*)

8. Casual dress in the 'Officers' Mess'. Mike Ramshaw in foreground with Paul Deakin behind. (*The Author*)

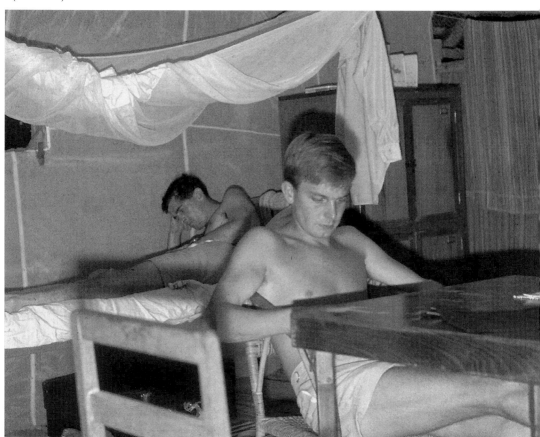

9. Typical helicopter landing site at approximately 5,000 feet on border ridge south of Long Jawi. Note backdrop of uncut trees to hide site from enemy territory beyond. (*The Author*)

10. 'Bonzo' at Nanga Gaat. (*The Author*)

11. Making close acquaintance with a slippery viper. (*The Author*)

12. Posing at Kuching after forced landing. (*Crown Copyright*)

13. Enjoying evening entertainment in local Iban longhouse. (*The Author*)

14. Result of my forced landing south of Brunei. (*The Author*)

15. Winchman, Dave Lloyd, consults with Mountain Rescue Team watched over by my navigator, Bill Gault – Stone Chute, Sgurr Alasdair, Skye. (*John Beatty*)

16. Rescue in the Stone Chute, Sgurr Alasdair, Skye a few minutes after previous photograph. (*John Beatty*)

17. Spot the winchman! Andy Ball dangles on 120 feet of tape during first authorised mountain training flight using the tape. (*Crown Copyright*)

18. Rare moment of relaxation while waiting for a refuel during tape winching mountain training. Author (left), Andy Ball (centre), navigator Brian Canfer (right). *(Crown Copyright)*

19. Winchman Dave Lloyd escorts rescued blizzard victims from their abandoned car.
(Brian Canfer – Crown Copyright)

20. Waiting for the mid-day express to Inverness! My Whirlwind temporarily parked on the only clear area for miles around. (*Brian Canfer – Crown Copyright*)

21. Stranded travellers at Slochd await arrival of urgent medical supplies. (*Brian Canfer – Crown Copyright*)

22. Recipients of Royal Humane Society Bronze Medal from the AOC. Left to right: Ray Sefton, Mick Anderson, AVM Kennedy, author, Bill Gault, Malcolm Carlyle. (*Crown Copyright*)

23. 'There will always be a place for you helicopter boys in a Scottish Air Force'. Local MP and member of the Scottish Nationalist Party, Winnie Ewing, makes a bid for Scottish independence to a mixed reception! (1977). (*Crown Copyright*)

24. Receiving the Queen's Commendation for Valuable Service in the Air from the AOC, AVM Kennedy. (*Crown Copyright*)

5. The Search and Rescue Training Unit becomes part of RAF Strike Command. (*Crown Copyright*)

6. Receiving the RAF Escaping Society Silver Trophy from Air Chief Marshal Sir Lewis Hodges. Left to right: Mike Dane, Sir Lewis, Mick Holloway, author, Carl Pollock. (*Crown Copyright*)

27. One of our Wessex helicopters from RAF Valley blows aircraft debris around as it finds a landing place at Lockerbie. (*Cumberland News Photographic Archive*)

28. Exhausted firemen take a break amongst the burnt-out cars on the A74 alongside Lockerbie. (*Cumberland News Photographic Archive*)

29. A policeman and fireman survey burning homes at Lockerbie. (*Robin Bryden*)

30. Aerial view of the devastation at Sherwood Crescent, Lockerbie. (*Cumberland News Photographic Archive*)

31. The Pan Am 747 cockpit in a field alongside Tundergarth Church. (*Bob Geddes*)

32. Close up of destroyed cockpit – the iconic image of the Lockerbie bombing. (*Robin Bryden*)

Eventually, we estimated that we had passed the freighter and were re-assured to receive a message from the coastguard saying that the crew had heard us pass in the distance. I promptly turned right and was soon gratified to detect the slight undulations of the bow waves, followed shortly after by a line of floating rubbish. So far, so good. Carefully creeping up this well-defined line, we soon detected the foaming wake from the propeller wash, followed very rapidly by the sheer black stern of the *Inagua Light*. The visi-bility was so poor that we could not see the stern rails or the deck above us, only the blank wall of steel. I quickly raised the Whirlwind's nose and reduced power to kill the final remnants of our closing speed, only to be startled to feel the aircraft settling in a gentle descent towards the sea despite the application of full power. Up to this point, my concern with our fuel status had related only to the higher than normal fuel consumption during the low-speed transit from our base and how long we would have for searching if we had initially been unsuccessful in finding the ship. A helicopter maintaining a hover requires high power settings, the requirement being proportionally higher if the aircraft is heavy. I had committed a cardinal error of failing to allow for the weight of the extra fuel when attempting to come to the hover; the aircraft was simply too heavy even for full power to hold us in a hover. In short, we were now in serious danger of settling ignominiously onto the sea surface, thereby failing in our rescue mission as well as losing the aircraft.

I quickly used the last foot or so of our descent to accelerate gently back into forward flight, gaining the advantage of an aerodynamic phenomenon known as 'translational lift'. I was now forced to fly a slow, tight circuit around the sides of the moving vessel while desperately trying to keep its indistinct bulk in sight. At the same time, Dave was rapidly calculating what fuel we would now need to complete the winching and continue on to Aberdeen with our casualty. With this figure established, I hit the fuel jettison switch to start dumping our excess fuel overboard to reduce our weight to a level low enough to have sufficient power to hover and lift the additional weight of our casualty. What the crew of the *Inagua Light* made of this per-formance I never discovered. I could imagine their anxious, puzzled faces lining the rails, straining to penetrate the fog, heads turning to follow the sound of our invisible progress as we circled their vessel close to its sides.

Eventually, the fuel gauge showed the calculated required fuel level and, switching off the fuel jettison switch, I stabilised the helicopter in a hover close by its port side, while Dave prepared to winch Tony over the side. With the gentle application of more power, we slowly rose up the side of the *Inagua Light*, past the line of curious faces at the railings and up into the densest fog, where only parts of the mast and superstructure were fleetingly visible as references. During this time, Dave had commenced his 'patter' – the con-tinuous stream of directions to me to achieve a position hovering precisely over the clearest area of deck, interspersed with a commentary on the frantic activity on the deck as the crew rushed to get the casualty to this area on a stretcher.

Normally, the choice of winching area, dictated largely by the proximity of masts and rigging, would have been communicated to the vessel by radio and any obstructions removed or secured before winching, but the lack of radio contact precluded any such preparation, leaving the crew ignorant of our requirements and intentions. Tony was quickly lowered onto the deck, carrying with him the helicopter's stretcher. This was a Neil Robertson stretcher which, being made of wooden battens and canvas, was specially adapted with slings to enable a casualty to be secured safely during winching. Tony worked quickly and expertly to transfer the casualty into this stretcher, while Dave continued his calm, unhurried patter.

'Steady . . . steady . . . height is good . . . winchman on the deck . . . right one . . . steady . . . winchman securing casualty in stretcher . . . steady . . . steady . . . height is good,' and later, 'Steady . . . height is good . . . ready to lift . . . steady . . . winching in . . . clear the deck,' and so on, until the winchman and casualty had been safely winched on board and were secured in the cabin.

I then manoeuvred the helicopter away from the ship until clear of the railings, before allowing it to descend slowly until we were once more just above the surface of the sea and in sight of it. Accelerating slowly, we departed the *Iguana Light* and set course towards Aberdeen, with Tony resuming his position at the cabin door reporting my height as on our outward journey. I called the coastguard radio to report the successful uplift of the casualty but, again, fate intervened – we had now lost all radio contact with them too!

*   *   *

At this point, I urgently needed to know what the weather was at Aberdeen. Was the fog as thick there as we were experiencing out at sea? This would prevent me from flying a 'blind' approach to the airport using only the aircraft instruments – I needed a minimum cloud-base of at least some 200 feet in order not to contravene the strictly enforced standards for operating into a civil airport. On present showing, I would be lucky to have 20 feet! We were therefore faced with the prospect of another slow, prolonged transit flight at low level, but this time with the added difficulty of making a landfall in very poor visibility on a cliff-fringed coastline. While I had sufficient fuel to fly far enough inland to be sure of reaching clear skies, the condition of our casualty was making it imperative that he reached a hospital as quickly as possible. In short, we were not in distress, but our passenger certainly soon would be. Accordingly, I made a transmission on the international distress frequency to the effect that I required urgent assistance. Although far too low to receive any land-based station, I received an immediate response from an airliner some 30,000 feet above me. The captain relayed my request for the Aberdeen weather and was soon able to report that the airport was basking in warm sunshine.

With this welcome news, I quickly put the helicopter into a climb and, after a few moments in the thick, swirling fog, we burst out into brilliant sunshine. Using the maximum speed, we soon reached the boundary of the foggy carpet and completed the rest of the flight to Aberdeen in excellent weather. Freed from the limitations of the weather, I was able to fly direct to Aberdeen Royal Infirmary and deliver my casualty to the medical staff waiting on the emergency helicopter landing pad.

Returning to the airport to refuel before our return flight to Lossiemouth, one of the first people to greet us was the local reporter from the *Aberdeen Press and Journal*. With a sharp nose for anything happening in his area, he had somehow heard from his various contacts of the recovery of the injured seaman. However, being totally unaware of the weather out at sea, he merely commented that we had had an exceptionally nice day for our mission and enquired if there was anything of interest to make reporting the story worthwhile! While Tony and I supervised the refuelling of our helicopter, my navigator, Dave, took the opportunity to acquaint him fully with the facts of the operation.

*   *   *

An amusing footnote to this story occurred some months later. BBC Television was running a drama series called *Oil Strike North* based on Scotland's booming off-shore oil industry. One of the episodes had featured a helicopter rescue that almost exactly reproduced our earlier experience and this had drawn a viewer's scathing comment in the *Radio Times* to the effect that the use of the ship's wake and dumped rubbish was 'far-fetched and unrealistic'. 'Modern helicopters,' he said, 'were now equipped with all modern aids, including radar, to enable them to effect rescues safely and easily in all weathers.' I wish! It was gratifying to read the producer's reply, which stated that the programme's events had been based closely on an actual rescue carried out recently in the North Sea off the coast of Scotland.

CHAPTER EIGHTEEN

MOUNTAINEERING IN WELLIES FOR BEGINNERS

Thursday 17 July 1975 was one of those perfect Scottish summer days – hot and sunny with only the gentlest of breezes to stir the windsock on the airfield at Lossiemouth. After taking over the search and rescue standby shift shortly after mid-day, I and my crew, navigator Flight Lieutenant Bill Gault and winchman Master Signaller Jim Clark, settled down to wait for what we thought would inevitably be a call for help from the Cairngorms, or possibly further afield. In good weather, the most frequent problems were with inexperienced or ill-equipped walkers who had been lured to the mountains by the warmth and good visibility, not realising that walking or scrambling up these giant chunks of granite demanded more than a pair of flip-flops for footwear, or they were completely unaware of the very significant temperature reduction with height. When these people encountered trouble, they became the bread and butter of the regional mountain rescue teams but, occasionally, complications such as the rapid onset of hypothermia or a broken limb would require our assistance for their recovery to a hospital.

The ground-crew had replaced the winch cable on one of our standby Whirlwinds and it now required rigorous checking and testing to ensure that the winch functioned correctly – after all, the winchman's very life depended on its faultless operation. This check involved winching a heavy concrete weight up and down while the helicopter was held in a hover. While Bill busied himself with entering the multitude of daily corrections and revisions to the maps and charts carried in the navigation bag, Jim and I got airborne to carry out this check. Some twenty minutes later Jim pronounced himself satisfied with the winch, little realising just how much he would rely on it later that day.

After a break for an evening meal, and with the prospects of being called out now appearing increasingly unlikely, Jim and I took off again to carry out some precision winching exercises, vying with each other to present ever more difficult challenges to test our skills. Again, we had no idea just how far we were to be tested in just an hour or so. I had then planned to round off the sortie with a series of engine-off landings – vital training that enabled us to put our 4-ton Whirlwind gently onto the ground without damage in the event of our single engine failing.

I had just completed a couple of these engine-off landings when the radio crackled into life; it was Bill warning us of a mountain job in the Cuillin Hills on the Isle of Skye. I quickly returned to the dispersal and, while waiting for Bill to join us, I kept the engine and rotors turning as the ground-crew topped up the Whirlwind's fuel tanks. Within minutes, and with everyone on board, we lifted off into the warm, calm evening air, relieved to be doing 'our job' at last. Staying low and just off the coast to avoid a Nimrod aircraft flying around Kinloss, we watched the 'Mexican Wave' as successive late sunbathers and picnic parties on the beach responded enthusiastically to our passage along the Moray Firth. Soon we were into the hills and mountains on our track to Skye, a route so familiar to us all that no formal navigation was required. Instead, Jim checked out the winching kit, harness, stretcher, rescue strop and first-aid kit, while Bill double-checked the accuracy of the plotted position of our reported casualty and briefed Jim and me on the situation. From his examination of the large scale map of the area, it soon became apparent that this could prove to be a bit more awkward than the average rescue. The map showed a massive, near-vertical rock face, Sron na Ciche, forming the eastern buttress beneath the peak of Sgurr Alasdair – at 3,254 feet the highest mountain on Skye. The casualty's position was reported at some 300 feet from the top of the 1,300-foot slab of rock.

With the sun slowly sinking in the west, the contours of the hills and mountains were thrown into stark relief, with the slopes facing the sun bathed in a brilliant golden glow, while other faces and corries were thrown into deep, impenetrable shadows. Wishing to avoid the risk of having to break off the operation because of shortage of fuel after our transit from Lossiemouth, I elected to take on a bit more fuel at one of our forward refuelling bases at Glenbrittle near the foot of Sgurr Alasdair. These bases also served as a useful rendezvous for the local mountain rescue teams and emergency services. While Jim supervised the setting up and testing of a couple of 45-gallon drums of fuel, Bill and I received an update on the casualty's situation. Having set off at the first alert, Gerry Akroyd, leader of the Skye Mountain Rescue Team, had just reached the casualty and was in radio contact with the rest of his team now assembled at the refuelling base rendezvous.

The casualty's situation was not good. His fall had been broken by his rope, but this had left him lying precariously on a narrow ledge barely 2 feet wide. To make matters worse, he had sustained serious head injuries as well as several broken limbs, and therefore needed urgent medical attention. His two climbing companions were roped to the sheer face just above him, but unable to help. The only feasible way for the mountain rescue team to get him off the mountain would be to lower him, secured in a stretcher, to the floor of the corrie over 1,000 feet below. With this in mind, Gerry Akroyd called for a couple of drums of long climbing ropes to be positioned above him for use by his team and I agreed to fly those up to the summit first, followed by the rest of his team. With refuelling completed, we again got airborne and headed towards the rock face a couple of miles away. Luck was on our side – the face was brilliantly lit by the setting sun. Despite this, it was very difficult to pinpoint the scene of the accident. This was a common problem in mountain rescue. Until the searcher's eye became attuned to the scale of the human figure within the scenery, it was easily possible to fly past a casualty while almost looking directly at him without seeing him.

*   *   *

We desperately looked for any climbers on the seemingly bare face of the huge cliff and soon our attention was attracted by the waving of Gerry at the casualty's position. I quickly manoeuvred the Whirlwind to what appeared to be a flattish area of rock at the top of Sron na Ciche buttress, directly above the casualty's position. With me holding the Whirlwind in a low hover, Jim and Bill heaved out the drums of climbing rope and then watched in disbelief as they both rolled slowly towards the cliff edge and plunged into the void. With the option of lowering the casualty down the rock face now lost unless more ropes could be found, it was time to revert to Plan B. I moved the helicopter until we too were over the sheer drop, before descending gently to place the casualty on our starboard side. Having established a steady hover several feet away from the cliff face, we assessed the casualty's situation. It was indeed as precarious as had been described to us on our earlier briefing – a narrow, thin ledge, already somewhat overcrowded with the casualty, his two climbing companions and Gerry Akroyd. My task at this stage was to maintain the hover to give my crew the best view of the situation while, at the same time, checking for suitable references that I could visually lock on to when it came to the precision part of attempting to winch Jim down to the casualty and subsequently recovering them both to the safety of the aircraft cabin. While Jim and Bill discussed our options, I calculated that I had a sufficient margin of power to be able to lift the additional weight of the casualty.

The plan was to lower Jim, complete with a lightweight stretcher and first-aid rucksack, to the casualty. Once Jim was secure on the ledge, I would then move well away to remove the noisy, disorientating and buffeting downwash from the helicopter's rotor onto the ledge, thus allowing Jim to communicate easily with the casualty and render any essential immediate first aid before securing him in the stretcher ready for winching.

Jim Clark was no climber. He had a strong dislike of heights and was much happier when being trawled through the rough, cold waters of the Moray Firth in the nautical part of our rescue work. Despite this, he had never demurred from being winched out onto all manner of cliff faces or mountain crags. This evening, however, was about to get a lot more exciting than he had bargained for, and his customary grimace, deep breath, eyes shut and tightly clenched teeth, would be more than justified as Bill attached him to the winch hook and swung him out of the cabin on the thin cable with over 1,000 feet of fresh air beneath his feet.

*   *   *

Picking up the commentary from Bill, I was guided to a position as near the vertical as possible above the casualty, while Bill continued to lower Jim on the winch. As I moved the helicopter gently sideways to my right, I lost sight of the casualty's position as it disappeared beneath me and transferred my attention to the thrashing rotor blades also closing with the rock face. I was reassured to see our Whirlwind's shadow etched clearly on the face, illuminated by the golden light of the setting sun. Crucially, I could see exactly how close the blades were getting to the rock as shadow and blades slowly moved closer together while Bill continued his commentary. In most circumstances, accurate judgement of blade clearances from obstructions had always proved notoriously difficult and, in order to provide an adequate safe clearance, the RAF's limitation on winching specified a minimum horizontal distance of 15 feet. The shadow of our blades was already showing a clearance of only a foot or so but, because of the near-vertical cliff, Jim was still almost a blade's length from the ledge and at the full 55 feet extent of the cable. Reaching out and grasping the top of the cable, Bill pushed and pulled at it to set up a pendulum motion to try and bring Jim closer to the ledge.

As the swings got bigger, so did my input on the controls to prevent the aircraft lurching sideways into the cliff face. Wider and wider the pendulum swung, until Jim was eventually able to kick off at each contact with the face, further increasing the arc of his swing. Suddenly, the aircraft lurched unexpectedly away from the cliff as Jim managed to grab onto a rocky outcrop but his hold was so tentative that another vicious lurch, this time towards the rock face, told me that he had lost his grip and was again swinging free beneath me. After several similar unsuccessful attempts, Bill directed me slightly lower and a little to one side of the ledge. Apparently Jim was becoming concerned about the proximity of my blades to the rock face and was indicating the clearance with his hands just a few inches apart, not realising that I was already only too well aware of the tiny distance separating us from the cliff. He also indicated to Bill that he wanted to try and make contact with a small rocky outcrop below the ledge. Again, Bill set up the gradually increasing pendulum, aided again by Jim kicking off against the rock face. The helicopter lurched again as Jim got a handhold but this time there was no corresponding lurch. Instead came a chilling call from Bill.

'Bloody hell, Jim's come off the hook!'

At the same instant, I had sensed the sudden change of trim and reduction in weight on the winch and, in horror, I quickly moved the Whirlwind sideways away from the face to regain sight of the situation, fully expecting to see no sign of Jim. I was therefore amazed at the sight that greeted me. Jim, in his winchman's yellow rubber immersion suit, complete with sealed-on rubber wellington boots, was precariously spread-eagled on the outcrop of rock some 25 feet immediately below the casualty with the valley floor a dizzying 1,000 feet below. His predicament was not helped in the least by the stretcher, which he was holding horizontally at chest height against the rock, nor by the bulky first-aid rucksack on his back threatening to pull him backwards off-balance.

Jim's situation was now dire. Realising that he would never be able to hang onto the rock with the weight of the heavy winch hook assembly (a fourteen-pound lead weight was permanently attached to the hook to ensure it normally hung vertically), Jim had made the brave decision to detach himself from the winch, his only lifeline. Bill and I watched in awe and dread as Jim tentatively tested his balance, his hands clawing at the rock-face while his wellington-clad feet scrabbled desperately for footholds. Then slowly, so slowly, he managed first to manoeuvre the stretcher to a vertical position and then, bit by bit, inch by precarious inch, feed it up the sheer cliff face towards the reaching arms of Gerry Akroyd. As the stretcher got further above his head, Jim's position appeared to get even more precarious – he still had to get himself up that near-vertical face. Scarcely daring to breath, Bill and I watched Jim's painfully slow progress, expecting any moment to see him wheeling off into space. Eventually, he was able to reach up and be grasped by Gerry on the ledge.

For someone who disliked heights so much, Jim's problems were far from over. He still had to administer basic first aid to the casualty and then secure him in the stretcher ready for winching back into the helicopter. Moving with quiet precision on the narrow ledge, Jim quickly did his job, only too well aware that a single slip or trip on the accumulation of ropes and equipment now littering the confined area could send him plummeting to certain death. It was with some relief that I saw Jim's arms, outstretched above his head, signalling that everything was ready for his recovery. Once again picking up Bill's commentary, I manoeuvred the Whirlwind to our previous winching position, while Bill winched out the empty hook towards the waiting group on the ledge. Again, Bill commenced the pendulum motion on the cable, aiming to place the swinging hook within Jim's reach. Unfortunately, the strength of the rotor downwash blowing against the cliff face served to hold it stubbornly out of reach. Further attempts were made using increased weight on the hook to try to increase the size of the swing, but all to no avail.

Stowed away under the cabin front seats of our Whirlwind was a waterproof bag that contained spare maps and all manner of miscellaneous pieces of equipment that might possibly prove useful in a rescue situation. Amongst this miscellany was a standard 200-foot climbing rope, tightly coiled and never used; it was this that now offered the best chance of extracting Jim and his casualty from their precarious situation. This would be the first occasion on the squadron that this rope, attached to the hook to give an effective winch length of just over 250 feet, would be used.

Bill quickly tied the requisite bowline loop in one end of the rope and attached it to the hook, then weighted the other with a helmet bag filled with several heavy items of equipment before paying it out under the aircraft. Repositioning once more towards the ledge, I was now able to hover so much higher that Bill was able to talk me into a position directly above the casualty while I could maintain a safer clearance of my rotor blades against the rock face. Jim had secured the rope to himself and the stretcher, and Bill winched them both clear of the ledge. Our next task was to find a suitable area nearby where we could place Jim on the ground, then either land alongside him to get the casualty into the cabin, or descend low enough for them to be winched aboard.

The problem that I now faced was that the bottom of the valley was in deep shadow, with the contrast between the brightly lit rock face and the dark valley bottom rendering the latter effectively in total darkness. As I slowly descended towards the valley floor, neither Bill nor I could accurately judge our rate of descent in order to give Jim and his casualty a soft landing. We decided to resort to descending in increments of just less than 50 feet. I came to a hover while Bill winched out all of the cable in the hope of landing Jim gently on the ground. When this did not happen, I descended a further 50 feet while Bill winched fully in. Coming to a hover again, Bill repeated the winching out process. This procedure was repeated several more times until, at last, Jim was placed gently on the ground. It was then only a matter of seconds for Jim to re-attach to the winch hook and to recover him and his casualty to the aircraft before delivering the injured climber to Broadford Hospital on Skye.

Twilight had now fallen and, as our operating orders prohibited a nighttime recovery to Lossiemouth through the mountains in our single-engined Whirlwind, we refuelled the aircraft from drums of fuel at the Broadford airstrip, then landed in a convenient field at Broadford conveniently alongside the Dunollie Hotel. The Hillditch family who ran this hotel were valuable friends to search and rescue crews who found themselves grounded overnight on Skye. If no bedrooms were available, the family were more than happy to sort out extra blankets and pillows and allow the crews to sleep on the barroom floor. They were also a reliable source of a meal whatever the time of arrival and, true to form, a hot meal was waiting for us by the time we had 'put our helicopter to bed' for the night, disconnecting the batteries, tying down the blades, and securing the cockpit and cabin.

* * *

We had just finished our meal when Bill took a telephone call for us from the Rescue Co-ordination Centre. A yacht on passage through the Western Isles had failed to make routine radio contact or respond to coastguard calls for more than twenty-four hours and there were now concerns for the safety of the two crewmembers. Would we be willing to carry out a quick search in the vicinity of Skye? Among the natural responses to the adrenaline rush following successful completion of a difficult or dangerous rescue are euphoria and overconfidence in one's abilities. It was in this light that we accepted the mission without question, never seriously questioning what our chances might be of finding a relatively small boat in a big sea, and with no recent position on which to base our search plan, with no radar, and a dark, moonless night. We prepared our Whirlwind and were soon airborne, initially heading off in the direction suggested by the Rescue Controller.

Flying solely by my instruments because of the lack of any external references, it was soon obvious that a conventional search of open sea was unlikely to yield any result. We therefore decided to concentrate our search around the coastline and bays of the several small islands lying to the east of Skye. Following Bill's directions, we picked up the first island in the sweep of our searchlight and proceeded to fly low and slowly around its coastline, before moving on and repeating the procedure around the next island. On a sweep of our third island we spotted a sailing boat lying at anchor in darkness in a tiny inlet. When the noise of our arrival and hover overhead failed to elicit any response from the vessel, we winched Jim onto an adjacent headland and then flew away while he attempted to hail the crew. Eventually, the crew stumbled onto the deck, confirmed the boat's name as that of the missing vessel, promised to make contact by telephone at the earliest opportunity and then promptly disappeared below deck. We winched up a slightly bemused Jim and flew back to Broadford, once again to put our Whirlwind to bed. The Rescue Controller was duly impressed when Bill rang to report that 'of course we found it!'

On our return to Lossiemouth the following morning, we were greeted by the local press and photographers – it had been D Flight, 202 Squadron's 100th rescue since being redeployed to Scotland from Southern England the previous year. Jim's part in the rescue only began to emerge as the fuss died down.

Several changes came about as a result of our report and recommendations following this mountain rescue. There was cautious acceptance of the use of the rope as a routine procedure to extend the Whirlwind's limited winching capability and eventually we were cleared to use it in training, initially only with inert loads, but later with live loads as confidence rapidly increased. The Lossiemouth crews carried out several more rescues using the rope, a particularly enterprising one being the night rescue of two injured youths trapped in a sea cave by the rising tide. The winchman was placed in an inflated dinghy secured to the helicopter with the rope then blown by the downwash into the back of the cave. With the casualties on board the dinghy, they were then towed out into the open sea by the helicopter and recovered normally by the winch. The long rope was soon superseded by two linked 60-foot lengths of drum-mounted tape, which allowed greater flexibility in use, as well as more rapid deployment. This equipment, in turn, became redundant with the introduction of a 300-foot winch on the newer Wessex helicopters. Also, in recognition of the dangers of being caught on a mountainside with inappropriate equipment, search and rescue helicopter crewmen were issued with climbing boots and better protective clothing.

Later that year, Master Signaller Jim Clark received the Air Force Cross from the Queen at Buckingham Palace for his courageous actions during that mountain rescue on the Isle of Skye. He also became one of a select band entitled to wear both the Air Force Cross and the Air Force Medal, the latter having been awarded during an earlier tour when, as a flight sergeant, he had distinguished himself as an instructor in search and rescue training duties.

CHAPTER NINETEEN

THE FLYING SNOWMAN

With Britain's major mountain ranges sited within our 'patch', it was inevitable that many of our search and rescue tasks at Lossiemouth involved assistance to climbers who had met with serious misfortunes. There appeared to be no regular season for climbing activities. Even mountains covered in ice and snow proved no deterrent, merely attracting more experienced and 'technical' climbers, the type who would think little of climbing straight up a frozen waterfall. Weather was always a major consideration when carrying out mountain rescues, with cloud cover and wind frequently conspiring to make life difficult for us. Winter brought the added problems of snow and more extreme weather to cope with. Two incidents serve to illustrate how some of these extremes could affect the conduct of a rescue.

*   *   *

The first of these occurred on 12 March 1976. I and my crew, navigator Flight Lieutenant Bill Gault and winchman Sergeant Dave Lloyd, had completed our duty shift at 1.00 pm and had stood down, only to be called back later that afternoon to assist the first standby crew. They had been scrambled to an avalanche at Coire an Lochan on the northern face of Cairn Gorm to recover six casualties, three on stretchers and three 'walking wounded'.

We landed at Glenmore Lodge, Scotland's National Outdoor Training Centre near to Aviemore, our usual rendezvous point for Cairngorms rescue operations, and, after a quick briefing from its Principal, Fred Harper, we followed our first Whirlwind, callsign Rescue 26, into the gloomy late afternoon. I had collected two members of the mountain rescue team to reinforce their colleagues already on the mountain but violent up- and down-draughts in the gusting 50-knot wind soon made it almost impossible to maintain safe control, forcing me to off-load them near a mountain refuge hut to reduce weight and improve my helicopter's margin of manoeuvrability. The team on the mountain had established a helicopter pick-up point at 3,000 feet near the base of the corrie. This had been used throughout the earlier rescues by the first helicopter, which was now in the process of loading more casualties on board before flying them down to Glenmore Lodge. I was able to catch brief glimpses of the other helicopter's flashing anti-collision lights higher up the mountain through the swirling snow as we waited on the ground by the refuge hut. A few minutes later Rescue 26 lifted off and passed close by us, advising us that there would be a delay of at least ten minutes before the final two stretcher cases were expected to arrive at the pick-up point from higher up the mountain. With the imminent onset of darkness and the weather now deteriorating rapidly, I decided to get airborne and attempt a pick-up from their current position. Time was also of the essence for at least one of these casualties who had sustained serious head injuries. I located the first stretcher case about 300 feet above the pick-up point and Dave was winched out to secure the stretcher to the cable. This lift went quickly and smoothly with only severe turbulence and frequent violent gusts of strong wind making it difficult for me to maintain a stable hover.

There was no sign of the second casualty, so I landed at the pick-up point to obtain an update on the situation. We had no direct radio contact with the team bringing the casualty down but the party at the pick-up point advised us of yet a further delay of about ten minutes. While sitting on the ground, my Whirlwind took on a life of its own, lifting a few inches off the ground before slamming down again, despite no control input from me. The conditions were now so severe that I should have abandoned the rescue operation at that point. However, we had a critically injured casualty tantalisingly close and we were determined to try our hardest to save him.

At long last, news came to us that the second stretcher was some 300 feet above us and approaching the point where we had made the first lift. Taking off once more, I was concerned to note the further deterioration in the weather that had taken place during our wait on the ground. The wind had strengthened beyond the initial 50 knots, with corresponding increases in the severity of the turbulence. This required me to make rapid and frequent changes of engine power, varying from idling to full power in order to maintain control. As I established a hover over the casualty's position on the steep mountainside, my visual references on the snow-covered rock-face just a few feet away were fading in and out of my view as swirling snow created white-out conditions, while the rapidly changing wind direction caused great flurries of snow actually to blow through the cockpit, temporarily blinding me, obscuring much of the instrument panel and clinging to my flying clothing. Dave Lloyd later recounted that, while being winched up with the second stretcher, he glanced up at the cockpit and was surprised to see the helicopter being flown by 'a bloody snowman!'

Despite the difficulty I had experienced holding the hover, the lift had proceeded fairly quickly up to this point. Suddenly, however, things went seriously wrong. The second stretcher became jammed in the entrance door, just as we were caught up in a mighty up-draught that thrust the 4-ton Whirlwind upwards, causing me to lose sight of all my visual references. My face had been frozen into a mask beneath the snow, but I was just able to shout a warning as we climbed rapidly. We were now in a dangerous situation – I had no power on, but our helicopter was still climbing quickly, a stretcher was stuck in the entrance door with two-thirds of it still outside and Dave was still hanging on the winch cable, bracing himself and the rest of the stretcher as best he could against the helicopter's side.

I turned away from the now invisible mountain face and transferred immediately to instrument flight, making frantic sweeps with my hand in an attempt to clear the snow from the instrument faces so that I could gain information on such vital aspects as which way up we were. As suddenly as the up-draught had started, we were gripped in a strong down-draught causing us to descend at a rate that even the application of full power did little to arrest. Fortuitously, I spotted a tiny break in the cloud below us and a flat-looking area at an apparent crazy angle to us. Rolling the Whirlwind to match the level surface, I landed on what was a small snow-covered frozen lake. Dave and Bill immediately set to work getting the second stretcher stowed safely on board while spindrift whirled about us and the helicopter shuddered and skittered about on the ice. When the stretchers were eventually secured side-by-side on the cabin floor, we continued our bumpy flight down to Glenmore Lodge where we landed at last light. Sadly, one of our casualties had died.

After refuelling at Aviemore, we flew our two casualties to hospital at Inverness before returning home.

*   *   *

The second of these mountain rescues took place under very different conditions, albeit at similar times and places. It was on 2 April 1978 when we were called to the assistance of two Royal Marines who had fallen on Ben Macdui, at 4,295 feet, the highest mountain in the Cairngorm range. The call had come in mid-afternoon and we took off into a clear sky with only the slightest southerly breeze discernable. As we approached the mountain, however, I could see a cap of thin wispy cloud over the snow-covered summit. The Cairngorm Mountain Rescue Team had located the two soldiers lying in deep snow in a small corrie (amphitheatre-like valley head) on the south-east side of the mountain. They had been skiing across the smooth, dome-shaped summit when they had inadvertently strayed onto a cornice of snow and, in poor visibility, had continued over its edge to fall some 100 feet into the corrie beneath. They had been extremely fortunate, having plummeted into some deep loose snow that had detached itself from the cornice some time earlier. Only one of the pair had sustained any broken bones.

An approach to a position overhead the two casualties for a winching pick-up was not possible. We would have been operating almost underneath the enormous overhang of snow of the cornice where the vibrations and turbulence from our rotor blades could have brought the cornice crashing down on us and on our casualties. The mountain rescue team had already recognised this problem and had devised a novel solution. I landed on the summit and waited while they moved cautiously in line-abreast across the smooth snow of the summit's surface, using their long, thin aluminium avalanche probes to map out the edge of the near-sheer rock-face above the corrie. Once they had done this, at one point getting me to move from a position perilously close to the newly-marked edge, two of the team started tunnelling down through the snow, secured with ropes by their team members. After what seemed a remarkably short time, they signalled me to bring my helicopter to land closer to the small hole in the snow and actually lower the winch cable through the snow hole. Using the helicopter's winch, we then raised each of the casualties in turn. As they were suffering from the cold, my navigator, Flight Lieutenant Brian Canfer, and I immediately flew them to Glenmore Lodge, where they could be assessed by a doctor and prepared for their onward flight to Inverness Hospital.

Having done this, Brian and I returned to the summit of Ben Macdui to start lifting down the mountain rescue team. It had always been my policy at Lossiemouth for our helicopters to provide whatever assistance we could to help rescue teams off the mountains at the conclusion of a rescue whenever possible. At busy times they might be called upon to return to the mountains two or three times in the same day or night, with the enormous expenditure of physical and mental energy that entailed. Returning for a final flight up to the summit to collect our winchman, Dave Lloyd, and the two remaining mountain rescue team members, I was somewhat dismayed to find that during our brief absence the wispy cloud had suddenly thickened into a thin solid layer that now totally obscured the summit. To add to my concern, the weak sun had already sunk behind the mountain range and dusk would soon be approaching. I made a couple of low passes above the cloud over where I thought the summit would be but saw nothing. I was soon rewarded, however, by the bleep of Dave's SARBE locator beacon, which gave me the direction towards his position, but no way of gauging accurately how far he was below us. The Whirlwind had no radio altimeter and its basic pressure altimeter was not precise enough to trust for this vital information. Descending too low too early could easily result in us flying into the side of the cloud-capped summit.

Suddenly, a wisp of orange smoke appeared, rising above the cloud top and becoming a steady plume, bending over slightly in the gentle breeze. I quickly assessed that, by following the line of the smoke down into the cloud, I should be able to fly the helicopter safely down a steady descent to Dave's position. It worked! Although sufficiently thick to obscure Dave as we had previously flown over him, the cloud was not as deep as I had feared and I was soon landing alongside him and the remaining members of the mountain rescue team who were choking in the flare's orange smoke being fanned by my rotors. Returning to Glenmore Lodge was now simply a matter of loading everyone on board and carrying out a vertical take-off through the cloud on instruments before flying sufficiently far away from the mountain to start a descent into clear air. Or was it?

Just as I was about to lift to the hover, Brian drew my attention to a small group of people who had just appeared out of the mist, stumbling towards us and gesticulating wildly. Dave was sent out to investigate and soon returned with the message that this was a group of four exhausted climbers who had become lost while trying to descend one of Ben Macdui's faces and had decided to climb to the top to seek a safer route down in what would soon be darkness. They pleaded with us to take them.

I calculated my helicopter's weight and realised that, even allowing for a maximum emergency all-up-weight, I would be well over this if I took these additional people on board. I had three choices – return for them after landing my winchman and mountain rescue team members, leave them with my two mountain rescue team members to be 'walked off' by them in the failing light, or dump fuel to get down to my maximum permissible weight. Reasoning that these exhausted people might well soon become casualties themselves if left behind, I decided to dump fuel. This would normally be easily and safely achieved by climbing away and hitting the fuel jettison switch while still above 2,000 feet, thus allowing the fuel to evaporate before reaching the ground. However, with the cloud still thickening and dusk fast approaching, trying to return to the summit after dumping the fuel would be a dangerous manoeuvre. Reluctantly, I jettisoned the required amount of fuel while sitting on the ground, hoping that it would have evaporated before the snow melted later in the year.

Finally, with everyone safely on board, I took off and headed back towards Aviemore, where we dropped off our 'casualties' before refuelling and returning to Glenmore Lodge to deliver our mountain rescue team members and collect our original two casualties for transporting to Raigmore Hospital, Inverness. We flew home from there in the dark.

* * *

Months later, during the following summer, I was chatting to one of the RAF Kinloss Mountain Rescue Team members when he announced that they had possibly discovered the site of another aircraft wreck. Like other remote high areas of Britain, the Cairngorms were littered with such sites where aircraft had come to grief on their slopes in the past. All remnants of wreckage were accurately plotted and recorded so as not to be misleading during any later searches for missing aircraft. He told me that some climbers had reported the strong smell of aviation fuel on the summit of Ben Macdui and had assumed it to be the site of a hitherto undiscovered wreck site. I confessed my part in the mystery. Apparently, some of the jettisoned fuel had found its way into crevices in the rock surface and had not yet fully evaporated.

I advised caution to smokers on the summit.

CHAPTER TWENTY

GOING FOR BRONZE

I apologise in advance for an apparently over-long and detailed chapter but this is the story of how two people were saved from almost certain death by the combined efforts of an unusually wide diversity of dedicated personnel – the police, the civilian and RAF mountain rescue teams, a Shackleton of 8 Squadron and our own search and rescue helicopter colleagues from Leuchars. It is also an example of how new techniques were evolved and adapted to overcome short-comings of the Whirlwind in the helicopter search and rescue role.

* * *

In common with most single-engined military helicopters, the Whirlwind had provision for the mounting of two Schermuly parachute flares for use in the event of an emergency landing following engine failure at night. As the helicopter auto-rotates, or 'glides', towards the ground, the pilot ignites the two flares in sequence using an electrical switch in the cockpit. The flares are fired clear of the rotors by rocket from their mounting, whereupon a small parachute deploys and the magnesium charge is ignited. Given sufficient height above the ground, each flare burns for eighty seconds as it drifts slowly downwards, producing a brilliant light of some one million candle-power. The aim for the pilot of the stricken helicopter is to position himself below the descending flares and then attempt a forced landing in the circle of their illumination. This was a tried and tested system. Indeed, it was a mandatory part of our routine training for each search and rescue pilot to fire at least two flares during night flying while rehearsing the engine failure drills.

Without the aid of powerful on-board lighting, our usual technique for reaching a casualty in the mountains at night was to fly very low and close to the mountain side so that we could maintain visual contact with the mountain using our searchlight. This was a slow procedure, probing into the darkness until our lights picked out rock faces in their beams, then creeping slowly along and up them, carefully manoeuvring around outcrops and obstructions, until eventually arriving at the casualty's position. While this was the only technique available for use in the presence of any fog or cloud around the mountain, it had occurred to me on several occasions that the illumination from the parachute flares could prove a useful tool in the rapid and safe

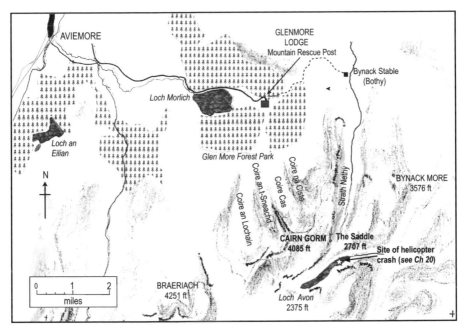

Map 7. Sketch map of the Cairgorms.

positioning of the helicopter at a casualty's position, with the whole of the immediate area of danger being temporarily bathed in the light from these flares. Provided that great care was taken to time the burn of the flares to ensure that a stable hover had been reached near the casualty before the lights extinguished, the remainder of the rescue and subsequent recovery could be accomplished by the light of the searchlight. One drawback to using our flares in this way meant that we would be left without any emergency illumination in the event of suffering an engine failure during the subsequent and some-times lengthy flight to safety beyond the mountains. A possible solution to this was to re-load with fresh flares whilst still airborne. While the normal position for the flare mounting was on the Whirlwind's starboard under-carriage leg, which placed it out of reach of the crew in the cabin, switching the mounting to an alternative location on the port leg and removing the port rear cabin window meant that the flares could be reached and re-armed from inside the cabin.

After several dummy runs on the ground followed by airborne trials, all the winchmen and navigators soon became adept at reaching through the hatch and replacing the spent flare tube with a fresh one in just a few seconds. Not only did this ensure that we could maintain continuous lighting over an emer-gency situation and still protect ourselves in the event of an engine failure, but we now also had the capability for a high-circling helicopter to maintain a continuous stream of burning flares in the air while a second helicopter beneath them carried out the actual rescue. Having streamlined the new technique in training by day and night, I was now keen to test it under operational conditions.

* * *

An opportunity presented itself a few months later when we were tasked by the Rescue Co-ordination Centre to recover a casualty from Coire an t'Sneachda, a glacial corrie or bowl on the north face of Cairn Gorm. The Cairngorm Mountain Rescue Team had been called out following reports of a young woman having sustained a serious fall and, on reaching the scene, they had initially assessed her as having sustained major injuries, including a possible broken back. A long, bumpy carry on a stretcher to Aviemore could prove prejudicial to her survival.

It was a dark winter's night with no moon. From my previous experience in mountain operations at night I was very aware that the total lack of any external visual references made flying the helicopter very demanding. With this in mind, I decided to call on a second pilot to monitor my instrument flying, thus allowing me to divide my attention between looking at the cockpit instruments and looking out to pick up external references revealed by the flares at the earliest opportunity.

Having completed the previous shift, Flight Lieutenant Malcolm Carlyle had stood down as second standby pilot as darkness fell around 4.00 pm and had returned to his home in Elgin. Landing at Elgin's football ground, I collected Malcolm and, with my two other crew members, navigator Flight Lieutenant Dave Pells, and winchman Sergeant Andy Ball, we were soon on our way to the Cairngorms. Making a rendezvous with the base party of the mountain rescue team at Glenmore Lodge, just outside Aviemore, we learnt that an updated medical assessment of the casualty had discounted a broken back, and rated her other injuries as non life-threatening. However, having got this far and only a few minutes flying time away from the scene, I decided to carry on with the rescue.

Using the Decca navigation system, Dave guided us in total darkness towards the unseen bulk of Cairn Gorm, while I swept the searchlight from side to side to try to get an early warning of any nasty surprises ahead. When we reckoned we were fairly close, we were reassured to see in the distance the pinpricks of lights from the rescue team's head torches before a bright red hand-held flare confirmed their location. Warning my crew, I gave a five-second countdown before firing the first flare and entering a steep descent. Simultaneously, Dave started a verbal countdown from his stopwatch to warn me how much of the eighty seconds burn time of the flare remained. We had quickly learned during our earlier night trials to curb our curiosity and look away from the flare as it was being fired – being temporarily blinded by the sudden blaze of light at this stage would have proved disastrous.

The flare, reflecting off the snow cover, threw the nearby mountain area into instant, magnificent and awe-inspiring relief. The first impression was just how close we appeared to be to the horseshoe of rock faces forming the corrie but, as my eyes adjusted to the new surroundings, the mountainside settled into proportion and I was able to plan a spiralling descent towards the bottom of the bowl. As the countdown reached ten seconds to go, I fired the second flare, and set the aircraft up for a steady final approach towards the casualty. As I got closer, I could make out the rescue team members kneeling in a circle around the casualty, bracing themselves for the icy blast of the helicopter downwash. All faces were towards me, making a bright circle of light from their head torches. So far, so good, but, as the leading edge of the icy downwash hit them, all the heads went down, obscuring their torches. We were surrounded by an instant swirling white fog of blown snow. Quickly stabilising in the hover some 20 feet above the rocky surface before the second flare burnt out, Andy was winched out. Working quickly and efficiently despite the virtual blizzard around him, Andy soon had the young girl secured in the stretcher and recovered to the cabin ready for the onward flight.

Keeping the airspeed low while Dave re-armed the two flare tubes, I set course for Inverness Hospital some 30 miles away, the remainder of the transit and subsequent return to our base at Lossiemouth proving something of an anti-climax after the earlier excitement.

My decision to continue with this mission despite the reduced medical urgency suggested by the updated medical assessment caused some controversy in retrospect. It was argued, with justification, that I had unnecessarily hazarded my aircraft and crew in pressing on in circumstances that were no longer urgent, and had used the situation to try out my new technique. I put my hand up to that and apologised to my crew. Proving the technique operationally, however, had added yet another tool to our range of available rescue procedures. The use of an additional pilot and the enhanced confidence that this rescue engendered in probing the Whirlwind's capabilities in night mountain rescues was to prove crucial in a later, much more difficult, night rescue in the Cairngorms.

*   *   *

'Scrambled to crashed helicopter – Loch Avon area Cairngorms – 2 rescued' is the cryptic entry in my Log Book for the night of 11/12 January 1977. Behind that brief entry was a rescue mission that took our crew and Whirlwind to the extreme limits of our capabilities. The call from the Rescue Co-ordination Centre was taken just after 6.00 pm by the Lossiemouth duty crew – pilot Flight Lieutenant Malcolm Carlyle, navigator Flight Lieutenant

Bill Gault, and winchman Master Air Loadmaster Mick Anderson – with the report that a helicopter operating out of Inverness Airport had been reported overdue at 5.15 pm while filming over Loch Avon, a large loch situated at over 2,300 feet above sea level and one of the most inaccessible lochs in the Cairngorms. The crew was put on immediate standby to prepare for action once more information was forthcoming. Apparent confirmation of something amiss came when a shepherd, who was looking in the direction of Cairn Gorm, had seen what he thought was a brief, faint red glow in the sky and had reported it to the police. This sighting was indeed fortuitous as it was already dark and, shortly after, the whole of the Cairngorm Range was covered by a blanket of thick, freezing fog with temperatures already well below zero, forecast to plummet towards minus fifteen degrees Centigrade in the mountains. The crew was tasked to position at Glenmore Lodge, the mountain rescue rendezvous point, as soon as possible and act as back-up for the RAF Leuchars' search and rescue Wessex and their local mountain rescue team, who had also been called. The Wessex was a much more capable search and rescue helicopter than the Whirlwind, boasting two engines, a basic autopilot and twice the lifting capacity.

Night search and rescue operations from Lossiemouth required my express authorisation as the Flight Commander. Any proposed mission would be discussed briefly over the telephone and I would ensure that all the various aspects such as weather, nature and location of the incident, together with crew capability, had been considered in relation to the specific mission. This duty crew was very experienced and I had every confidence in their ability to tackle almost any task that might face them. However, the freezing fog put the visibility well below the prescribed minimum required level for operations during daylight, let alone for the much more stringent conditions required for night rescues. I felt, therefore, that I could neither expect nor authorise them to commence an operation already so far outside our operational limits.

The only way I could see around the problem was for me to assume that responsibility and take over the duty shift. Having previously used a second pilot to increase our safety margin and flexibility during the night mountain rescue described earlier, I had no hesitation in recruiting Malcolm Carlyle for this task. He had been with me on that occasion and I knew that we had worked well together in those difficult circumstances. While the ground-crew completed preparations on the aircraft, I drove to the Flight crew-room and joined the crew there for an update on the situation and the latest weather from our Meteorological Officer, particularly the disposition of the freezing fog. This information was far from encouraging, with the fog thickening and the temperature falling further.

In good weather, the route from Lossiemouth to the Cairngorms was a well-worn and familiar track, taking in minor hills and undulating moorland.

We would normally fly direct to Glenmore Lodge, near to Aviemore, but because of the dense fog reported in the area we decided to follow the general line of the Spey valley and fly via Aviemore, some 6 miles to the west of Glenmore Lodge. Although the fog might be slightly denser near the valley floor and in close proximity to the river, this would keep us clear of the higher ground and would give us the chance of picking up the lights of the town and provide us with a safer entry point into the more mountainous and dark terrain. Despite its familiarity, we studied the route carefully, not knowing at what point we would run into the fog and whether it would be possible to continue at very low level when we did so.

We took off at 6.30 pm and made good progress until just before the half-way point where we encountered the bank of fog. From there we slowed down and dropped lower to stay in visual contact with the ground, rattling over the outskirts of Grantown-on-Spey at roof-top height at little more than walking speed. At this point the omens for conducting a successful rescue operation in these conditions were certainly not looking good.

The lights of Aviemore eventually became dimly discernable ahead of us. Trying to cause as little disturbance as possible, I edged my helicopter through the town and out towards the road leading to Glenmore Lodge. Still barely at walking speed, we crept along this road, sweeping the powerful landing light mounted on the bottom of the aircraft from side to side while straining to pick up sufficient guidance in the fog to allow us to keep moving forward. Suddenly a police car appeared, flashed its lights and took up position in front of me with its blue light flashing. The driver seemed to have sensed our predicament and, with great initiative, was now leading us the remaining half-a-dozen miles to Glenmore Lodge with me formating on his rear. We landed there after an hour's flying and shut down for further briefings.

The RAF Kinloss Mountain Rescue Team was already present and, shortly after, we were also joined by Flight Sergeant Ray 'Sunshine' Sefton, the RAF Leuchars Team Leader. Gathering all the available information, we now had a tally of three mountain rescue teams – one at Leuchars, two helicopters – the Wessex at Leuchars and our Whirlwind at Glenmore Lodge – and a Shackleton of No. 8 Squadron from Lossiemouth, circling high overhead looking for flares. The Shackleton crew was in radio contact with the RAF teams through the comprehensive communications equipment carried in their vehicles.

*   *   *

Just after 9.00 pm the vigilance of the Shackleton crew was rewarded by a brief glow of a red flare on the ground. Several more flares followed, which enabled the position of the casualties to be established with some accuracy, putting its origin approximately one mile north of Loch Avon, at the high southern head of the long valley of Strath Nethy. Now that it was certain there was at least one survivor in a known position, the Rescue Controller decided to use the Wessex helicopter to lift the Leuchars Mountain Rescue Team to conduct the rescue operation and ordered us to stand down.

Having just resigned ourselves to being remote witnesses to the drama unfolding just a few miles away from us, we were surprised to hear from the Rescue Controller that the Wessex had turned back in the dense freezing fog and was returning to Leuchars. The new plan was for the Leuchars team to travel by road to Glenmore Lodge to join the other teams there in order to make a combined ground attempt to reach the casualties. Time was now becoming pressing. The survivor or survivors had been exposed to sub-zero temperatures since their accident some seven hours earlier and, with no means of communication, there was no way of knowing what physical state they were now in. With temperatures falling steadily towards minus fifteen degrees Centigrade, doubts were being voiced on their ability to survive at least the additional four or five hours that a ground party would take to reach them and recover them to Glenmore Lodge. The Lodge staff, experts on the local snow conditions, were also expressing serious concerns over the high risk of avalanches in the area and were reluctant to send out a ground party. Not only would this put the ground party at high risk but it would also impede their progress because of the extreme care they would have to take to avoid triggering a snow fall. In the event, one team had already been sent out but their current whereabouts was unknown.

Taking Ray Sefton with us, I took my crew off to a quiet classroom where we could consider the position quietly and carefully. No new information was forthcoming, only confirmation that the missing helicopter had two people on board. The pilot was young, fit and healthy, but little was known of his cameraman passenger. Nor had any information been gleaned either on any survival equipment carried on board the missing helicopter, or on the crew's ability to use it. It was not even known whether the helicopter had crashed, maybe causing injuries, or whether the pilot had made a controlled precautionary landing because of the deteriorating weather. All we knew at this stage was that at least one survivor was alive and had fired several emergency flares.

*   *   *

With only a minimum of discussion, we were unanimous in our resolve to mount an airborne rescue attempt, so we settled down to work out exactly how we could maximise our chances of success. We studied the large-scale Ordnance Survey maps of the area and were dismayed to realise the implications of all the contours and spot heights being shown in metres. We had only recently upgraded from the old one-inch-to-the-mile Ordnance Survey maps on which heights were defined in feet, the same unit used on all British aircraft altimeters. As accurate height information was likely to be one of the main indicators of our position along a rising mountain valley, Bill, my navigator, set about marking imperial conversions clearly on his metric map. By now there was total cloud cover over the area, as well as the freezing fog. Nevertheless, I requested that the Shackleton crew drop parachute flares on my command once we were in the search area. This they agreed but, in the event, the cloud cover prevented any useful light penetrating to our position. Realising that we were going to need everything on our side to counter the anticipated difficulties, we also elected to wait until moonrise at midnight in the hope that the waning half moon might provide a glimmer of light. Unfortunately, when the time came, the cloud would deny us even this slight help.

Our basic plan was to use a police Land Rover to lead us through the featureless and densely wooded area surrounding Glenmore Lodge and point us along the track towards Bynack Stables, an emergency mountain bothy near the northern end of Strath Nethy. From there we would turn to fly up Strath Nethy and try to locate and lift the survivors and return them to Glenmore Lodge. If, at any point, we could proceed no higher up the valley, Bill would attempt to winch Mick and Ray down, together with survival equipment, and they would continue on foot to the casualties, administer first aid and set up an overnight camp. In this respect, I was extremely fortunate in the composition of my crew. Ray, as Leader of the RAF Leuchars Mountain Rescue Team, was one of the most experienced mountain rescuers in Scotland and a veteran of many successful rescues carried out under the most arduous of conditions, while Mick was happiest when undertaking long expeditions in the mountains, on one occasion walking and climbing from coast to coast in an almost straight line through the centre of the Cairngorms, sleeping out on the mountainsides every night. Not only had they scaled most of the Scottish peaks in all weathers but both had spent many nights huddled in bivvy bags in foul conditions. Also, if the worst came to the worst and we forced landed or crashed, Bill was also an experienced mountaineer who would be able to look after Malcolm, my co-pilot, and me. The presence of the Shackleton circling overhead would be another reassuring factor; once airborne, we too would be in radio contact with it.

We decided on our crew seating and lookout positions. Malcolm would fly alongside me, concentrating exclusively on the instruments and ready to take control from me if I inadvertently put the aircraft into a dangerous attitude. Bill would be positioned by the open door with an Aldis hand-held searchlight to augment the spotlight mounted in the bottom of the helicopter fuselage. He would assist me in illuminating the scant ground references during our transit up the steeply rising valley. Mick and Ray, positioned on each side of the cabin, would be responsible for checking the clearance of my rotor blades from the numerous rocky outcrops on the valley sides, especially as we approached the head of the valley where it became steeper and narrower. I had elected to fly as low as possible in the bottom of the valley in the hope of picking up traces of the burn that ran there under the deep snow cover. By flying slightly to the left of this, both Bill and I would have the best chance of spotting its course in our combined lights.

With our planning complete and summarised in a final briefing, I had a final update on the weather from the Shackleton and then went out to our Whirlwind. After the warmth of the Lodge, we were immediately struck by the biting cold which, together with the apprehension we all felt, soon had our teeth chattering and our breath forming ghostly frozen clouds around us. The other impression was of the incredible silence, with the fog acting as a thick, icy, muffling blanket. We quickly completed our checks on the aircraft and I pressed the engine starter button. To my dismay, the usual whine of the rapidly accelerating gas-turbine engine was absent, replaced by a painfully slow increase in rotational speed towards the minimum possible for the engine to be self-sustaining. The engine computer would be monitoring what was happening and, at the correct engine speed, would start spraying fuel into the combustion chambers and firing the igniters to start the engine and accelerate it to idling speed. Although fully charged, the battery was only producing a fraction of its normal power in the intense cold. I tried every trick in the book to encourage the engine into life, switching from computer to manual control and selecting continuous operation of the igniters while I cautiously opened the throttle as quickly as I dared, bypassing the automatic safety circuits. If I got this wrong, then at best the engine would fail to start, while at worst I risked burning the engine out and ruining our rescue attempt. After what seemed an age, I heard the reassuring roar as the engine lit up and carefully adjusted the throttle to control the rapidly rising temperature. Once everything was stable, I re-engaged the engine computer – I would have my hands full just flying the aircraft without having to control the engine manually as well.

Lifting quickly into a high hover to escape the swirling, blinding maelstrom of snow that our rotor blades had whipped up all around us, I moved across towards where the police Land Rover was waiting for us with all its lights flashing. Taking up station above and behind it, we were led out of the grounds of the Lodge and through the snow-covered forest, the lights of the Land Rover cutting a flickering swathe through the trees and marking out the route for us. All too soon, however, the Land Rover could proceed no further because of the depth of snow and we were cast adrift over the near featureless dark snowfield to feel our way towards our first navigational checkpoint, Bynack Stables mountain refuge hut. In better weather, the hut would have been a conspicuous feature but, in this night's conditions, we got within 20–30 feet of the building before it showed up in our lights. Here we passed the ground party. They had made good progress, but still had several miles to go and a long climb ahead in avalanche conditions.

*   *   *

Turning right up Strath Nethy, we commenced the most difficult phase of our flight towards the casualties' position. The depth of the snow had obliterated most of the features, and the meandering burn on which we were depending for guidance was running beneath the snow, affording us only momentary glimpses through occasional holes in the thick snow cover. As planned, Bill operated the hand-held searchlight from the open cabin door, giving calm, precise directions when he sensed me drifting away from the stream bed, while I operated my landing lamp to sweep the area ahead. My eyes were streaming in the freezing draught from the open cockpit window but I didn't dare blink for fear of losing the minimal visual cues on which we were relying. Flying just a few feet above the ground, I had to maintain a speed sufficient to keep us just ahead of the swirling snow thrown up by our rotor blades, yet slow enough to see and avoid the rising ground ahead of us at the limit of our vision in the fog. Malcolm, alongside me, devoted all his attention to the dimly glowing cockpit instruments, mentally flying the Whirlwind so that he could immediately make a seamless transition to instrument flight and initiate a full power climb through the fog to safety if required, At intervals he would call out the altimeter reading, marking each increment of 50 feet through which we had climbed, thus enabling us to gauge approximately how far up the ever-steepening valley we had progressed. Other than the spoken corrections and heights, the intercom was absolutely quiet, with each concentrating to his utmost to maintain safe progress.

Suddenly, at about 2,000 feet above sea level, we were surprised to emerge clear of the densest fog. While we were still in a critical position, I now had slightly more freedom on the heights and speeds I could use. I was disappointed to note that there was a solid layer of cloud above us that was obscuring the hoped-for moonlight. I contacted the Shackleton, still circling above, and called for a succession of parachute flares to be dropped near our position. Unfortunately, none penetrated the cloud to give us any useful illumination, so we resigned ourselves to making do with our hand-held searchlight and the aircraft lights. I continued along the valley, matching our climb with the rising valley floor. Strath Nethy terminated at a saddle at 2,707 feet above sea level and formed a hanging valley emerging immediately above Loch Avon.

As we approached this saddle, we saw the brief red flash of a flare off to our right and some 200 feet above us. I carefully flew the Whirlwind to place it alongside the point from which the flare had been fired and Bill's searchlight soon picked out the two survivors, huddled together amidst the snow-covered large boulders that comprised the steep valley side at this point. It was with a great sense of relief that we saw both of them wave back at the aircraft.

It was decided to get Mick and Ray to them to assess their condition before preparing them for winching. Not knowing how secure the survivors' position was, nor wishing to subject them unnecessarily to an icy blast from our rotor downwash, Bill talked me into a suitable position slightly lower down the slope where I could balance one main wheel on an outcrop of rock and let Mick and Ray climb out. Once we had achieved that, I put the aircraft in a hover near their situation where Bill could illuminate the site with his search-light while I concentrated on maintaining a steady hover. We watched as Mick and Ray climbed towards the survivors' position, picking their way care-fully amongst the icy, boulder-strewn, steep slope. A slip or fall on their part at this stage would add a major complication to the situation. Also, time was now of the essence – our fuel state, after the long, slow climb at high power, had eaten well into our planned reserves. After a brief conference with the two survivors, Mick soon gave a 'thumbs up' indicating that they were ready and fit enough to be lifted. Under Bill's directions I repositioned the helicopter directly overhead with the winch cable and strops dangling underneath us. Both survivors were rapidly winched aboard in turn, paired up with Ray and Mick, and at last I was able to climb clear of the close confines of the narrow valley into the sudden darkness away from the glare of our lights reflected off the snow. I climbed on a safe heading away from the invisible bulk of Cairn Gorm for a brief respite before tackling the problem of getting back onto the ground beneath the fog with our low fuel state.

* * *

Initially there was some confusion over our first glimpse of lights that sparkled tantalisingly in the distance. From our new perspective at a height of some 4,500 feet I thought at first that they were the lights of Aviemore and that the fog had magically disappeared. However, when Malcolm spotted dim lights almost underneath us we all realised that these were from Aviemore and the bright lights were those of Inverness almost 30 miles to the north-west. Mick's preliminary assessment of our survivors' condition had revealed only minor injuries but both were suffering from hypothermia, one of them in a state of confusion and uncontrollable shaking. Ideally, we would have taken them direct to the hospital at Inverness, but I knew that we had insufficient fuel even to attempt that relatively short journey. This left us the only remaining option of a return to Aviemore.

In preparation for a 'blind' approach, using only the aircraft instruments, Malcolm set up the Decca navigation equipment as accurately as possible, while Bill prepared to plot our letdown into Aviemore. A phenomenon of thick fog is that, while horizontal visibility can be reduced to just a few yards, it might still be possible to make out bright lights vertically below. This is rather like being able to see the moon a quarter-of-a-million miles away on a foggy night, while having difficulty seeing only a few yards in any direction at ground level. It might logically be supposed that all I needed to do in this situation was to come to hover directly above Aviemore, then descend vertically through the fog onto the dimly discernable lights of the town.

Whilst a vertical descent would be possible in a helicopter equipped with fully automatic flight controls, autopilot system and advanced hover instrumentation, the Whirlwind had none of these. We were therefore committed to flying a long, straight descent, losing height progressively as Bill counted off the range to the selected touch-down point, the main car park in Aviemore.

He selected an approach from the north-east that would bring us along the low-lying valley of the River Spey, keeping us between the rocky outcrops of high ground on either side. Having double-checked the Decca – the slightest error on this could have us flying into the side of one of these rocky outcrops – Malcolm began reading out the co-ordinates displayed on the equipment, while Bill plotted them carefully in the cabin and passed corrections for me to fly. After a very tense quarter-of-an-hour, we were all greatly relieved to see the sudden loom of lights glowing all around us as we approached the main car park in the centre of Aviemore. Bill recalled seeing the shocked expression of a policeman as we emerged from the fog and landed at the side of our emergency refuelling hut situated at the car park. I shut down the helicopter but then realised that I could not release my right hand from the control column. The combination of extreme cold and tension had frozen my hand almost solid. As I struggled to release my grip, Mick reported a similar problem; he had been holding the Aldis searchlight at the open cabin door ready to assist with extra lighting for my landing, but now could not let go of it. Putting the cabin lights on revealed a chaotic scene – our two survivors looking the worse for wear, surrounded by maps, torches and climbing gear and the cabin floor a solid, slippery sheet of ice from all the snow brought aboard.

We were soon collected and taken to the Police Station for a de-briefing and a most welcome mug of hot tea. By this time we were all shivering so violently that it was impossible to hold our drinks without spilling them. It was only then that we heard the full story from our survivors. The helicopter, a Bell JetRanger piloted by John Poland, had been hired by a film company to film remote winter scenery for a film *The Land that Time Forgot*. Flying low over Loch Avon, with the renowned cameraman Peter Allwork filming from the open door, the helicopter had suddenly lost its tail rotor, sending it spinning uncontrollably onto the frozen surface of the loch. Having extricated themselves from the wreckage, they recognised their predicament; no one knew precisely where they were and there were only a few hours of weak winter daylight remaining. The fog had not yet made an appearance so they made reasonable progress over the surface of the frozen and snow-covered loch. Attempting to enter the southern end of Strath Nethy, however, they faced a gruelling climb through waist-deep snow to reach the saddle some 400 feet above them. Although shocked and slightly injured in the crash, they achieved this but, having just passed over the high saddle into Strath Nethy, they were overcome by exhaustion and the intense cold and collapsed on the boulder-strewn slope. John Poland had then fired a series of red, emergency flares, one of which had been seen by the shepherd so many hours ago and triggered off the rescue mission.

*   *   *

After a fitful night at Glenmore Lodge, the following morning found us still in thick fog. However, a check with our meteorological officer at Lossie-mouth indicated that the fog was not as widespread as during the previous night, with broken patches to the north of us leaving Lossiemouth in weak sunshine. We returned to Aviemore and refuelled our Whirlwind from the fuel stock held in the hut, before completing our pre-flight checks for our return to base. However, on pressing the starter button, I was greeted with just a soft moan as the engine barely started to rotate. The long exposure to the extremely low temperature during the night had finally taken its toll of the battery's output and no amount of coaxing or ruses was going to persuade it to start the engine. We were now grounded until a replacement battery could be delivered from Lossiemouth. We retired to the warmth of a café and treated ourselves to a leisurely breakfast while mulling over the events of just a few hours ago. One of the waitresses came to our table to say that there was a telephone call for the helicopter captain so, following her through into the kitchen, I took the call, expecting it to be my base with news of the replace-ment battery. It took a few seconds for it to dawn on me that it was BBC Radio Scotland on the line and that I was now being interviewed about the night's rescue. Caught totally unawares in the steamy kitchen and surrounded by the rattle of plates and shouted food orders, I mumbled my way through my replies, remarking at one point that the operation had had 'a few very interesting moments'!

Our ground-crew eventually arrived by road and fitted the new battery. This time, with a reassuring whine, the engine rapidly wound up when the starter button was pressed and, shortly after, the rotor blades thrashed into life, creating an icy blast that made the crowd of curious onlookers quickly turn their backs on us. The return to base was flown in companionable silence. We had only just begun to realise how tired we were after all the excitement and lack of sleep.

*   *   *

Each year, every RAF unit has a formal visit or inspection from the Air Officer Commanding its particular formation. Before these visits, however, there are a series of 'pre-inspections', when every aspect of a unit's activities is scrutinised and reported on by specialists on the staff of the AOC's headquarters. The previous day, now almost a lifetime ago, I had been preparing for an engineering inspection of my Flight, and had been due to meet the HQ staff that morning. It came as something of a surreal experience, therefore, to find myself within moments of landing being grilled on engineering practices and manpower problems by the HQ staff who were impatient at being kept waiting all morning. Seeing that I was almost asleep on my feet, the current Duty Pilot, Flight Lieutenant Carl Mason, took it upon himself to remonstrate firmly with them, telling them to come back another day.

Before leaving for home, I was ushered into the hangar to be confronted by a barrage of lights set up in front of a Whirlwind and a BBC Television News camera crew. After stumbling through another interview, I was eventually allowed to leave. It was probably fortunate that returning fog delayed the recording sufficiently for it to miss the early evening news slot and I was long asleep by the time of the later news bulletins. While driving home, however, I had a strange moment of *déjà vu*. Tired and pre-occupied, I became vaguely aware of someone on the BBC Radio programme, *PM at 5 PM*, describing an 'interesting' night-time rescue in the Cairngorms. It took several seconds for me to realise that this was, in fact, a replay of the recording I had made that morning in the café at Aviemore. Shortly after, I was having to repeat it once again to Marian, who had been unaware of what had happened.

*   *   *

A few months later we were surprised to be informed that the four of us in the helicopter crew had been awarded the Bronze Medal of the Royal Humane Society.

CHAPTER TWENTY-ONE

LITTLE GREEN MEN?

The scene: a military airfield near Berlin during the First World War. A young fighter pilot ace is demonstrating a new *Eindecker*, an early monoplane, with an enthusiastic display of aerobatics. Suddenly, something goes seriously wrong, and the aircraft plunges to the ground and explodes in front of the horrified spectators. Then the scramble bell rings. I grab the red telephone and answer in my mock-German accent, 'OK, we've got it! One *Eindecker* crashed, 5 miles south of Berlin – we're on our way.'

The Rescue Co-ordination Centre Controller obviously had not been watching the Sunday late-night movie on television. My reference to the *The Blue Max* was met with impatience, 'Stop messing about, I've got a job for you,' was his response, before going on to say that a light aircraft appeared to be in difficulties just to the north of us and was 'flying the triangles'.

This reference got my immediate attention. If an aircraft is in difficulties above cloud and requires assistance to enable a safe recovery but is unable to communicate normally by radio, it can fly a series of triangles, which will probably be observed on the radar display of a ground controller. The direction and time of each leg would convey important basic information to the ground controller. Triangles flown in a clockwise direction would mean that the distressed aircraft had a serviceable radio receiver but could not transmit. In this event, the ground controller would pass instructions on the standard aeronautical distress frequency to the aircraft, which would have tuned to that frequency. By observing the aircraft's response on his radar screen, the ground controller would talk the aircraft to the nearest suitable available airfield. If the distressed aircraft was a light, low-speed aircraft, then each leg of the triangle would be flown for two-minute periods, whereas if the aircraft was a jet, the legs would be only one minute in length. If, however, the distressed aircraft flew the triangles in an anti-clockwise direction, this would signal to the ground controller that it could neither transmit nor receive messages on its radio, and would therefore require another appropriate aircraft to be sent up to find it and shepherd it back to an airfield. Our aircraft was flying two-minute, anti-clockwise triangles and a fighter controller at a northern RAF radar station had observed this pattern on his display and had alerted the Rescue Co-ordination Centre.

Having struggled into our cumbersome rubber immersion suits, we were soon airborne and climbing out over the Moray Firth to the north. It was now the early hours of 1 May 1978. I was directed to contact the radar station and, after a few radio exchanges, the fighter controller there confirmed that he had me identified on his radar screen and also that he still had my 'target', the distressed aircraft, on his screen. The fighter controller's normal job was to direct RAF fighter aircraft to intercept suspicious aircraft approaching the boundaries of the protected national airspace around the UK. By giving precise directions to the pilot of an intercepting fighter and a commentary on the target's movements and height, he would aim to effect a rapid interception. This he now proceeded to do for me.

'Rescue 26, this is Buchan Radar. Target indicating Flight Level four-zero, range 30 miles. Come left onto three-three-zero. Maintain climb.'

The fighter controller continued to give me directions to close with the unseen aircraft while I climbed to its reported height approximately 4,000 feet above the sea while correcting to a north-westerly heading. During the climb, we passed through a thin layer of cloud at about 3,000 feet, which obscured most of the ground features along the Moray Coast, now off to our left side.

'Rescue 26. Come further left three-one-zero. Target now twelve o'clock, range fifteen, maintaining Flight Level four-zero.'

As I made the small heading adjustment, I and my navigator, Flight Lieutenant Taff Rees, peered ahead into the darkness, straining to catch the first sight of our target. Nothing. While we should have been able to pick up the navigation lights of our target at much more than this range, I was not too surprised. If our distressed aircraft had suffered a total electrical failure then not only would its radios be inoperative but also its navigation lights would not be working. Slowly we got closer to the target.

'Target twelve o'clock, range ten, same height. Confirm visual.'

'Negative.'

'Roger 26. Maintain heading.'

* * *

As we continued to fly westward along the Moray Firth towards the target, I could make out the brighter lights of Inverness penetrating the thin cloud beneath us and casting a pale reddish, yellow glow on the cloud ahead. I was now puzzled. The distressed aircraft had sufficient visual references to get itself safely below cloud and probably into Inverness Airport without my assistance. However, it was possible that there may have been other complications on board. Maybe the pilot was having eye problems, perhaps he was incapacitated and the aircraft was now being flown by a passenger who was not confident enough to get the aircraft through the cloud layer without help. However, someone had flown reasonably consistent, accurate and identifiable triangles. The possibilities were numerous. I gently weaved the nose of the Whirlwind so that my winchman, Master Air Loadmaster Bill Payne, could also have a good look towards the area in which our target should appear. The next transmission certainly got our full attention.

'Rescue 26. Target half-twelve, range five, same height, come right ... Standby! We have just had a reported sighting from a police sergeant in Inverness who is watching a bright light through the cloud to the north of him and he can also see your red anti-collision lights near to it. Confirm now visual!'

'Negative. I am now climbing to try to highlight the target against the backdrop of the Inverness lights.'

'Rescue 26. If no contact, come hard left; I say again, hard left. Your blips are merging. Acknowledge!'

By now, the hairs on the backs of our necks were prickling and I was getting seriously worried. The last thing I wanted was to collide with the unknown aircraft but I could not see anything to avoid. Turning hard left and applying full power to climb above our target's height, I frantically swivelled my head around, expecting any second to feel the impact of a collision. Nothing!

'Rescue 26. The police sergeant is still on the line and has just reported seeing your flashing lights merging with the bright one. Are you visual?'

I considered that it was time to get well away from our target and start all over again. Homing in from a different direction might present the target from a different aspect and show something previously obscured from us.

'Negative. Take me out to 5 miles, then vector me back onto target.'

The fighter controller acknowledged and I continued to fly away from the unseen aircraft's area to re-assess the situation. The policeman on the ground reported that he could now see my flashing lights coming towards him at Inverness, with the bright light still in approximately the same position as before. Reaching 5 miles from this position, the controller instructed me to turn until the target was again dead ahead of me. We were now approaching the target from almost the same direction as the police sergeant on the ground was observing it. Sure enough, he confirmed that he had watched my lights turning in the sky ahead of him until I started moving towards the target. Nothing! We were now totally mystified and getting very uneasy about the whole situation.

Suddenly, 'Did you see that? Rescue 26, the target has now split into two parts ... one is proceeding north-east at very high speed; the other part is moving west!'

Simultaneously, the police sergeant had reported that the bright light had now disappeared, leaving just my helicopter's red flashing lights in view.

'Buchan Radar, Rescue 26. Still nothing seen ... vector me to track the slow-moving target.'

'Roger 26. Come left two-eight-zero. Target tracking west, speed approximately 120 knots, and descending, range twenty. Other target has now faded 150 miles north-east of you.'

I turned quickly onto the given heading and adjusted to my maximum speed of 95 knots, realising that we would now be unable to catch the target if it maintained its speed.

The situation had now changed dramatically and, for the first time in this sortie, we began to speculate on the possibility that this was an unidentified flying object, a so-called UFO. While the target's behaviour up until a few moments ago had been somewhat bizarre and the anomaly with its 'invisible' lights seemed inexplicable, at least it had displayed performance characteristics consistent with a conventional light aircraft. With the split into two distinct parts and the incredibly rapid acceleration of the part disappearing towards the northern tip of Scotland, this was a new experience for all of us. While our unease increased, even to the point where we questioned whether we should even be there, our curiosity was even more overwhelming. Were we about to make the first acquaintance with an alien being? What was the recommended protocol for dealing with aliens from outer space? How could we indicate lack of hostility? Were we about to make world history – and at what price?

As I followed the still invisible target somewhere ahead, the fighter controller continued with his directions but this time he was also counting down the target's height as it continued its descending trajectory. We dropped through the thin layer of cloud, the lights of Inverness now clear and bright to our left. Down and down we went, the target now descending more rapidly and its forward speed reducing. Soon we had passed over the Black Isle and Dingwall – 2,000 feet, 1,000 feet in the descent, still with the invisible target on our nose.

'Rescue 26, target has faded. Lost contact, half-twelve, range ten.'

Making a small heading correction to my right, I continued descending with all my external lights on and sweeping my searchlight from side to side to avoid any obstructions. The area we were now over was on our regular low level route to our frequent mountain rescue missions on Skye, so I was reasonably familiar with the terrain and happy to go down to ground level. The position given by the fighter controller coincided with the village of Strathpeffer.

As we moved slowly over the tree-tops between Dingwall and Strathpeffer, we were all suddenly startled to be caught in a brilliant beam of white light pointing vertically up at us from the ground. For a split second, we thought that the strange, alien quarry that we had been tracking down for most of the preceding hour had suddenly found itself cornered and was now retaliating on its pursuers. For my part, I confess to being momentarily paralysed with heart-stopping terror before self-preservation kicked in. I applied full power and turned violently in an attempt to evade the malevolent beam, but it held us steady. I corkscrewed round to my right in a steeply banked turn, desperately trying to peer beyond the light's origin to catch a glimpse of what I was sure must be an alien craft.

As suddenly as it had come on, the light disappeared, leaving us temporarily disorientated. However, my own searchlight was still on and I now brought its beam to bear on the spot where the strange light had come from. With a mixture of relief and disappointment, not to say anti-climax after the build-up of tension, we found ourselves looking down on a couple of chaps holding a small, powerful searchlight. I quickly descended and came to a hover, looking for somewhere to land near to them. Once we were on the ground, Bill, our winchman, quickly ascertained that *they* had seen nothing of any UFO and were somewhat disconcerted to be woken in the early hours by our noisy helicopter moving very low and slowly overhead with all its lights on.

We got airborne again, reporting the incident to the fighter controller who was unable to offer us any further information. I climbed, then we quartered the area for several more minutes, looking for fires or signs of wreckage, but all to no avail. I reported this to the radar controller and, shortly after, he relayed a message from the Rescue Controller instructing us to return to base.

*   *   *

We landed back at Lossiemouth at about 2.00 am, fully expecting to be called again at first light to resume the search for the mystery craft. However, the total lack of any further action was almost as mysterious as the events of the previous night. No further search was ordered and there was no follow-up to our mission report. We were told not to discuss the matter but we were sure there would be something about it on the local television or radio during the next few days. However, we heard nothing more of the incident and put this down to the prevailing official reticence of the time neither to acknowledge nor deny the possibility of UFOs.

Months later, the local television news was full of reports of balls of light hurtling at low level along Loch Ness towards Inverness. These went on for so long that they were captured by television news cameras as well as by amateur photographers. Again, no official comment or explanation was forthcoming.

*   *   *

In December 2009 the Ministry of Defence reported that it had closed its department to which all reports of UFOs had been directed and had shut down its dedicated UFO hot-line answer phone service and internet address. It also reported that all the files it held on such occurrences would be made public through the National Archives. Having failed to find any reference within these files to my incident, I wrote to the Ministry of Defence with a brief description of the circumstances on that night. In reply I received a 'standard' letter, repeating the fact that the Ministry 'had no opinion on the existence or otherwise of extra-terrestrial life'. The letter went on to say that 'in over fifty years, no UFO report has revealed any evidence of a potential threat to the United Kingdom'.

CHAPTER TWENTY-TWO

AGAINST ALL SODS!

It might be supposed that the RAF's search and rescue helicopter units would receive all possible support and encouragement from their masters, who would be content to bask in the reflected glory of some of the more spectacular and publicised rescues. Alas, no! Towards the end of my tour, scarcely a few weeks went by but I was contacted by my Wing Commander, the senior officer in overall command of the two search and rescue helicopter squadrons, to question and criticise my judgement and that of my crews over the manner in which we conducted operations in our area. From my point of view, much of the comment was ill-informed and failed to take into account fully the challenging nature of that area, particularly in the numerous mountainous zones and extremes of weather we regularly experienced. It also failed to recognise the expertise and strategies my team had carefully evolved to cope with them.

While there was much ignorance of our working methods, partly because of the infrequent visits by my senior officers of the geographical remoteness of Lossiemouth, on balance this worked in our favour and led, in practice, to remarkably little interference. Most rebukes and 'rockets' were usually delivered by telephone, which allowed me to exploit the 'crossed-line gambit'. While my wing commander was mid-rant, I would pick up the other telephone on my desk and, after dialling a random number, would place both telephones end-to-end in my drawer and leave the unwitting recipient of my call to untangle the situation. When all noises in my drawer ceased, I simply replaced the handset.

Typical of the criticism was that levelled after a mission to recover a critically injured young boy who had cycled off a bridge in thick fog and fallen into a gulley near to Cape Wrath, the most north-westerly point of the UK mainland. The call had come from the local coastguard who had been alerted by a walking party in the area. With the greatest of luck for the boy, this party included a neurosurgeon who, on assessing the boy's head injuries, had emphasised both the urgency of the pick-up and the specialist nature of the treatment that was essential if he was to have any chance of recovery. At a distance of 240 miles and a time of seven hours by a tortuous road journey, Aberdeen Royal Infirmary was the nearest hospital with the required facilities. The same journey by air was 150 miles and, even allowing for the hour it would take the Lossiemouth helicopter to reach Cape Wrath, the time to get the boy into hospital would be less than half the time for the road journey. However, the coastguard reported one problem – the whole of the area was wreathed in dense fog.

The duty crew, captained by Flight Lieutenant Dave Carey, then one of the most skilled and experienced search and rescue helicopter pilots and on temporary loan to me, set off immediately. The plan was that they would get as far as possible while I contacted the resident jet training squadron to ask if they could divert one of their Jaguar ground-attack aircraft to carry out a quick reconnaissance of the weather in the Cape Wrath area for me. While not routine, or even official, such requests for assistance were invariably acted upon by both the Jaguar and Shackleton squadrons at Lossiemouth and their willing co-operation was sometimes vital in providing essential communications links or, as in this case, a timely weather report. The message soon came back that the fog cover was complete and extensive, reaching half-way from Cape Wrath to Lossiemouth. However, the fog was only a hundred or so feet thick, with a clear, sunny sky above. This was relayed to the helicopter crew who then followed their plan to get into close contact with the ground and then creep carefully along in the fog, just a few feet above the remote country roads towards Cape Wrath for as far as the visibility allowed. If, at any stage, the pilot was forced to climb above the fog layer, the mission would have to be abandoned.

Although slow, progress was steady and the boy, together with the neuro-surgeon in attendance, was eventually picked up. Again, the crew was able to benefit from the Jaguar pilot's weather report and, with confidence, climbed above the fog layer for the return journey at maximum speed. The helicopter required more fuel to continue to Aberdeen and also to pick up the medical supplies that had been requested by the surgeon. Forewarned of these requirements, I contacted Lossiemouth's Senior Medical Officer, who arranged to meet the helicopter with the medical supplies and also volunteered to accompany the casualty to provide a helping hand. Meanwhile, my ground-crew were standing by to carry out a 'rotors-turning' refuel, an emergency procedure that incurred a minimum of delay on the ground.

All went smoothly, and the boy was safely delivered to the specialist neurological unit at Aberdeen where, we were later delighted to hear, he made a good recovery.

Not so delighted was my new Squadron Commander, now based at RAF Finningley near Doncaster. On hearing of this incident, he remonstrated with me over the crew's flight in such poor conditions, saying that 'there was more than one way to skin a cat'. My riposte that I thought they had made a pretty good job of skinning this particular cat was not well received.

* * *

Another such incident occurred one winter's afternoon when a large bulk-ore carrier, *Anglia Team*, radioed for assistance in getting an injured crew member to hospital. The ship was on passage in the Atlantic approximately 30 miles west of the Hebridean Isle of Lewis and some 170 miles from Lossiemouth.

After a brief consultation with Lossiemouth's duty Meteorological Officer, the crew took off and headed west along the Moray Firth at low level. The weather was not good, with frequent snow showers and low cloud hampering their progress. Also scrambled was a Nimrod maritime patrol aircraft from RAF Kinloss, 10 miles to the west of Lossiemouth. For the more remote tasks out at sea, it was standard practice to have a Nimrod in attendance both to assist in guiding the helicopter towards a distant ship, and to provide a reassuring presence and radio link for our vulnerable single-engined helicopters.

The crew refuelled their Whirlwind at Stornoway for the flight out over the Atlantic, by which time it was dark. As they set off to find the ship the Decca Navigator, the sole on-board navigational aid, failed, leaving Flight Lieutenant Bill Gault the unenviable task of calculating the interception with the moving ship using only basic techniques. There was a further unwelcome occurrence when the Nimrod had to return to base with an engine fire.

By this time the pilot, Flight Lieutenant Martin Cocksedge, had spotted the blazing lights of the ship penetrating the gloom. The winchman, Sergeant Andy Ball, was winched onto the deck and the casualty quickly recovered to the Whirlwind's cabin for the return journey to hospital at Stornoway. Without the Nimrod, Bill Gault again had the task of making an accurate land-fall on the Isle of Lewis using only the most basic navigation techniques. This he achieved without fuss.

While Martin later recalled the size of the Atlantic swell, and Andy confessed to having felt somewhat isolated and exposed once the Nimrod had left them, none of the crew thought of the mission as being particularly noteworthy for the north of Scotland in winter. However, something had alerted my senior officers. Shortly after 8.00 am in my office the next morning, I was following my crew's final leg of their flight home when my telephone rang. It was the Air Officer Commanding 18 Group. The Air Marshal told me he had just received his morning briefing from his staff during which he had been appraised of the activities of all of his Group's aircraft during the night. My Flight's night-time excursion into the Atlantic had apparently featured prominently and he questioned me closely on the circumstances. I described the flight as factually as I could, playing down the weather aspect and the lack of navigation aids. However, there was no fooling him. *He* told *me* what the weather had been, reminding me that he had also received a comprehensive meteorological briefing from his staff. He then surprised me by telling me he was ringing to give his apologies for the premature departure of the Nimrod during the mission. Emboldened, I confessed that the Whirlwind had carried out a crucial part of the flight without any functioning navigation aids. There was a brief silence on the line before he replied, 'Please give the crew my heartiest congratulations on a job very well done.' Replying that it would be my pleasure, I put the telephone down, only for it immediately to ring again.

It was my Wing Commander and the conversation could not have been more different from that of a few moments before. Phrases like 'cavalier approach', 'flagrant disregard of limitations' and 'gross irresponsibility' squeaked out of the earpiece, now held at arm's-length. The tirade abated momentarily, presumably waiting for some response from me.

'Can I add your congratulations to the crew to those of the AOC's for a job very well done, Sir?' I enquired sweetly before replacing the receiver.

* * *

Occasionally, trouble would arise from an unexpected source – the Rescue Co-ordination Centre. The controllers there were responsible for the allocation of rescue missions to the helicopter flights within their region and, in that capacity, we normally enjoyed a close working relationship with them. However, things could quickly turn sour when the more senior controllers became involved.

When both helicopters were serviceable, the second standby crew would occasionally be brought in for VIP tasks, ferrying royalty, senior officers and politicians on local engagements. However, our orders made it clear that these flights must never prejudice the response of the first standby aircraft. It followed, therefore, that if only one aircraft were available, then this must be reserved for emergency use. Unfortunately, the odd senior controller, thinking perhaps to protect his career, sometimes ignored this rule with embarrassing results.

On one occasion, I and my crew, as second standby, were detailed to collect the Chief of the Defence Staff, Marshal of the RAF, Sir Neil (later Lord) Cameron, from RAF Kinloss and fly him to an appointment at Aviemore, barely 40 miles south of us. As head of all the British armed services, officers did not come any more senior. I was somewhat disappointed, therefore, when the duty crew suddenly disappeared over the horizon for a rescue mission on Skye. My crew and our Whirlwind were now on immediate stand-by. The VIP flight was off; or at least it should have been. One of the senior controllers, a Wing Commander, had other ideas. Calling me, he ordered me to carry out the VIP task as planned, telling me that I would retain first stand-by status while *en route*, despite the fact that I would probably be beyond reliable radio range for much of the time. I protested, claiming that this was a potentially dangerous precedent that he was creating. My protests fell on deaf ears and I duly found myself flying south with the Chief of Defence Staff in my cabin and about 10 miles to run to Aviemore.

Suddenly, the coastguard radio burst into life. A fishing boat was sending a 'Mayday' distress message, reporting that it was taking in water in the Moray Firth just a few miles north of Lossiemouth.

'Shit!' I exclaimed, not for the first time in my career. 'Here we are running a bloody taxi service while one of Lossie's boats is sinking.' I started turning north towards Lossiemouth.

'Is there a problem, Captain?' came the calm voice of my passenger. I hadn't even realised that he had been connected to the helicopter's intercom system.

'Yes Sir.' I replied. 'One of Lossiemouth's fishing boats is sinking just a few miles off-shore.'

'What do you propose to do?' he asked.

'I'm already turning back, Sir. This is the first standby helicopter and we're needed there. I can take you with us, or I can drop you off at Lossiemouth on our way.' To my surprise, he asked if I could drop him on the main A9 trunk road and call for a vehicle. I agreed, and moments later I waved farewell to the lonely figure at the side of the main road not, I confess, without some misgivings on my part – squadron leaders do not normally abandon the Chief of the Defence Staff in the middle of nowhere.

I then called Kinloss on the radio and requested that a staff car be sent to the specific grid reference on the A9 to collect our VIP.

'You've done what?' was the incredulous response from Kinloss. I explained that I was now engaged in a search and rescue operation and didn't have time for explanations. Shortly after, we were overhead the stricken vessel, now wallowing low in the water. Other fishing boats in the area had responded immediately to the distress call and had taken the crew off. Being so close to their home port, they declined to be winched up, preferring instead to supervise the salvage of their boat.

Verbal repercussions were swift and I spent the next few hours answering extremely critical telephone calls, including one from the irate Senior Controller.

'Are you mad?' he demanded. 'How can you possibly think of doing something so stupid?' Initially I attempted to defend my decision, pointing out how it would have looked in the local and national press if the boat had sunk with loss of life and it had been discovered that the only available local rescue helicopter was away on a VIP flight. I was wasting my time. Soon my own Wing Commander weighed in with his criticism of my actions. Eventually, I had to avoid the telephone. I was so angry that I was afraid of what I might say. So much for support!

The following day I was called to the telephone by one of my crew.

'It's a Group Captain from CDS's office for you.' he said ominously. I resigned myself to yet another haranguing, but was unprepared for his message. He said that the Chief of Defence Staff had become aware of the adverse reaction to my actions the previous day and wanted me to know that he fully supported my decision and apologised for the situation in which I now found myself. I was told that the CDS had also made it clear to all my critics that I had behaved entirely correctly and he now considered the matter at an end.

I didn't doubt that I had won few friends over this vindication, particularly at the Rescue Co-ordination Centre. The opportunity for revenge from that quarter was not long in coming.

* * *

One fine summer Saturday morning, my crew and I were alerted by the coast-guard to a sinking cabin cruiser just off the coast of the Moray Firth near to Inverness. There had been an explosion and the small boat, with three people on board, was now burning fiercely. Leaving our ground-crew to call the Rescue Co-ordination Centre to advise them of our departure, we ran out to our waiting Whirlwind. This was standard procedure when the emergency call had originated from an agency such as the police or coastguard and where speed was vital.

Within a few minutes we were airborne and heading towards the ominous plume of black smoke in the far distance. As we passed Kinloss, I was surprised to receive a radio call ordering me to return to Lossiemouth and stand by for an inbound Jaguar. As this was a Saturday, Lossiemouth would normally be closed and no notification had been given to us of any un-scheduled movements over the weekend. I asked Kinloss to enquire what the Jaguar's emergency was. The reply puzzled me – the Jaguar was not in any sort of emergency and would be making a normal approach and landing following a delivery flight from a maintenance unit. I was again ordered to return to Lossiemouth. Again I queried the order. Here I was, *en route* to a burning boat with casualties on board, now being ordered to return to watch a perfectly serviceable Jaguar land. Kinloss continued to relay the repeated order until I switched the radio off so that we could concentrate on dealing with the emergency on the water now just a short distance ahead of us.

By the time we arrived, the Cromarty lifeboat was alongside the smoulder-ing and sinking cabin cruiser and the final casualty was being transferred by stretcher. A doctor was present on the lifeboat and he advised that, in view of the short time it would take to put into port, he would prefer to monitor the casualties' condition aboard the lifeboat rather than subjecting them to the further trauma of being winched into our Whirlwind. I escorted the lifeboat to port before returning to Lossiemouth where the Jaguar had landed un-eventfully several minutes ahead of me.

'You've really done it now, Geoff!' was the warning from one of the sympathetic controllers from the Rescue Co-ordination Centre. 'He's out to get you this time and he's already talking about a Court Martial.' This event, coming on top of the fiasco over the VIP flight had obviously hit a nerve with the Senior Controller. Over the next couple of weeks I received hints of administrative action being carried out preparatory to a Court Martial. This would include the taking of a summary of evidence that would form the basis for any charge. If a case was established, a convening order for a Court Martial would be signed by the AOC.

Shortly after, I was attending the first Search and Rescue Wing dinner, held in the Officers' Mess at RAF Finningley where the Wing and both Squadrons' Headquarters was located. The AOC was Guest of Honour. At the dinner I found myself seated next to a Wing Commander who was the AOC's Personal Staff Officer. Turning to introduce himself, he commented on my glum appearance.

'Cheer up. It may never happen,' he declared cheerily.

'It already has,' I replied, introducing myself. 'You must be aware of the situation I'm in.'

'I know who you are – *and* I know all about your problem,' he said. 'You can rest assured that there will be no Court Martial. The AOC has thrown the charge out.' He went on to say that the controller had been wrong in trying to call me away from an on-going emergency incident and that the AOC was intending to clarify the orders. The following week, he issued a directive emphasising that the dispersed helicopter flights were 'area assets', and their role did not include an obligation to assist any particular RAF station at which they just happened to be sited.

*   *   *

It was to prove a recurring theme throughout my RAF career that I invari-ably found the most senior officers in the chain of command to be the most courteous, considerate and down-to-earth. Regrettably it was the middle-ranking officers above me with whom I seemed to have most of my problems.

*   *   *

It should not be thought that life running a search and rescue flight was one endless series of confrontations. By way of compensation and as an antidote to the often distressing situations in which we inevitably became involved, there was much humour on the flight, from the good-natured banter amongst col-leagues to the black humour surrounding our job.

On one occasion, one of our crews had been called to a major accident aboard a fishing vessel 20 miles north-west of Cape Wrath. A trawl had parted and the broken hawser had whipped across the deck, cutting one of the crew in half and seriously injuring three others. The winchman, Sergeant Dave Lloyd, had been lowered into the open hold, almost waist-deep in slippery fish and awash with blood and body parts. Working to secure the two most serious casualties in the helicopter's stretcher, Dave's orange immersion suit had quickly become covered in blood and fish scales to the extent that he now resembled some exotic, shimmering merman.

Leaving the third casualty to be picked up by a RN Sea King that had arrived to assist, Dave's crew delivered their two casualties to hospital at Stornoway. While subsequently returning to Lossiemouth, they were diverted to go to rescue a fallen, injured climber on Skye. The initial call to the trawler had come just as the crew were starting their lunch and, working on the principle that you never knew where or when your next meal might be, Dave had stuffed himself injudiciously with crisps and Mars bars. With all his exertions on the ship and the appalling carnage there, he was now starting to feel somewhat nauseous. The mountain casualty was located quickly and Dave was duly winched out on the end of the 120-foot tape to be placed alongside him. After the briefest of inspections of the casualty, Dave was forced to turn away and part with his lunch.

'Am I going to die?' asked the semi-conscious climber.

'No,' replied Dave, 'but I am!' and promptly threw up again. It later transpired that the casualty, in his dazed state, had seen this shimmering, golden apparition approaching him from the sky and thought that it must be an angel come for him. When the 'angel' had turned away from the casualty in apparent shock at his appearance, he thought that his time had definitely come.

Some angel!

CHAPTER TWENTY-THREE

BLIZZARD

Many of our search and rescue tasks were inevitably carried out in appalling weather. Indeed, it was frequently this factor that had precipitated our involvement by helicopter in the first place, particularly in winter when the days were often too short to permit complex mountain searches by ground parties alone. However, nothing had prepared us for the ferocity and duration of the storm that hit the Scottish Highlands during the night of 29 January 1978. That evening, Marian and I had attended a concert at our eldest child's school just at the rear of the Married Quarters at Lossiemouth. During the concert, we were not the only ones exchanging worried looks as we heard the wind start to increase from its relatively normal gale-force to a new level of intensity that tore round the building, rattling windows and doors in its ferocity. At the end of the concert, we struggled home, pulled and buffeted in all directions, thankful that we did not have far to go. By now, heavy flurries of snow were being whirled around, rapidly adding to the previous falls, while a temperature plummeting to minus ten degrees Centigrade added to the misery.

I went into work early the next morning to find the Duty Crew had already called in the second standby crew in anticipation of a busy day. There had been little change in the weather overnight and our frustration mounted as the list of urgent requests from the police steadily lengthened. High on their list was the search for a man missing overnight near Inverness. Eventually, I decided to attempt to get airborne.

In strong winds, starting the 25-foot long, flexible rotor blades of helicopters of the Whirlwind's era was always potentially hazardous and a maximum wind speed for emergency starting was set at 45 knots for a steady wind but only 30 knots if gusting. The northerly wind was now gusting well over 60 knots (70 mph), a violent storm in meteorological terms, and therefore considerably in excess of our starting limits. One option for protecting the blades in strong wind conditions was to start up inside the hangar before taxiing out into the blast. I had used this method previously but now, with the combination of the wind strength and its direction across the open hangar doors, my helicopter would be slammed against the side of the hangar as it emerged. I therefore elected to have the Whirlwind towed out onto the airfield, well clear of all buildings and associated turbulence, before attempting a start. I also had the Crash Crew in close attendance in case the blades flailed sufficiently to chop off the tail.

As I engaged the rotor blades following engine start, I watched helplessly as each blade passed in front of me in turn, flapping wildly up and down as the wind generated unwanted and unpredictable lift before the blades gained their rigidity through the powerful centrifugal forces generated by their rotation. When the blades reached flying speed, I quickly completed the take-off checks and lifted to the hover. Immediately, we were blown rapidly *backwards* before the controls could take effect and hold us in a stationary hover while the helicopter was effectively flying forward into the 60-knot wind. I thanked my lucky stars that the decision to start well out into the airfield meant that we had not been blown backwards into a hangar or other obstruction.

Setting off towards Inverness, nearly 40 miles south-west of our base, we found ourselves crabbing along sideways with an enormous angle of drift and with me looking left across the cockpit to see where we were going. By this time, the thickening blanket of snow was already being blown into deep drifts by the storm-force wind, forming a moving and undulating sea of white beneath us, while the continuous snowfall put us in a swirling, featureless white world with no discernible horizon – the dreaded 'whiteout' conditions.

Arriving in the area where the man had been reported missing, we commenced our search along one of the minor roads running south from Inverness. Coming across an isolated house, my winchman, Sergeant Dave Lloyd, was lowered to ensure that the missing man had not sought shelter there. By unfortunate coincidence, this was the missing man's home and his wife quickly confirmed that he was not there. Continuing our search, we soon spotted an ominous mound of snow in the centre of the road some few hundred yards further on. Again Dave was winched down and, scraping away the snow, discovered the dead body of the missing man. Winching him aboard our helicopter caused some difficulty as he was rigidly frozen in the posture in which he had fallen at some time during the previous night, face-down with his arms above his head. Once Dave and our casualty were in the cabin, we set off to return to Inverness but our direct route was now blocked by further heavy snow, forcing us to head for the relative safety of Loch Ness. As we approached the Loch, we noted a snow-covered car on a road. Once again, Dave was winched down to investigate, this time discovering a couple and their child inside. They had been there for many hours and were extremely cold and hungry. I managed to land almost alongside the car, while my navigator, Flight Lieutenant Brian Canfer, manoeuvred the still-frozen body to the rear of the cabin and covered it with a blanket. With everyone loaded safely aboard, we set off once again towards Inverness. We frequently flew winter rescue missions with the helicopter's heating turned off. If we picked up a severely hypothermic casualty, any sudden external warmth could easily result in a fatal drop in blood pressure. Brian and Dave ascertained that our new passengers were merely very cold and so the full heating was switched on. Shortly after, I was aware of the most horrendous screaming over the noise of the engine and rotors. The frozen body at the rear of the cabin had started to thaw and his arms slowly lowered to displace the blanket. The child had been terrified by the sight and had reacted accordingly!

Having unloaded our casualty and the rescued family at Inverness Police Station, we were soon heading south again to deliver urgently needed medical supplies to another isolated house at Slochd, a few miles along the road north of Carrbridge. Here a reported sixty-three travellers had sought sanctuary after the road had become impassable. With our Decca navigation equipment proving less than reliable, we were having some difficulty establishing an accurate position and, on several occasions, we resorted to winching Dave down to wipe snow from road-signs. At one point we came up against a line of high tension power cables strung across our route. The tops of the pylons were hidden in the low cloud-base barely 50 feet above us, while the cables appeared to loop down alarmingly close to the surface of the deep snow beneath us. Despite flying for some distance along the line of cables I could find nowhere giving any greater clearance between wires and ground. With a 60-knot wind behind me, I could not risk an attempt at flying beneath them at a high ground-speed. Instead, I turned the Whirlwind into wind, coming to a hover with the cables behind me. Choosing a line that took us as close to one of the pylons as possible and therefore the highest point of the cables atop it, Brian then talked me *backwards* under the cables while Dave kept a very sharp lookout for any sight of them above. Just brushing the snowy surface with the helicopter's wheels and with the snow billowing up from our rotor downwash being blown clear behind us, we inched our way through to safety on the far side.

Continuing on our way, we came across a cottage almost completely engulfed in the snow, where we spotted a red telephone box nestling in its lee. I landed on the road outside, just as another heavy fall of snow commenced. Doubled-up against the driving snow, Dave set off towards the cottage, sight of his bright orange immersion suit soon being lost as the visibility abruptly reduced to less than the length of the rotor blades. The Whirlwind had been shuddering and shaking in the severe buffeting when I suddenly became aware of the compass slowly rotating. Thoughts of an unserviceable compass were quickly dispelled when I realised that the four-ton Whirlwind was being blown bodily down the road and rotating slowly in the process despite the locked brakes. The next moment, Dave came sliding past on his back, having been blown over in the storm.

Eventually, all reunited on board, we set off to a revised location. Dave had needed all his powers of persuasion to get the telephone operator to put him through to the Rescue Centre Controller as an emergency free call. The Controller had identified his position from the telephone box's location and had given us further guidance to reach our objective. As quickly as it had arrived, the storm blew on past us and we soon located the house, marked with a black 'X' in the snow, together with its trapped, but safe, travellers.

On our return flight to refuel at Inverness Airport, we had just winched up two lorry drivers who had been stranded miles from anywhere when there was a sudden muffled 'thud' from the engine followed by a continuous, ear-splitting banshee wail. Something was obviously seriously amiss but, quickly scanning the engine instruments, there appeared to be little loss of perfor-mance. Rather than carrying out an immediate precautionary landing in the white wilderness we were currently traversing, I elected to try and continue to Inverness Airport where we could have the engine examined in detail. Every-thing continued to work and soon I was landing at the airport watched by curious observers who had been drawn out of the offices and buildings to investigate the source of this awful noise. The airport management allowed me the use of a near-empty hangar in which I could park the Whirlwind out of the continuing heavy snow showers. The hangar was dark and unheated, all power having been lost since the previous night. We examined the engine by torchlight and were horrified to discover the extent of the damage to the tiny blades in the intake area of the jet engine almost certainly caused by the ingestion of a chunk of ice or snow. This was going to need a complete engine change. I contacted Lossiemouth and spoke to my engineering ground-crew who assured me that they had a spare engine and would send it out with a team as soon as possible.

Later, two of my ground-crew arrived. The Motor Transport Section at Lossiemouth had declined sending any vehicle out in the blizzard conditions, so the engine had been loaded into the back of one my ground-crew's own van and the two of them had slipped and slithered their way for nearly three hours through thick snow and ice along the 30 or so miles from Lossiemouth – a fine effort. On arrival, they set to immediately to change the engines over, aided by Dave and me holding torches and spanners for them as they struggled with frozen fingers to complete the multitude of intricate connec-tions. In the meantime, Brian had been loaned to British Airways Helicopters to help navigate their larger Sikorsky S-61 around an area unfamiliar to them, their usual flying being out of Aberdeen Airport, ferrying workers to and from the North Sea oil platforms.

* * *

With the new engine installed, I carried out a series of ground runs so that my groundcrew could carry out essential adjustments before telephoning the squadron's engineering headquarters at Finningley to request clearance to carry out a limited engine airtest at night, a most irregular procedure. There was now a huge demand for helicopters and reinforcements were flying in to meet the ever-mounting number of tasks. As well as the Sikorsky S-61 from Aberdeen, there were search and rescue helicopters from Leuchars, Boulmer and Leconfield and Finningley, and Sea Kings from Prestwick. Nevertheless, we could ill afford to waste a single Whirlwind. I was surprised when clearance was received and I took off into a relatively fine night for a series of climbs and autorotations to test the engine. All appeared well and, reclaiming Brian from British Airways, we flew to the Police Station at Inverness to receive our next list of urgent tasks. Arriving there at the same time as two RN Sea Kings, we were regaled with horror stories from their crews of their struggle along Loch Ness to get to Inverness. They were amazed to hear that we had been going up and down that route all day while they had sat on the ground waiting for an improvement in the weather. They were even more surprised when they heard that we were about to set off on another series of emergency missions while they were intending to go to bed.

*   *   *

Our first job was to deliver emergency medication to Tomintoul, at 1,132 feet the second highest village in the UK. The weather had improved to the extent that the cloud cover was now around 4,000 feet, the snow was only intermittent and the wind had abated to a relative zephyr of 40 knots or so. It was, however, incredibly dark. As we approached the estimated location of Tomintoul there was not the merest glimmer of lights. Brian checked and re-checked the Decca Navigator and cross-checked with his map, each time with the same result – Tomintoul should be directly beneath us, but there was just a blank darkness below. Suddenly there was a tiny pin-prick of light – then another – and another. As I circled, the number of lights below slowly increased, eventually forming a magical sparkling carpet on the snow. I carefully spiralled down, all of us alert for any unexpected obstructions, before setting up an approach onto the square in the centre of the village now beautifully lit by torches and candles in many of the windows. The square was bisected in both directions by roads with trees along the road sides and I selected what I thought was the clearest quadrant. Coming to a hover over the centre of the quadrant, I descended slowly under Brian's directions. Suddenly I realised that we weren't descending anymore. Simultaneously Brian called,

'Up! Up! Up!' the call for an emergency climb. I had perched my Whirlwind like a four-ton canary on the only wire running diagonally across the quadrant, snow-covered and invisible in my landing lights against the backdrop of more snow. Fortunately, my next very circumspect attempt into an adjacent quadrant was more successful and our precious load of medicines was delivered safely to the local doctor.

Although many power lines were down and power blackouts were widespread, one fortunate aspect of these blizzards was the fact that the telephone system had escaped relatively unscathed. It was by this means that a farmer near Bridge of Brown, barely 4 miles north-west of Tomintoul, had reported that he and his family were totally cut off and had burnt the last of their furniture in an attempt to keep warm. On board we had food and a large cylinder of butane gas for him. Leaving the welcoming lights of Tomintoul, we once more ventured into the all-enveloping darkness. The frantic flashing of a torch in our direction quickly identified the isolated location in a valley but the position was complicated by a line of high tension power cables running across it just beyond the farm. After several careful orbits, gradually getting lower and lower, we decided that an approach in total darkness into wind and over the cables could not be conducted safely, so I elected to drop the supplies from a very low down-wind pass. Lining up on the pin-prick of light from the farmer's torch, we thundered past, dropping his supplies right alongside him before I had to apply full power and climb steeply to clear the power cables ahead of us.

*   *   *

Returning to Lossiemouth in the early hours of the morning after almost six hours of flying in extremely trying conditions, I tried to take stock of the confused and chaotic situation. Neither of my other two Whirlwinds was there. One was at Wick having been heroically engaged in helping evacuate two trains that had become de-railed in the drifting snow, while the other had been grounded by continuous blizzard conditions just north of Loch Shin and the crew had taken refuge in the Crask Inn at Lairg. During the afternoon and evening, more helicopter reinforcements had flown into the area. In addition to the Sea Kings at Inverness and the Sikorsky S-61 encountered earlier, a Wessex had flown up from RAF Valley in Anglesey and one of Boulmer's two search and rescue Whirlwinds was also detached to help us. Another civilian helicopter, a JetRanger, had also been made available but was now stuck overnight at Wick,

I discovered that my ice-damaged engine had not been the only casualty of the day's operations. The only serviceable Wessex from Leuchars had been abandoned in a whiteout at Loch Laggan, east of Fort William while attempting to reach a stranded climber on the slopes of 3,700-foot Creag Meagaidh, its crew themselves being rescued by the Wessex from Valley and taken to Fort William. The Whirlwind from Boulmer had, like us, also suffered an ice-damaged engine that required changing.

The following morning, everything was on the move again. In place of the rather piecemeal responses of the previous day, largely dictated by the atrocious weather, improving flying conditions meant that a more co-ordinated and reliable response could be made to calls for assistance. Invaluable in this was the contribution made by the faithful Shackletons of 8 Squadron, our neighbours at Lossiemouth. While maintaining a continuous airborne presence over the north of Scotland, they kept a plot of the location of all the widely dispersed helicopter assets, relaying tasking messages from the Rescue Controller at Edinburgh and the Police Control Room at Inverness, and providing a vital and reassuring radio link to our helicopters, which were often operating in isolation over very inhospitable and remote terrain. As the emergency progressed, the Rescue Co-ordination Centre devolved its authority to the Inverness Police Control Room, now manned with an RAF liaison officer in the person of Squadron Leader Alex Sneddon, the Officer Commanding our sister search and rescue helicopter unit, 22 Squadron. His role became essential as the number of military helicopters sent into the area from as far afield as the south of England continued to increase steadily during the morning, eventually reaching a total of twenty-two.

My crew's tasking for the day was again south of Inverness and consisted largely of road searches, checking all the vehicles found for occupants, and taking food and other essential supplies to isolated farms and villages. It was reassuring to note the self-reliance and independence of many of these people in some of the remotest areas. Accustomed to being cut off and isolated for lengthy periods during most Highland winters, they had prepared accordingly and, in several cases, actually declined our proffered emergency rations. We returned to Lossiemouth after another five hours flying and finally met up with some of colleagues to hear their stories of their rescue operations at the opposite end of the huge affected area.

A particularly difficult time had been had by Flight Lieutenant Martin Cocksedge and his crew. After my first couple of hours flying on the first day, I had radioed a message to my Flight Operations Room to the effect that I considered that the conditions were just flyable, albeit while exercising extreme caution. Acting on that, Martin had got airborne with his crew, navigator Flight Lieutenant Bill Campbell and winchman Master Air Loadmaster George Muir, initially in response to a police request for assistance at Wick, but subsequently changed to helping police search for any vehicles trapped in the snow on the A9 immediately north-east of Helmsdale where the road rose steeply through the narrow pass in an area known as the Ord of Caithness. Here, the snow had drifted to a depth of more than *20 feet* giving rise to concerns that there might be vehicles buried there. Many vehicles were indeed located and their occupants air-lifted to safety in spite of the almost impossible flying conditions.

Returning to the area after refuelling, Martin and his crew were diverted to help air-lift some eighty-four passengers from two trains that had become derailed and embedded overnight in deep drifts between Forsinard and Altnabreach, a particularly bleak and remote area where the railway line looped inland from Helmsdale across the exposed moor. While helping to fly these passengers to safety in atrocious conditions and with the onset of darkness imminent, Martin had been receiving intermittent radio messages requesting help for the police still searching at the Ord of Caithness. Although initially assisted by the British Airways Helicopter S-61 and a Bristows Helicopters JetRanger, it was touch-and-go whether the evacuation could be completed before nightfall. When the S-61 departed to refuel, the situation became even more critical, leaving Martin facing a terrible dilemma. At the train, some of the passengers had decided to attempt the 5-mile walk to the nearest station at Altnabreac, rather than spend a second freezing night in the train without food or light. With extremely deep snow drifts and an effective wind chill temperature of minus thirty degrees Centigrade, this was an almost certain recipe for death from exposure in their ill-equipped state. At the Ord of Caithness an unknown number of people were possibly still trapped in their vehicles beneath the snow. With the weather conditions so bad that it was by no means certain Martin could even reach the new location, he elected to stay with the trains, eventually completing the evacuation in darkness. It was a decision that he was later called upon to justify at a Scottish Fatal Accident Inquiry after three bodies were discovered the following day in two buried cars at the Ord of Caithness. The Sheriff at the Wick inquiry agreed with his decision. Even in ideal conditions, he could not have been in two places at once. In the appalling conditions prevailing at the time, the question that should have been asked is how on earth Martin and his crew managed to be flying anywhere in the area at all.

Two days later, another buried car was discovered, this time with its occupant still alive. He was a travelling salesman from a company in Wick and had used his stock samples of ladies' tights to wear and wrap around himself to stave off the bitter cold, a fact made much of by the media. I picked him up and flew him to hospital at Wick.

*   *   *

After the first two hectic days, the search and rescue aspect was effectively over, leaving a multitude of more mundane but, nevertheless, essential tasks to be undertaken – ferrying doctors on their rural rounds, transferring patients to hospital, transporting engineers on their mission to restore the many downed power lines, delivering feed to farming livestock – all co-ordinated and directed from the Police Control Room from where instructions were relayed to us by a succession of ever-circling Shackletons of 8 Squadron.

Sadly, the storm had claimed four lives but, given the severity of the pre-vailing conditions and the extent and remoteness of the area affected, this was a remarkably small number. Northern Constabulary records show that well over 300 hours had been flown by twenty-two helicopters and some 392 persons had been rescued from life-threatening situations, almost a third of whom had been picked up by my Flight's three Whirlwinds in the first hectic day.

It had been one of the largest military peacetime operations in support of the civil powers in the UK on record. It had provided a stimulating and memorable experience for those of us at the heart of it, and had required some extremely challenging decisions to be made by my crews.

CHAPTER TWENTY-FOUR

FAREWELL TO 'LOSSIE'

During the early part of 1978, I started losing members of my Flight as they were posted to join the Sea King Training Unit at the Royal Naval Air Station at Culdrose in Cornwall. There, along with other experienced pilots and crew members drawn from other search and rescue and support helicopter units, they would learn to fly and operate the RAF's latest search and rescue helicopter before returning to Lossiemouth to form the first Sea King Flight. Their loss left a big gap in my Flight's strength and one that was only partly filled by crews on loan from other Whirlwind Flights around the country. Few had experience of operating in a mountainous environment and they required careful teaming up to ensure a satisfactory level of combined experience and local knowledge in each crew. The problem was compounded by their relatively short detachments to Lossiemouth. No sooner had they started to feel comfortable operating in their new area than they were returned to their units to be replaced by more newcomers. Despite this, however, the Flight managed to maintain its enviable record of success in search and rescue operations.

*   *   *

Right out of the blue, I was promoted to Squadron Leader in the July list. This came as a huge surprise to me as none of my previous periodic career interviews or one-sided conversations with immediate superiors had given any hint of it. After the initial novelty of getting used to the new rank and taking the inevitable ribbing from my colleagues, the reality of my situation hit me. Up until this point, I had been provisionally earmarked for the next Sea King course and was destined to take command of the second newly-equipped search and rescue Flight at RAF Boulmer, near Alnwick in Northumberland. Now, as a Squadron Leader, I was ineligible for that Flight Lieutenant post. I might reasonably have hoped to take command of one of the two search and rescue Squadrons, but neither incumbent was due for posting. I did not have long to wait to find out what my next posting would be – Officer Commanding Bristol University Air Squadron. Yet another abrupt lurch in my career!

*   *   *

In mid-1978, the first RAF Sea King had been delivered to RAF Finningley by Westland Helicopters, the manufacturers, and I was later invited by my

Squadron Commander to join him in flying this helicopter up to its new home at Lossiemouth. This was certainly the newest military aircraft I had ever been in, let alone flown. It had fewer than seven hours recorded in its Log Book – the time taken for Westland's test pilots to complete the initial check flights and deliver it to Finningley. We each took it in turns to fly the helicopter while the other experimented with all the new navigation equipment that the Sea King carried, the Aircrew Manual open on our knees as we tentatively pressed and turned all the switches and knobs. As we approached Lossiemouth, our two Whirlwinds joined us in formation as we made a circuit of the airfield and local town to mark our arrival.

*   *   *

By the time the Sea Kings took over I had been in this post for four years. During that time, I considered that I had had one of the best and most satisfying jobs in the RAF. The serious shortcomings of the Whirlwind described earlier were treated as challenges by my crews, who relished extracting every ounce of performance from its ageing airframe, using novel and innovative techniques to overcome its limitations while operating in the most demanding and unforgiving search and rescue environment in the UK, as well as in some of its worst weather. They enjoyed being able to pit their wits and flying skills against the elements and the wide variety of situations presented to them to bring help to people in distress, achieving many notable rescues in the process. I find it disappointing to note that many current search and rescue crews have little idea of the history of the role and the vital part that the two main squadrons, 22 and 202, had played in evolving the techniques and equipment in use today. (One recent Sea King Squadron Commander has been reported as saying that the Whirlwind was such a basic helicopter that it could only have been of very limited use in the Scottish mountains. I leave the reader to judge just how 'limited' that use was and how much its crews had strived to extract every ounce of performance from this undoubtedly basic helicopter.)

I also counted myself most fortunate in the crews that I had been privileged to command. Despite the lack of confidence in them sometimes shown by some senior officers, I had put great trust in their judgement and abilities, and had been rewarded by their unfailing loyalty and support.

*   *   *

Following the formal parade to mark the handover of the search and rescue standby from the Whirlwind to the Sea King crews, the AOC took me aside and enquired what I thought of my forthcoming posting. I told him that I was pleased that it was to be another flying appointment but disappointed that I hadn't been able to stay in the rescue helicopter world. He then asked if

I would allow him to use his influence to get my posting changed, adding that he didn't want to lose me. I agreed with alacrity, suddenly hopeful that I might yet stay in the job to which I had grown so firmly attached. Just a few days later I was informed that I was going to take over as the Officer Commanding the RAF Search and Rescue Training Squadron at RAF Valley on Anglesey, the unit primarily responsible for the specialist training of all RAF helicopter search and rescue crews and also for providing basic rescue training to all RAF helicopter pilots during their initial helicopter courses. There was only one problem. The post required me to be a Qualified Helicopter Instructor, a QHI – yet another course was in the offing for me.

In the meantime, I was detached to the search and rescue flight at RAF Coltishall, near Norwich, where I spent several relatively relaxed shifts, freed from the additional responsibilities of running a flight. My time there, however, was rudely interrupted by a telephone call one Monday morning.

'What the hell are you doing at Coltishall, Leeming? You're supposed to be starting the QHI course today. I want you here first thing tomorrow morning!' With that hearty welcome ringing in my ears, I patiently explained to the Chief Flying Instructor at RAF Shawbury that I had not received any joining instructions to report to the Central Flying School (Helicopters) there. Furthermore, I was still on search and rescue standby for the rest of the week and couldn't just drop everything and leave Coltishall. After some negotiation, it was decided that I would join my course one week late on the following Monday. It had been reasoned that my previous experience as a fixed-wing flying instructor could be taken into account and that I would not suffer unduly from missing some of the early lectures on instructional technique and lesson planning.

Later that week I slipped and slithered my way north to Lossiemouth on treacherous, wintry roads to collect my kit before driving all the way back to Shawbury to join my course.

CHAPTER TWENTY-FIVE

PRACTICE DROWNING

RAF Shawbury in Shropshire was now the home of RAF helicopter training and it was to there that I reported, one week late, to commence the helicopter instructor course. The course progressed well and I enjoyed it much more than the equivalent fixed-wing instructor course that I had undertaken twelve years earlier. I also had my previous instructional experience to draw upon, so it was perhaps not surprising that I won the Llangollen Trophy for the academic aspect of the course. Also, all the flying was carried out in the delightful Aerospatiale Gazelle. Compared with the venerable Whirlwind, the Gazelle was like driving a sports car.

Ironically, the only aspect of flying that caused any hiccups for me was mountain flying. As with my earlier helicopter training, this was carried out in the beautiful surroundings of the mountains of Snowdonia, but I had some difficulty in curbing my enthusiasm for advanced techniques learnt and evolved during my many search and rescue missions in the loftier and more rugged Scottish mountains. My instructor had to keep reminding me that I had to teach the 'standard' approach to mountain flying, leaving all my operational experience and ideas behind. I decided to bite my tongue and be a good student.

* * *

After travelling to Angelesey I arrived at the Search and Rescue Training Squadron, commonly known by its more manageable acronym as SARTS, on 1 April 1979 and immediately began my specialised training to qualify in teaching all aspects of search and rescue. While the procedures and techniques were all very familiar to me, I now had to adapt to flying all the exercises from the left-hand cockpit seat where I was blind to much of what the student would be seeing. What is more, every part of the exercise had to be flown to the very high standard demanded for demonstration to a student.

On completion of this training, I took over command of my new unit from my predecessor, Squadron Leader John Davy, with whom I had served in Singapore and Borneo. He disappeared off to the Ministry of Defence.

* * *

The start in my new job was inauspicious, resulting in yet another king-sized rocket. One of my early projected tasks was to provide the helicopters and crews to remake the instructional search and rescue training films used during classroom lessons. A Ministry of Defence film unit was due to carry out the filming, but was concerned about the continuity and light levels being affected by the changeable weather. Because of this unpredictability, I realised that the time forecast to complete the filming would make significant demands on my limited resources over an extended period of time. I therefore started planning how best we could continue working with the film crews while avoiding any disruptions to the courses. The solution came indirectly from a signal via the Ministry of Defence asking for help in providing a winchman to meet an unexpected short-term manning crisis on 84 Squadron, which was based at RAF Akrotiri in southern Cyprus and provided the search and rescue cover for that part of the island. Needless to say, I was not short of volunteers, but I could ill afford to lose any instructors with the filming task about to begin. With a stroke of logic, my erstwhile predecessor, John Davy, suggested that I could perhaps send both a spare winchman *and* the film crew to Cyprus where the filming could be carried out in a very short time in the more predictable Mediterranean climate. I quickly obtained agreement from the Squadron Commander in Cyprus that, in exchange for the loan of a winchman, he would undertake to provide a helicopter and crew for the filming. John and I soon sorted out all the details, with him obtaining the necessary authority of an air vice-marshal at the Ministry of Defence for the air passages of the personnel to and from Cyprus.

With that task satisfactorily disposed of, I turned my attention to the busy routine of flying training that I had inherited. One day later, the telephone rang and I found myself in familiar territory. Even with the telephone at arm's length I could still clearly hear the Station Commander from RAF Shawbury as he blasted my impertinence in going behind his back, making unauthorised detachments of his personnel and obtaining air passages by dubious means. Protestations, apologies or attempts at explanations on my part were to no avail. He ended by saying that he had cancelled the whole enterprise and that I should tread very carefully while getting on with the task I had been given. Stopping the project caused immediate reactions that soon escalated to exchanges at the highest levels, the result of which was that my plan was considered to have been well-founded and would go ahead!

At first sight, the involvement of the Station Commander of Shawbury might seem odd until it is explained that he was my 'Boss', SARTS being a detached unit of Shawbury. He was furious at having had his decision countermanded. Two days later, a Gazelle helicopter landed on our dispersal and out stepped the Chief Flying Instructor from Shawbury. Ushering me into my office, he proceeded to give me a succinct summary of the complaints against me made by Shawbury's Station Commander, who had sent him to deliver his message. The interview was very civilised and I suspected that he sympathised with my position, recognising that I had been trying my best to resolve a problem efficiently and, in my enthusiasm, had only been guilty of the discourtesy of not keeping my distant 'Boss' fully informed.

* * *

The next problem was not far behind – our supply of students practically dried up overnight. Our students were drawn from two main sources. All *ab initio* helicopter students passing through Shawbury came to us for a two-week course to learn the basic skills required for using the helicopter as an emergency search and rescue aircraft, irrespective of the role in which they would eventually be operating. These formed the regular and numerical bulk of our training task. The majority of the remaining students came for advanced search and rescue training to equip them as pilots and crew members manning the assigned RAF search and rescue helicopters. While the latter came through in a steady trickle, it was the loss of the former students through an unforeseen hiccup earlier in the training 'sausage machine' that had caused the sudden impact on our workload.

In order to protect my instructors from being farmed out during this hiatus, I and my two excellent Flight Commanders, Flight Lieutenants Dick Foster and Dave Holmyard, devised a plan to keep us all busy and ready for the resumption of normal training: we would cross-train each other – pilots would learn to be winch operators and winchmen, while navigators and winchmen would train as pilots. My instructors set to with a will and, as well as being challenging and tremendous fun, it produced major benefits in the better understanding of each other's problems during tricky winching operations. Thereafter, I frequently flew as winchman on training flights, a habit that was later to be of some benefit.

As sure as night follows day, the student shortage ceased, only to be re-placed with a surplus, or 'bulge' in the system as full training resumed. Because of our preparation, we were able to move back smoothly and quickly into our normal instructional roles. However, the student numbers were such that we instructors were frequently carrying out five or six instructional flights each day. In true RAF 'can do' style, my instructors took all this in their stride, even competing for a 'Hog of the Year' tankard for the most hours flown by an individual instructor. Because of my additional administrative and super-visory duties as the Officer Commanding, I only appeared on my unit's estab-lishment as half an instructor, in other words I would only be expected to fly half the number of instructional flights when compared with my instruc-tors. Despite this, however, my Log Book summary showed a total of over 300 hours in my first year, rising to 450 hours in the next. And I was not even in contention for 'Hog of the Year', being beaten by a significant margin by most of my instructors.

This hard work came in for unexpected criticism from the Station Commander at Valley. During an annual appraisal of my performance in the job, he declared that he had never before witnessed a unit working so hard and so efficiently in peacetime and, what was more, maintaining such high morale. Before I had time to reflect on this very favourable assessment of my unit, he went on to say that it was my fault that they were having to work so hard and that, as their Commander, I had failed to protect them from it. It was like a slap in the face. I pointed out that I had, on several occasions, raised my concerns with RAF Shawbury over long-term under-manning in my instructor posts, reminding him that I had sent copies of all the relevant correspondence to him as a courtesy. While acknowledging this, he observed that there had been no positive results from my efforts but neglected to offer advice on what more I could have done. Once again, I felt at odds with the current ethos of the RAF that I had joined and for which I had always tried to give my best efforts.

The Station Commander then compounded the problem by putting me in charge of the annual cadet flying at Valley. This involved flying members of the Air Training Corps and similar organisations during their summer camps at Valley. For this task I was loaned two Chipmunks and a handful of engineers to maintain them. My pilots were drawn from Volunteer Reserve members of the RAF, generally experienced Chipmunk pilots, as well as several young instructors from the resident Hawk fast-jet trainers. With the introduction some years before of all-jet training in the RAF, many of the latter, while very keen, had no experience either of piston-engine flying, or of landing an aircraft with a tail-wheel. Consequently, they required instruction from me to convert to this new configuration before flying cadets. I was no longer current as a fixed-wing instructor but this omission was soon rectified by a high-speed dash in a Hawk to and from the Central Flying School, now located at RAF Leeming, near Northallerton in North Yorkshire, interspersed with a very intensive one-day refresher and examination on the Chipmunk to revalidate my fixed-wing instructional category. At that moment, I probably became the only RAF flying instructor current and active on both fixed-wing and helicopter aircraft. Because of the high utilisation of Valley's airfield by the Hawks, all Chipmunk flying had to take place during the long summer evenings and at weekends. The physical demands of working all hours was only partly off-set by the pleasure in renewing my acquaintance with the splendid little Chipmunk.

My Chipmunk flying reaped an unexpected bonus when, as a favour, I was asked to collect an aircraft from RAF Woodvale, near Liverpool, and deliver it to RAF Binbrook, near Grimsby. Binbrook had only been allocated one Chipmunk for their cadets' summer camp and, as this had now become un-serviceable, a replacement was urgently required. That particular day was a Friday and a Dining-Out Night had been organised in the Officers' Mess at Valley for that evening to bid farewell to several officers leaving, amongst whom were two from my unit. I had emphasised to the chaps at Binbrook that the price of my help was a guaranteed flight back to Valley and had received assurances that a Jet Provost would be available for that purpose. I duly delivered the Chipmunk, only to be told that the Jet Provost was now un-serviceable and that attempts to procure another aircraft were not looking good. I was not too pleased at the prospect of being stranded at Binbrook over the weekend with no kit, or of missing the formal dinner at Valley.

'I don't suppose you'd accept a trip in a Lightning?' queried the harassed officer at Binbrook. 'It's all we've got, I'm afraid.' I could scarcely believe my ears. During those early years when I had flown Valiants on refuelling missions for Lightnings, I had made many fruitless journeys to one of their bases in the vague hope of a trip in their rare two-seater version and now it was almost presumed that I would refuse. The unit at Binbrook was the Lightning Training Flight and had several of the latest two-seater Lightnings.

Half-an-hour later, I was sitting on the end of the runway at Binbrook, strapped alongside Squadron Leader Henry Ploszek in the cramped cockpit of the Lightning.

'I'll show you a full re-heat take-off,' said Henry, 'then it's all yours.' As the twin Rolls-Royce engines reached full power against the brakes, the aircraft pitched gently nose-down as the nose-wheel undercarriage was compressed. Then, brakes off and, with a lurch, we were suddenly hurtling down the 9,000-foot ribbon of runway with a mighty force pushing at our backs. At 160 knots, Henry eased the fighter airborne, holding it low over the runway as he retracted the undercarriage and allowed the aircraft to continue acceler-ating rapidly. In seconds the runway had almost disappeared when Henry suddenly hauled back on the control column, sending the Lightning into a vertical climb. I had often witnessed this spectacular manoeuvre from the ground and marvelled at the acceleration of a rapidly receding Lightning riding on the end of plumes of flame from its afterburners. The initial acceler-ation far exceeded that of a moon rocket, and now I was experiencing it for myself.

'You have control,' said Henry, releasing his grip on the controls. We were still pointing vertically upwards with the push in our backs seemingly un-abated and rapidly approaching the speed of sound. Henry was busying himself with the Lightning's radar, peering into a 'shufti-scope' on the left-hand side of the cockpit.

'Start levelling off and come onto west,' he instructed. When you are pointing vertically upwards, which way is west, I thought. Eventually I got the Lightning level and set course for the return to Valley. Henry was still busy with his radar; there was a lot of thunderstorm activity about which it would be prudent to avoid, and I was given heading changes to fly round the denser areas of storms. Suddenly I noticed the Mach meter was indicating that we were now travelling well in excess of Mach 1, the speed of sound. Being unfamiliar with the aircraft and its instrument layout, I had inadvertently gone supersonic. The subsequent approach to land at Valley proved to be something of a 'white-knuckle ride' when the airfield suffered a total electrical failure in a thunderstorm that had arrived inconveniently overhead. Using my intimate knowledge of the local coastline, gleaned from spending many hours hovering alongside it, I was able to guide Henry towards the runway in the temporary absence of any air-traffic services. We landed at the second attempt, with the rain lashing down and the afternoon prematurely dark from the storm, the absence of runway lighting causing major problems in spotting the runway threshold as we thundered towards it. I had been waiting for this flight for twenty years and a bit of Anglesey rain wasn't going to detract from my enjoyment.

*   *   *

The earlier altercation over loaning a winchman to the Cyprus squadron had led me to think that my unit would be more logically placed under the direct control of Number 18 Group, the formation responsible for all UK search and rescue and maritime aircraft. After all, this was the recipient of our newly qualified students as they joined their operational helicopter units. I duly wrote a Service Paper, a reasoned argument for such a transfer and was pleasantly surprised when the proposal was accepted in its entirety. In December 1979 we exchanged our red and silver Whirlwinds for the more familiar iconic yellow ones, at the same time changing our name from SARTS to SARTU, the Search and Rescue Training Unit. The new arrangement worked well. I was now back in a familiar environment and several of my instructors benefited from easily-arranged informal exchanges with the operational Flights.

Another advantage was that I was able to introduce the concept of Staff Pilots and Winchmen to ease our workload. These were experienced operators in the search and rescue role but were not qualified as instructors. They could, nevertheless, be employed on flights in a capacity that did not require an instructor. For example, a staff pilot could pilot a helicopter for flights that only involved the training of a winchman or winch operator. Similarly, a staff winchman could be employed when pilots were under instruction from a pilot instructor. The first of my staff pilots was a former fellow-pilot from Lossiemouth, Flight Lieutenant Frank Pole, whose exemplary flying provided compelling evidence in support of the concept and made it a permanent feature of the unit's composition.

*   *   *

Since 1975, major changes had taken place in the search and rescue helicopter force. Following an all-Whirlwind force, we now had alternate flights around the coast equipped with the twin-engined and more capable Westland Wessex helicopter. At the same time, 22 Squadron assumed control of all the Wessex flights, while 202 Squadron took on the remaining Whirlwind flights pending their imminent re-equipping with the even more capable Westland Sea King. With the Whirlwind era rapidly drawing to a close, it was a natural progression to re-equip my unit with the Wessex during February and March 1981. We received our Wessex helicopters and set about an intensive programme of in-house conversion, using those of our instructors with previous Wessex experience to teach the rest of us. We also had to attend a course at Shawbury on the technical aspects of our new helicopters, and pass a written examination on them. I was proud to note that my crews again responded magnificently to the challenge. Through sheer hard work and long hours, they succeeded in a smooth transition to the new aircraft without dropping a single course or student. I found flying with my first student on the Wessex a surreal experience – he had more than twice as much experience on the Wessex as I had.

*   *   *

On 18 November the previous year, the search and rescue world had been shocked to hear of the death of Master Air Loadmaster David Bullock. Dave was a popular member of any crew, a typical cheerful, cheeky chappy, whom I had got to know during his detachment to my Flight at Lossiemouth, and several shared shifts at RAF Coltishall. Dave had been the winchman on a Sea King scrambled from Coltishall to go to the assistance of a USAF pilot who had ejected over the North Sea off the Norfolk coast following the mid-air collision of his Lockheed A10 Thunderbolt with another USAF aircraft of the same type. The other pilot had also ejected but was safe on land. Arriving on the scene, the crew of the Sea King found the American pilot still attached to his parachute, which was dragging him through 15-foot waves, powered by gale-force winds. An extract from the citation for the subsequent posthumous award to Dave of the George Medal summed up the situation:

> In the most appalling weather conditions, more hazardous than any he had previously encountered during his two years in the Search and Rescue role, Master Air Loadmaster Bullock was winched down to a helpless pilot. Despite the unique and considerable difficulties, created by the

inflated parachute, he calmly went about the business of attempting to recover the pilot to the helicopter as quickly as possible. He was close to success when the cable broke. Well aware of the very dangerous situation created by this catastrophic turn of events, he had every opportunity, over a period of three or four minutes, to disconnect himself from the pilot and save his own life. However, consciously and with conspicuous courage, he chose to remain with the pilot in the hope of saving him. The selfless sacrifice of his own life while trying to save another totally accords with the very highest traditions of the Royal Air Force.

(*London Gazette*, 4 August 1981)

The RAF Board of Inquiry convened to investigate the circumstances of this tragic accident focussed on the 'unique and considerable difficulties' created by the inflated parachute and recommended further exploration of these problems with a view to developing a procedure to deal with them should they recur in future rescues. I was charged by 18 Group with carrying out that exploration. I set up a select team of my most experienced winchman instructors under the guidance of Flight Lieutenant Mike Dane, now a SARTU Flight Commander. Sent to assist in establishing the precise circumstances of the accident was the Sea King's winch operator on that ill-fated flight, Master Air Electronics Operator John Reeson. John had been a most experienced winchman and had been an instructor on SARTU when I first arrived. He was no stranger to dangerous winching situations, having also been awarded the George Medal for rescues carried out in rough, oily seas when the BP offshore drilling platform, *Sea Gem*, collapsed and sank in the North Sea in December 1965. I included myself on the team as a winchman, drawing on the earlier training I had received at the start of my tour. My reasoning was that if I, as a very inexperienced winchman, could cope with any new technique, then a fully trained winchman of average ability should have no problem.

We started by obtaining a USAF parachute, complete with a typical body harness and fastenings, which we fitted to an accurately weighted mannequin or 'dummy'. We enlisted the help of the local RAF Marine Craft Unit based at Holyhead. Their routine job was to patrol up and down the coast near Holyhead in their powerful motor launches and provide a regular platform on which our students could practice all aspects of winching onto the decks of ships. They were only too happy to break the monotony of their routine and become actively involved in our trials. Over a period of a few days, we made many attempts to 'fly' the parachute and dummy, first towing it behind the boat to inflate the parachute before releasing it from the boat to observe its behaviour. On each occasion, however, the parachute merely flopped into the sea, with just the odd panel lifting listlessly in the wind. We were beginning to despair of ever replicating the accident conditions when, on one particularly blustery day with a heavy sea running, the parachute remained inflated after release and promptly took off across the Irish Sea.

'That's it!' exclaimed John Reeson, sitting alongside me in the open cabin doorway of our Wessex. 'That's exactly how it was.' The rest of us watched, mesmerised by the sight of the malevolent-looking, mushroom-shaped parachute 'bouncing' over the sea surface and the dummy being dragged remorselessly behind it, slamming from one steep wave to the next, and frequently being submerged beneath the surface. As one, we were imagining all too clearly what Dave Bullock had been confronted with when he lost his life.

The boat eventually recovered the parachute and dummy, and thereafter we were able to reproduce the situation with some consistency in suitably rough weather. Our first trials focused on trying to deflate the parachute either by damaging the parachute itself, or by hooking the canopy and dragging it to one side to spill the wind in it, thus presenting the rescue crew with a stationary parachute lying on the surface of the sea. While the latter proved possible, it was also time-consuming and entailed carrying a very sharp and potentially dangerous grapnel in the cabin. Trying to destroy the canopy by tearing or setting fire to it by firing pyrotechnics at it proved futile. We also attempted to cut through the multiple nylon shroud lines of the canopy, or through the parachute risers, the webbing straps connecting the pilot's harness to the shroud lines, using a knife on a line dangled from the helicopter. Again, this proved impractical.

We reluctantly concluded that the only reliable method was to place the winchman precisely with the rapidly dragging survivor and maintain his position in contact by accurate instructions from the winch operator to the helicopter pilot. We replicated this situation by dragging the dummy and harness behind the Marine Craft Unit launch, with the winchman maintaining a physical grip on the dummy's harness.

We took turns in being dragged behind the launch, taking our share of the cold, choking, watery battering until exhaustion forced a change around. For safety purposes, a quick-release mechanism on the launch was manned by one of our team and an inflatable boat was run alongside the dummy, manned with two more of the team to provide immediate assistance should things go wrong. And go wrong they did. First of all, normal knives, however sharp, proved difficult to control in the ensuing torrent of water and ineffectual in cutting the thick webbing of the parachute risers. Secondly, the combined shapes of the winchman and dummy being dragged through the rough sea at speed proved potentially unstable. On one occasion I watched in disbelief from the inflatable boat as the winchman, Master Air Loadmaster Carl Pollock, and the dummy flipped over and totally disappeared from sight beneath the sea surface while being dragged. The tow emergency release was operated immediately but there was no sight of my winchman. We occupants of the inflatable peered into the water for what seemed ages, searching for any sign of him. At long last, the form of his orange-coloured immersion suit became faintly discernible way below us, slowly, so slowly, rising to the surface. We jumped overboard to help haul Carl into the inflatable, choking from swallowing sea-water and gasping for breath.

We gradually evolved a reliable method of slicing through the webbing risers to which were attached the numerous shroud lines running up to the parachute's periphery. This was by making use of a particular commercially available industrial packing safety knife on which the sharp blade was almost hidden in the bend of the J-shaped knife, while the T-handle allowed a good grip on the equipment. While hanging on to the dummy and making a sweeping motion across the risers, the jaws of the knife would locate and guide the webbing onto the sharp blade, severing it at a single stroke. It was only necessary to cut one of the two risers to destroy the integrity of the parachute canopy, causing it to collapse almost immediately.

Mike Dane and I drove to HQ 18 Group at Northwood in North London and presented our findings to a group of senior officers who approved our solution and tasked us with amending our training syllabus to include the new techniques. Back at Valley, we devised an exercise, 'Cutting and Dragging', where the student helicopter rear-crew members would be subjected to the experience of being dragged behind a launch while trying to cut through the webbing tow on a dummy in a similar manner to our trials, albeit in more benign circumstances. The exercise was not popular with the students, quickly being re-named by them as 'Practice Drowning', but at least they were better prepared to tackle the type of extremely difficult and dangerous situation that Dave Bullock had encountered.

A few months later, I was informed that our work on the trials had been recognised by the RAF Escaping Society, which awarded my unit their Silver Trophy. Instituted in 1958 'to perpetuate the memory of the outstanding risks and sacrifices made on behalf of the RAF and Allied aircrew', the trophy later became an annual award for 'the best individual feat of combat survival or comparable feat or challenge and achievement carried out by a member of the RAF during operations or recognised training'. This was the first occasion that a unit, rather than an individual, had been honoured by this award.

*   *   *

The final couple of months of my tour passed in a busy whirl of activity as I prepared to hand over to my successor, Squadron Leader John Corby. In the middle of this I was appointed a member of a three-man Board of Inquiry into an RAF helicopter accident where a visiting search and rescue Whirlwind had crashed on the Belgian Air Force airfield of Koksijde, about 10 miles east of

Dunkirk. The pilot of the helicopter had lost control after it had suffered a total failure of the tail-rotor. The Whirlwind had been destroyed in the ensuing crash that had also injured its crew.

My involvement with crashed helicopters was to be far from over. After handing over to my successor, I reported for duty with the Inspectorate of Flight Safety at the Ministry of Defence in London in early August 1981 to commence another ground tour.

CHAPTER TWENTY-SIX

CLIPPED WINGS

The Russian KGB guard stood rigidly to attention in front of me as I inspected his smart blue ceremonial uniform – hat straight, tie tightly knotted, tunic buttons all fastened and so on, right down to his long black boots. I gave him a curt nod of satisfaction before crossing to his companion and repeating the procedure. I was 'inspecting' the Guard of Honour positioned on each side of the entrance to Lenin's Tomb in Moscow's Red Square and was now enjoying myself after taking nearly two hours of humiliating and embarrassing queuing to get there. I had just completed the second inspection when I was confronted by a young officer who proceeded to berate me in Russian. I looked him straight in the eye, smiling politely, and drew out my passport.

'British officer', I declared affably, 'Splendid turn-out. Well done. Carry on please,' and stepped smartly back into the bemused, watching queue, leaving him staring speechless after me.

*   *   *

It was August 1982 and I was in Moscow to attend the World 18th Ornithological Congress with which the Bird-Strike Committee Europe had been temporarily amalgamated, and was scheduled to give a paper later in the week to this assembly at the Moscow State University. My place as a delegate to this annual meeting of the Bird-Strike Committee was part of my new job at the Ministry of Defence working in the Inspectorate of Flight Safety. While my responsibilities at the Inspectorate were primarily related to all aspects of safety and accident prevention on helicopters, my secondary role was the collating of all material on RAF aircraft accidents caused by collisions with birds, and monitoring and reporting upon measures to reduce the tragic and costly consequences of such collisions. This aspect of my new job had assumed greater importance as a result of these accidents, as well as sending me to interesting places.

I had arrived in Moscow a couple of days before the start of the Conference, and had teamed up with my opposite number in the Civil Aviation Authority John Thorpe, with whom I sometimes worked on joint military/ civil bird-hazard projects. Together, we decided to explore the city and had promptly headed for the Kremlin. This was still the era of the Cold War and standing in the centre of the fifteenth-century fortified enclosure of the Kremlin was a surreal experience. Not only was the name synonymous with the Soviet Government but this spot would have been Ground Zero, the aiming point for any nuclear attack on the city. After we had explored the magnificent gilded, onion-domed churches within the Kremlin, we had decided to join the queue to view Lenin's body lying in his mausoleum by the Kremlin walls overlooking Red Square. John, a keen photographer, had duti-fully deposited his camera bag as instructed at a kiosk in the History Museum before we entered the checkpoint to the vast, empty, cordoned-off area that took in most of Red Square. Empty, that is, apart from the long, silent queue that was lined up, arrow-straight, to the entrance of the mausoleum, where it made a right-angled turn to mount the steps to the entrance. Eagle-eyed soldiers patrolled this line like surly sheepdogs, snapping at anyone who dared to put a foot out of line. We eyed this performance with mild amusement until a stony-faced soldier suddenly appeared alongside me and started gestic-ulating and shouting loudly right in my face in Russian. The queue imme-diately in front and behind us silently shuffled away to distance themselves from this performance, clearly not wishing to be associated in any way with us. I pulled out my passport and repeated the word 'British' to him, hoping that he would perhaps find an interpreter amongst his many nearby col-leagues. The rant continued until John, searching the faces of the nearest members of the silent queue in bewilderment, noticed a man discretely gesticulating to him.

'I think he wants you to take your hands out of your pockets.' John suggested. As soon as I did so, the tirade ceased.

'Why didn't you say so in the first place?' I enquired politely. The guard wasn't satisfied. As I withdrew my hands, he resumed his shouting. Again John sought clues from the man in the queue.

'He wants you to empty your pockets.' John ventured. The guard had spotted the slight bulge in my pocket where I had stowed a miniature camera. With a triumphant roar and theatrical gesture, he ordered me off the Square. I walked back to the checkpoint, aware of the hundreds of silent, disapproving stares.

I deposited my little camera at the kiosk and returned to the checkpoint, naively assuming that I would be able to re-join John, who by now was nearing the mausoleum entrance. Instead, I was forced to start queuing again from the checkpoint. After five minutes or so, I thought I would try my luck, sidling up the side of the queue on the guards' blind-side. I had reached almost half-way when shrill blasts of whistles warned me I had been spotted. As before, the queue swiftly parted, leaving me isolated as a handful of guards came running over. I tried to explain my situation, pointing and waving at John up ahead. He responded and was immediately the centre of his own little storm. Clearly, these guards were not accustomed to having members of the public stepping out of line, or having their authority questioned. I resigned myself to a solo visit to Mr Lenin. When I eventually reached the Guard of Honour, the temptation to make a small gesture of rebellion against these overbearing guards and restore something of my injured pride proved too much to resist. Hence my 'inspection' of the guards.

*   *   *

Despite this experience, my visit to Moscow was certainly the highlight of my Ministry of Defence tour and it was not one without humour. The Bird-Strike Committee held its plenary sessions in a large lecture theatre in the university, with hundreds of seats in tiers and the delegates seated alpha-betically by nation. It was an odd national grouping, with almost all Warsaw Pact and NATO member countries being represented alongside such countries as Azerbaijan and India. At the end of my presentation, I invited questions from the audience. From the furthest left corner of the lecture theatre came a question, not one word of which I could understand. I asked for the question to be repeated. Suddenly, a small dapper Indian gentleman, sitting in the first row immediately in front of me, politely announced himself as Dr Grubb of Bombay University and informed me what the question had been. I asked the questioner if that was correct and received a vigorous head-nodding in confirmation. I answered the question, whereupon he asked a further one with an equal lack of comprehension on my part.

'Dr Grubb?' I appealed, and again had the new question put to me. At this point I stole an envious glance up at the UK delegation half-way up the auditorium on the right-hand side, wishing I was sitting there with them. Instead of support, I was disconcerted to see them contorted with suppressed laughter, handkerchiefs and fists stuffed in mouths to stifle the noise. To add to my discomfiture, 'USA', sitting next to 'UK', joined in, closely followed by 'USSR' alongside.

*   *   *

Interesting visits aside, much of my bird hazard work was more mundane but, nevertheless, led down some unexpected and interesting paths. One area I would never have imagined becoming involved in was that of Town and Country Planning, where I spent a significant time discussing planning clear-ances for the creation of such local amenities as water parks and landfill sites. The significance of areas like these was that they were extremely attractive to birds such as gulls for roosting and for feeding. They could encourage vast numbers of birds flying between the two on a regular daily commute and an injudicious juxtaposition of areas such as these and the flight paths associated with an airfield were a recipe for disaster. Assisting me in advising various local authority planning officers on these matters was an expert three-man team of scientists working for the Ministry of Agriculture, Fisheries and Food. It was this cheerful and friendly team, the Aviation Bird Unit, that had the dubious privilege of receiving all the fragments of bird remains collected from bird-strike accidents and incidents for the purpose of forensic examination to determine their species. Knowing the bird type enabled them to give me an accurate estimate of its weight which, in turn, allowed aircraft engineers to calculate what kinetic energy had been expended in the collision and thereby relate it to the damage caused.

When a particular aircraft appeared to be sustaining a disproportionate amount of damage for a given level of impact energy, the designers would produce remedial modifications that were then subjected to practical testing. Enter the chicken gun. Not, as might be thought, a gun for shooting chickens, but a gun that used a chicken as the 'bullet'. This contraption, located at the former de Havilland's airfield at Hatfield, took the form of a very wide-bore air-gun into which a chicken carcase of appropriate weight was loaded. The gun was charged with compressed air which, when the gun was fired, projected the chicken at a pre-determined speed to hit the sample specimen of aircraft structure under test. The whole procedure was filmed by high-speed camera for later analysis.

Witnessing these firings was a salutary experience, particular when the test subject was a cockpit canopy. A senior RAF officer flying at low level in the front seat of a Hawk trainer had recently experienced such a collision. In this, a large gull had penetrated the canopy and hit him in the face, its bloody remains jammed beneath his Perspex visor temporarily blinding him and almost suffocating him. Only the presence of another pilot in the rear cockpit averted an immediate crash. It was to prevent recurrences of such accidents that this work was carried out. Armed with the data from these firings, the engineers and designers were able to add appropriate strengthening where required. This was serious business. During the previous year alone, the RAF had lost two Harriers, a Jet Provost and even a Nimrod, the latter killing the two pilots. All of these were the result of bird strikes.

* * *

As the helicopter expert at the Inspectorate, one of my most important jobs was overseeing the investigation of RAF helicopter accidents, monitoring the progress of the ensuing Board of Inquiry and ensuring that it had all the assistance required. When the findings of the investigation had been delivered and commented upon by senior officers in the chain of command of the unfortunate unit sustaining the accident, it was then my job to summarise the findings into a formal Aircraft Accident Report, together with its associated summaries and press releases.

I also lectured on bird hazards to the regular courses held at the Inspectorate of Flight Safety and escorted course members on visits to the Air Accidents Investigation Branch in their headquarters at the famous Farnborough airfield, now a centre for business aviation. Here, using the recovered wreckage of recent accidents painstakingly laid out in the extensive hangars, the Branch's inspectors led the course members through the meticulous detective work of tracking down the cause of each accident and the lessons to be drawn from them. As well as conducting the inquiries into all civilian aircraft accidents in the UK, these same inspectors also provided their expert services in assisting RAF Boards of Inquiry with the detailed technical investigation of military aircraft wreckage. One of the inspectors, Mick Charles, had been a fellow course member with me throughout basic flying training. Years later, as a senior inspector, he was to lead the biggest air crash investigation in UK history, the destruction by terrorists of Pan American Flight 103 at Lockerbie.

In April 1982, Britain went to war with Argentina over sovereignty of the Falkland Islands. Several of us quickly volunteered to return to our former operational squadrons where, we thought, we could be of immediate use either in reinforcing the Task Force, or by temporarily replacing those aircrew already on their way to the South Atlantic. Our offers fell on deaf ears and we resigned ourselves to following the progress of the campaign in the curiously expressionless nightly reports on television from the Ministry of Defence spokesman, Ian McDonald. Our staff also manned the twenty-four-hour RAF casualty information hot-lines, ready with the card-index system and a bank of telephones to deal with the anticipated flood of enquiries. In the event, our services were not required. Despite having had three Harriers shot down during the conflict, the single RAF fatality was the result of an accident when a Navy Sea King helicopter crashed into the sea during a night transfer between two warships.

* * *

On completion of my ground tour at the Inspectorate of Flight Safety I was hoping to resume my career in search and rescue by taking over one of the Sea King flights, all now commanded by squadron leaders. I was therefore bitterly disappointed to receive a follow-on ground tour. I was to be the General Service Training Officer on the Flying Training School at the RAF College, Cranwell.

Before taking up this appointment, there was inevitably another course to be completed, this one to qualify me as a Combat Survival and Rescue Officer, authorised to conduct escape and evasion exercises and instruct in land and sea survival techniques. The two-week course was held at the RAF School of Combat Survival and Rescue based at Mountbatten, near

Plymouth. In retrospect, my abiding memory of the first part of the course was of crossing and re-crossing Dartmoor on foot, once by daylight and twice at night, on the last occasion being pursued by Royal Marines. The course involved much discomfort, including burying myself alive to evade capture by the Marines and enduring several hours of interrogation in what was termed Conduct after Capture training. There was also the dubious pleasure of bobbing around in tiny liferafts in the English Channel by day and by night, and struggling to disentangle oneself from beneath a parachute canopy float-ing on the surface of the water.

*   *   *

As well as supervising similar survival training exercises at Cranwell, my new post of General Service Training Officer covered a multitude of different activities, all aimed primarily at developing the officer and leadership qualities of the students on the Flying Training School at Cranwell.

At the lowest level was the teaching of Service Writing, the 'house style' for all military communications, from telegram-type signals to formal and informal letter and report writing. At the other end of the scale came the Leadership and Survival Exercises where, over a six-day period, the students were assessed on their abilities to survive and evade capture under adverse conditions of weather and terrain in an abbreviated and simplified version of my Mountbatten training.

This latter aspect of my duties was by far the most enjoyable, allowing me the freedom of the Yorkshire Dales and making me virtually inaccessible to the tedium of daily routine at Cranwell for the duration of the exercises. I continued a close and friendly liaison that had been built up over the years with many of the farmers in the Dales upon whose co-operation we depended for the use of their land on which we conducted our exercises.

One exercise was the creation and use of emergency location aids, includ-ing the firing of distress flares and building rapidly-ignited fires arranged in an internationally-recognised triangular shape. Whenever possible, I would arrange for one of Cranwell's Jet Provosts to carry out a brief search of the exercise area and assess the effectiveness of the students' signalling efforts before making a very low pass on its departure. On one particular occasion, I was aware that the farmer's elderly mother was bed-bound and not expected to live much longer. The escape and evasion exercise on his land went ahead at his insistence, but I had abandoned the Jet Provost's participation in consideration for his mother's frail condition and the proximity of the field to the farmhouse. My students duly lit their fires and fired their flares. Shortly after, the farmer came hurtling towards us on his quad-bike.

'It's Mother', he shouted, much to my consternation and fearing the worst, 'she wants to know where her plane is.' I explained why I had cancelled the fly-by, whereupon he told me that his mother had struggled out of bed and was, even now, standing at the window looking for 'her' Jet Provost. He gave me a lift to the farmhouse where I made an urgent call to Cranwell Air Traffic Control, explaining the circumstances and asking if they could possibly divert a Jet Provost to my location. A short time later, a Jet Provost roared overhead, much to the relief of the farmer and the delight of his dear old mother.

Near the bottom of my list of enjoyable activities was taking a weekly early morning parade on which, with the help of drill instructors, I put my students through the intricate choreography and shouted commands in the various key posts of Parade Commander, Squadron Commander and so on. Having run through a complete rehearsal of the General Salute and marches past, we would be joined by a senior officer from the staff at Cranwell who would take the salute on a second run through before the students were dismissed to their normal duties at 8.00 am. Rain or shine, light or dark, these parades proceeded regardless, only being cancelled in the most extreme weather conditions. The sight of spectral marching columns looming out of the gloom of a cold, foggy Lincolnshire morning is not amongst the fondest memories of my time at Cranwell.

My intimate knowledge of the parade sequence did, however, stand me in good stead on one occasion. I had been detailed as escorting officer to Air Vice-Marshal Stuart-Paul, our Air Officer Commanding, during his annual formal visit to Cranwell when, during the short journey to the dais from where he would review a parade in his honour, I was discretely informed that one of the parade's Squadron Commanders had collapsed. I made my excuses and dashed around the side of the hangar to where the full parade had formed up in preparation for marching onto the parade ground itself and where the College Band was already on the move. As the incapacitated officer was being loaded onto a stretcher, I managed to relieve him of his ceremonial sword and belt. Then followed an almighty tussle as I fought to fasten the belt around my waist, there being no time for the complicated adjustment that was required to fit my stockier physique. With the assistance of the Drill Sergeant, I eventually managed to fasten the ornate buckle, leaving me gasping in the belt's unrelenting grip. I just had time to straighten my hat and draw my sword before shouting the command for 'my' squadron to march on. Fortunately, the parade went without any further hitches, the only surprise being Marian's. Seated amongst the spectators alongside the dais and unaware of the frantic behind-the-scenes changes, she received a discreet wink from me as I marched past, 'Eyes Right,' sword at the salute.

*   *   *

Just over half-way through my tour, and anxious that my next appointment should be a flying one, I started putting out feelers as to what I might expect. The feedback was not promising with few, if any, of the Sea King Flight

Commander posts becoming available at a time that would coincide with me completing my current tour. I therefore sought an interview with the Air Secretary's Branch, the RAF department responsible for all officer appointments. Unlike the Army or Royal Navy, the RAF did not offer any routine face-to-face discussion with one's 'poster', with the result that new appointments almost always came as a surprise and often seemed to take little account of the annually-declared personal preferences.

'You seem to have got yourself away from your specialisation,' declared the young group captain interviewing me, 'and that makes it difficult to find you a suitable posting.'

'I've got myself away from my specialisation!' I exploded. 'Just show me where, in that pile of annual confidential reports in my file, I have made a single request over the past ten years for other than helicopter search and rescue?'

Admitting that this was the case, he tried to placate me by offering a promotion to Wing Commander in the Fighter Control Branch, which operated the chain of radar stations around the country to guide fighter aircraft onto their targets.

'How long would that be for?' I queried.

'Oh, that would be a permanent transfer to the General Duties Ground Branch,' he explained, 'there would be no changing back to flying duties.' I was appalled.

'Exactly which specialisation have I supposedly got myself away from?' I demanded, 'Helicopter search and rescue? Qualified Helicopter Instructor? Qualified Flying Instructor? Take your pick, Sir!' At this point he started talking about my reported lack of tact and diplomacy.

'If I'd wanted to be a diplomat, I would have joined the bloody Foreign Office, not the RAF!' I retorted. Giving me a look that seemed to say I had just confirmed the critical reports on my lack of respect for authority, he brought the interview to an end. It had not gone well. In anger and frustration, I elected to transfer from the General List, the RAF's career path to promotion, to the role of Specialist Aircrew in which I would retain my rank, but would be employed almost exclusively on flying duties.

In short, I would be flying helicopters again, but I had said 'Goodbye' to any opportunity for further promotion to Wing Commander or beyond, and would remain in the rank I had now held for almost ten years.

I had asked to be transferred to a flying unit as quickly as possible after making this decision and, a few months later, found myself back at the Search and Rescue Training Unit at Valley, which I had commanded only a few years earlier. It was a step down in status, but I was back on flying and back in the familiar world of search and rescue.

I was happy again.

CHAPTER TWENTY-SEVEN

ENDGAME

After four years of very limited opportunities for flying because of two consecutive ground tours, I was now back where I wanted to be – well, almost. I had wanted a posting to one of the search and rescue helicopter flights but, as an experienced instructor in the role, I had to accept that I would be most effectively employed again as an instructor at the Search and Rescue Training Unit at Valley. After a brief refresher course both on the Wessex helicopter and the whole range of exercises I would again be teaching, I started what would turn out to be the final tour in my RAF career. It was to be a long tour, a busy and interesting tour but, ultimately, a very sad tour, marred by a major terrorist atrocity and by the loss of one of our own instructional team.

* * *

Soon after reaching Valley, I suddenly found myself in temporary command of the Search and Rescue Training Unit in place of the current Squadron Commander who was away on detached duty. His absence coincided with a major Press Day to highlight the RAF's search and rescue services and I was put in charge of organising it. As well as the usual detailed briefings and presentations to the members of the press, I and my colleagues had great fun putting together a practical display that would demonstrate many of the aspects of fixed-wing, helicopter and ground rescue operations. The location chosen for this display was Holyhead Range, our regular cliff winching training area sited on the rugged coastal strip at the north-west end of the broad sweep of Trearddur Bay.

Following the briefings, we flew the journalists to a vantage point on a small island on the Range. Looking in one direction, they were confronted just a few hundred feet away by a typical mountain rescue scenario – injured climbers trapped on a rocky outcrop and being prepared by Valley's Mountain Rescue Team for winching up in stretchers into one of our Wessex helicopters. Looking in the other direction, they were presented with a deteriorating nautical situation. One of the RAF Marine Branch's seagoing pinnaces was wallowing in a choppy sea with voluminous clouds of smoke pouring from her, the result of a simulated engine fire while *en route* to picking up the occupants of a couple of single-seat dinghies, now bobbing about in the sea a few hundred yards away. Soon, a Nimrod maritime patrol aircraft arrived on the scene, making a majestic low-level pass across the bay before accurately dropping additional survival equipment to the dinghy occupants. Shortly after, the air appeared full of rescue helicopters, with each one demonstrating a particular capability for dealing with cliff, sea and ship rescues. The whole operation proceeded without a hitch and some very complimentary write-ups appeared as a result.

*   *   *

Amongst several notable detachments that I carried out on this tour was one to the 1988 Farnborough Air Show where two of our Wessex helicopters provided the airborne crash cover for the week-long programme of displays and demonstrations. For someone who had been so thrilled to attend these airshows as a schoolboy, it was a fascinating experience to witness the activities from the opposite side of the airfield to the spectators and to rub shoulders with the cream of Europe's test pilots during the daily meteorological and display briefings. We also took part in the parade that heralded the start of each day's flying displays, our Wessex helicopters proudly processing slowly down the length of that famous runway in formation behind the many fire trucks and rescue vehicles on call to deal with any emergencies. Casting my eyes over the sea of spectators, I recalled how many years it had been since I had last stood there as a teenager, eagerly anticipating another memorable demonstration of all the latest wonders in British aviation. Before commencement of the flying display, we had a secondary role ferrying VIPs to and fro between Farnborough and RAF Odiham, the nearest airfield open to visitors arriving by air. During one of these regular shuttles, I was privileged to fly Prince Philippe, Crown Prince of Belgium.

*   *   *

While the Search and Rescue Training Unit was specifically devoted to providing trained crews for the operational units, unlike them, it had no formal standby commitment. However, being made up of some of the RAF's most experienced helicopter search and rescue instructors, it could be called upon at short notice to assist our regular operational colleagues. Such was the case one mid-summer Wednesday afternoon. Holyhead Sailing Club held races every Wednesday evening and Flight Lieutenant Ken Park and I regularly sailed an RAF Squib, a 19-foot sailing boat, in these races. The previous day I had been visited at work by a young student on the Hawk fast-jet training aircraft, Pilot Officer Simon 'Tommo' Tompkins. Tommo was keen to join us racing the Squib and I had made arrangements to meet him at the sailing club after work on the Wednesday. That afternoon, both Ken and I were called to assist with ferrying guards by helicopter to provide security cordons around the wreckage of two of Valley's Hawks that had collided and crashed near the coast at Borth, some 8 miles north of Aberystwyth. I made a quick telephone call to try to warn Tommo that we might be late but had to leave a message when told he was unavailable. Returning much later, having deposited my guards near the still-smouldering crater where one of the young student pilots had been killed, I was shocked to discover that Tommo had been that young pilot.

* * *

Occasionally, we took over full search and rescue standby duties when the resident unit was deployed elsewhere. One of these was to RAF Manston in Kent whose Sea Kings had been detached for a month to the very north of the British Isles to cover a major air defence exercise. The detachment to Manston was very popular, being one where we could fully immerse ourselves again in the day-to-day routine of the job we all loved. As Detachment Commander, I ensured that all the local rescue agencies were aware of our presence and capability and soon the demands for our services were flooding in – missing windsurfers off the coast, a crashed light aircraft on the beach near Hastings, a petrol tanker on fire in the Channel, a fishing boat missing in thick fog – the list of jobs successfully undertaken mounted rapidly. We also took the opportunity to acquaint ourselves with the various cross-channel ferries and found our enthusiasm reciprocated by their crews. We winched our off-duty crew-members on and off these ships almost daily, much to the entertainment of their passengers and, in return, we were privileged to witness their procedures for weaving across the busy Channel shipping lanes from the vantage point of the ship's bridge.

* * *

One unusual task that we inherited from the absent Sea King crews was to take part in the production of a publicity film for the RAF Association. This film, designated for general release in cinemas to coincide with the Association's annual Wings Appeal, focused on the work of the Sussexdown Nursing Home situated just north of Worthing and had the actors Nicholas Lyndhurst and Richard E. Grant providing the narratives. We quickly completed filming the required flying sequences, then sat back to watch with much interest as the film crew went about their business, laying lengths of track across the manicured lawn, and festooning the area with lighting rigs and microphone booms. Eventually, all was ready and, with our highly-polished yellow Wessex helicopter as the main prop, Nicholas Lyndhurst, now dressed as the pilot with my flying kit, walked slowly from its tail towards the cockpit while delivering his lines. His timing was evidently causing some problem as he consistently arrived at the steps too early and before he had finished his piece to the camera.

'You right plonker, Rodney,' came the call from our own resident comedian, my winchman, Flight Sergeant 'Barny' Barnes. 'You need a longer "chopper"!' With that, the whole situation rapidly descended into farce. As take followed take, the repartee flowed, reducing Nicholas and the rest of us to helpless fits of laughter, rolling on the grass with tears streaming down our faces. Mindful of the tight schedule, the director eventually threatened to banish us from the set unless we behaved ourselves. During intervals in filming, we discovered that Nicholas was due to take the written examinations for his Private Pilot's Licence in the following few days, so a crammer session was quickly organised, with Flight Lieutenant Phil Boothby, my navigator, giving him the benefit of his extensive experience. A good day had been had by all.

*　*　*

Several more detachments followed in support of our operational colleagues, but nothing had prepared us for the scale and the horrors of the events of the night of 21 December 1988.

CHAPTER TWENTY-EIGHT

LOCKERBIE

Ironically, my very last operational search and rescue flight came while I was still on the staff of the RAF Search and Rescue Training Unit at Valley. It was to take me well away from my normal operating area and to a place whose name was soon to be indelibly etched on the minds of people throughout the world as a by-word for tragedy and atrocity.

I had taken leave for the period running up to Christmas 1988 and, in anticipation of all my family arriving the following day for the festivities, I was attempting to re-plaster a length of wall in a spare bedroom. It was just after 7.00 pm and frustration was setting in as yet another application of pink plaster slowly peeled off the wall and slumped to the floor. My heartfelt curses were interrupted by my wife, Marian, calling me to the telephone.

'Have you been drinking?' was the abrupt question, put without any preliminaries by a voice I recognised. Flight Lieutenant Ken Park, one of my colleagues on the Search and Rescue Training Unit, had been attending its annual Christmas 'Coffee' event, at which the opportunity was taken to invite and thank those many people at RAF Valley who had supported us over the past year. The aim was to ply them with coffee, generously laced with alcohol.

'No, Ken. And a Happy Christmas to you too!' I replied. His response and tone of voice immediately removed any jocularity from the situation. There had been an extremely serious incident near the Scottish Borders, he stated tersely, and all available crews were to report to work as quickly as possible. Pausing only to wash the wretched plaster off my hands and throw on a spare flying suit, I rushed into work. On arrival I was greeted by my colleagues, many of whom had not had the opportunity to return home, or be picked up by their wives or girlfriends following the Coffee Party. Although shocked into sobriety by the prospect of a major job, most were ineligible to fly as crew for at least eight hours in order to comply with the very strict rules governing flying and the consumption of alcohol; hence the premium on available crews who had not imbibed that day because of their absence on leave. It should be mentioned that, unlike the operational helicopter search and rescue squadrons, who maintained continuous standby rescue cover throughout the United Kingdom, the Search and Rescue Training Unit was specifically devoted to providing trained crews for the operational units and, as such, had no formal standby commitment. However, as mentioned earlier, its expertise

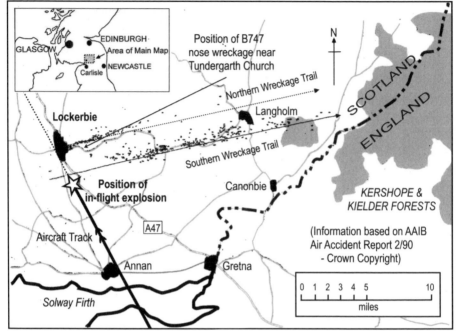

Map 8. Lockerbie area indicating the distribution of aircraft wreckage.

could be called upon at times of major emergencies to assist our regular operational colleagues.

Scratch crews were soon made up to man the two Wessex helicopters, with me being nominated as one of the aircraft captains and with a crew of Flight Lieutenant Phil Boothby as navigator and Master Air Loadmaster Graham Andrews, together with a second aircraft captained by Flight Lieutenant Steve Garrod carrying the unit's Squadron Commander, Squadron Leader Chris Gibbons, as his navigator. The non-operating crews were divided between the two aircraft to provide additional relief crew members in the event of a lengthy detachment. Routes to the Lockerbie area were plotted while we waited for more news to filter through to us, and for the order to scramble, which would come from the Rescue Co-ordination Centre, which was attempting to clarify a chaotic situation.

*   *   *

At about 9.00 pm, the order to go was received and our two Wessex helicopters beat their way noisily into the night sky. During the intervening period, little more had been gleaned on the nature of the incident towards which we were flying, other than that a large aircraft was believed to have crashed in the hills near Lockerbie. Perhaps more surprisingly, there was no indication of the number or type of casualties we were likely to be searching for. As we approached the half-way point, now flying below low cloud in a steady drizzle, we were diverted to Manchester Airport to meet an incoming civilian flight and pick up a ground-rescue team. They were just returning from a mission to Armenia searching for the victims of a major earthquake that had occurred there earlier in the month. With them safely on board, we continued our flight to Lockerbie.

The first indication of the task ahead of us appeared as a dull red glow piercing the gloomy sky. As we got closer, this glow became increasingly intense until, when overhead, it resembled looking down into the crater of an active volcano near the heart of the town of Lockerbie. The surrounding countryside had been plunged into almost total darkness by the destruction of the power lines, and the only lights readily visible were the pin-pricks of scattered blue flickering and flashing strobe lights of the emergency vehicles, and the headlights of an occasional slow-moving vehicle tentatively probing the dark and wreckage-strewn roads.

With no communication with anyone on the ground, our urgent task was to find somewhere to land safely and make contact with the emergency services. In order to speed up this process, Steve and I had split up to search different areas. Each time I set up an approach into what looked like a black, empty hole, I was repeatedly thwarted at the last moment as my landing lights picked out obstructions – trees, overhead cables, unlit buildings or, most shockingly, bodies seemingly strewn everywhere. After several anxious minutes of searching, all the time conscious of the proximity of the raging inferno nearby, I managed to land as close as possible to the centre of activity to offload my ground-rescue team. Meanwhile, Steve had located a school on the northern side of the town – Lockerbie Academy. He had landed on the school's playing field and switched on his bright, white, flashing anti-collision lights to indicate his position to me. A Royal Navy Sea King from Prestwick, apparently the first helicopter on the scene, was already parked in a corner of the field but there was no sign of the crew. I landed shortly after, and we found that a police mobile major incident unit caravan was parked in the school grounds. I reported to the police officer in the incident vehicle and was given a very sketchy briefing to the effect that a large aircraft had been circling the area, probably trying to land with some sort of emergency, and had struck the higher ground to the east of the town. From what we had seen during our earlier attempts to land, this seemed improbable but, until the receipt of later information and the arrival of the pale light of a winter dawn, the full extent and nature of the disaster could not be appreciated.

By now, steady, persistent rain was falling and my concern was to get my crews under some sort of cover so that we could get maps together and decide on some plan of action. Until then, they had gathered around the headlights of the police incident vehicle to study their maps. My request to use the school was refused because the caretaker was not available to unlock it. My suggestion that we would gain our own entry was met with dark mutterings about criminal damage. A request for large-scale local maps was also refused because the shop would be shut until the morning. This attitude was to be a recurring feature when dealing with most of the local authorities during the early stages of this disaster. The event was completely unprecedented and proving overwhelming, not only for the local authorities, but also for the townspeople. One moment they had been watching early evening television, preparing the evening meal, putting young children to bed – all the hundred and one activities of a normal daily routine. The next, their world had been turned to horror and chaos. The lights had gone out and wreckage had rained down on their town with a dreadful thunder, bringing death and destruction to their midst. In short, and unsurprisingly, most of the residents of this small town were in a state of shock.

The arrival in the incident vehicle of the Secretary of State for Scotland, Sir Malcolm Rifkind, did nothing to clarify either the initial assessment of the situation or of any subsequent developments. I was ignored while Sir Malcolm was given the same unlikely story that I had already heard. He also declined to assist us in gaining entry to the adjacent school.

Leaving the incident vehicle in frustration, I found an RAC van parked alongside. Using his radio, we eventually managed to establish a tenuous link with the Rescue Co-ordination Centre, from where we learnt more of the true nature of the situation. We were relieved to hear that RAF mountain rescue teams had arrived at Lockerbie, one from RAF Leeming having been delivered by Sea King helicopter, while the other had been driving north along the M6 trunk road towards Lockerbie at the time when the wreckage of the doomed aircraft rained on the town. They were setting up a Control Room and would be co-ordinating the available helicopter resources.

More helicopters had now arrived at our landing area, having also failed to find anywhere else to land. Now parked on the playing field were Sea Kings from RAF Boulmer, near Alnwick in Northumberland, from RAF Leuchars in Fife, from Leconfield, near Hull, and from Prestwick, together with our two Wessex helicopters from Valley. We were instructed to find our way to a school gymnasium near the centre of the town. We walked along the darkened streets, illuminated only by the flashing lights of emergency vehicles, picking our way carefully though the mass of debris – chunks of aircraft wreckage, a huge turbo-jet engine half-buried in the road, fire hoses snaking in all directions and torrents of running water. Hanging in the air, along with the smoke from the burning crater, was the pervasive and distinctive raw stench of the remains of some 100 tons of aviation fuel.

Reaching the gymnasium, we joined other rescue personnel assembled there – harassed policemen, exhausted firemen with haunted faces and, in the midst of seeming chaos, the welcome sight of WRVS ladies cheerfully dispensing tea and sandwiches. The continuing steady rain and very low cloud precluded any further flying that night, so we hunted round for somewhere to grab a few hours of sleep. No sooner had we started to make ourselves as comfortable as possible in a fairly quiet corridor, than the helicopter crews were identified by the police, and invited to follow them to the homes of local residents who had volunteered to look after us. I and one of my crew, Graham Andrews, were taken in by Alan and Edna Eelbeck who, despite the late hour, insisted on feeding us before surrendering their own bedroom to us. Then followed a surreal night – the two of us laid on the bed in our flying kit, wide awake, and only too aware of the malevolent, red glow beyond the curtains and the ever-present flickering blue lights. We tried to rest as best we could, aware that the following day was likely to be very demanding in all respects.

* * *

We were roused by the smell of cooking bacon and eggs and, once again, our kind hosts insisted on feeding us. What was more, they had prepared packed lunches to sustain us during the coming day. This spontaneous kindness and hospitality under such traumatic circumstances was typical of the response of the people of Lockerbie and was later to be extended over the following weeks, months and years to the bereaved families of the victims of the atrocity. During the night, teams of television and radio reporters had set up their equipment at vantage points along the road outside the Eelbeck's bungalow. It was on a slight rise to the east of the town centre and commanded a panoramic view overlooking the town's worst affected areas.

Well before first light, we were collected by a police car and taken for briefing at another school hall near the town centre where the mountain rescue teams had located themselves. There, I was surprised to be greeted by a familiar face. Squadron Leader Bill Gault had been my deputy as Flight Commander on the search and rescue flight at RAF Lossiemouth ten years earlier, and had been my navigator on numerous rescue missions in northern Scotland. Earlier on the day of the incident he had been at the Ministry of Defence in London taking over as the new Inspector of Land Rescue, the post responsible for all the RAF mountain rescue teams, and had been driving north to his home in Greenock for Christmas leave. He had just passed a mountain rescue team's lorry also heading north on the M6 motorway when he heard the first news of the incident on his car radio. With great presence of mind, he waited for the lorry to catch him up, and flagged it down. Leaving his wife to drive on alone, he boarded the lorry, identified himself to the surprised team and ordered them to proceed immediately to Lockerbie. Arriving just over an hour later, he found the team from RAF Leeming already there. Over the following few hours, with the help of the team members and another RAF helicopter navigator, he established an Operations Room in the gymnasium, and set about collating all the available information and preparing briefings for the helicopter crews. Where I had failed to acquire a single map, he and his teams appeared somehow to have commandeered the town's entire stock. The team's specialist vehicles were equipped with long-range High Frequency radios with which they could communicate directly with the Controllers at the Rescue Co-ordination Centre, an essential asset in the absence of any telephone lines until BT installed an emergency link during the night. They also carried VHF and UHF radios for talking to the helicopters. Bill had sent his teams out to make their own reconnaissance and assessments of the situation, liaising with the police and accurately plotting significant occurrences. This information was annotated on large-scale maps, each marked up into sectors for aerial searches and allocated to specific helicopter crews at the briefing. During those first chaotic and confusing hours Bill's expert guidance proved crucial in maintaining the closest liaison between the police and the Rescue Controllers, keeping the helicopter crews informed and making the most effective and efficient use of those resources. He and his team had become a *de facto* Forward Rescue Co-ordination Centre.

Joining my crew of Graham Andrews and Phil Boothby, I now had Master Air Loadmaster Jock Menmuir and Flight Sergeant Sean Ekberg. We received our briefing from the mountain rescue team and set off in the early dawn light to find our helicopter. We were soon airborne and heading towards our assigned area, flying over scenes of utter and shocking devastation adjacent to the still smoking crater. Broken bodies and limbs lay in profusion on roads, in the gardens of many of the houses, draped across walls and fences and even within the shattered roof spaces of some of the houses. Aircraft wreckage was scattered liberally over the whole area. Houses had been destroyed and the shells of burnt-out cars littered a section of the southbound carriageway of the A74, the main route north from London to Glasgow before its upgrading to become the A74(M). Until now, the only information available to us on the extent of the wreckage site had been gleaned from the search parties on the ground during the night. This reconnaissance had suggested that the wreckage was confined within a relatively small area between Lockerbie and the small farm settlement of Tundergarth, 3 miles to the east of the town. However, it was now apparent from our aerial perspective that the area affected was considerably more extensive. Just how far the wreckage trail actually extended was still to be discovered.

*   *   *

Approaching our assigned search area, we spotted the detached white and blue section of the crumpled forward fuselage and nose of the Pan-Am Boeing 747 lying on its port side near the centre of a large field adjacent to Tundergarth church, its name *Maid of the Seas* clearly visible below the cockpit. This was to become the iconic image of the tragedy. As we carried out a quick reconnaissance of the field, my gaze took in a scene seemingly of absolute stillness. The area appeared as a surreal graveyard with the many bodies widely scattered at random around the field, each guarded by a policeman. In their black raincoats, the police seemed like dark, grim-visaged effigies, standing their silent, motionless vigils for the blanket-shrouded corpses at their feet. Other casualties were draped across nearby boundary walls and lying in another smaller field next to the church.

Those lying in the open fields were each accompanied by a shallow scoop in the soil marking the initial point of impact after their fall before bouncing *back* into the air and finally coming to rest a few feet further to the east and away from Lockerbie. The significance of the direction in which the bodies had fallen and the distance between first impact point and final resting place was not apparent to us until the release of the Air Accidents Investigation Branch report into the tragedy. Although the Boeing had been travelling on a northerly track at the time of the explosion, the disruption to the aircraft's structure and flying controls was such that a violent nose-down pitching movement had accelerated the rapid disintegration of the aircraft. The nose and forward fuselage section had broken away almost immediately, tearing off one of the inboard engines and striking the tail as it separated from the rest of the aircraft, spilling its passengers into the thin night air 30,000 feet above Lockerbie. To all intents, the forward motion of the Boeing had virtually stopped but a very strong westerly wind, a jet-stream, of some 120 mph had then exerted its influence. While heavier items such as the engines and centre fuselage plunged almost vertically down onto Lockerbie, lighter objects, including the bodies of some of the passengers, were immediately caught up by this wind and carried in an easterly direction during their estimated two-minute fall to earth. By the time of impact, these bodies had gained a significant easterly velocity, giving rise to the strange markings we had observed on the ground.

In marked contrast to many of their fellow passengers who had fallen nearer to the town centre, some of these bodies appeared at first sight to be unmarked, with some appearing merely curled up on the grass, peacefully asleep. There was much speculation, both at the time and since, as to whether at least some of these victims might have been alive up until the point when they hit the ground. During training, many RAF pilots, me included, had been regularly subjected to explosive decompression to the equivalent of 48,000 feet, well in excess of the 30,000 feet at which this aircraft had been blown apart. It is suggested that the decompression of the aircraft breaking up should therefore have been survivable, especially by the younger and fitter passengers and crew. However, the immediate lack of oxygen at those heights would most probably have rendered them unconscious within the first few seconds of their fall, with perhaps a regaining of consciousness once lower levels with more breathable air were reached. Indeed, one witness who had arrived on the scene within minutes claimed to have found one female passenger with a pulse that lasted for a short time. Horrific, distressing details.

*   *   *

As we widened our search from the field containing the nose section, we encountered what at first appeared to be a shepherd sitting against a low wall and surrounded by his sheep. We waved to him in passing but, on getting absolutely no response, I decided to take a closer look and gently manoeuvred my hovering aircraft towards him. Still no reaction. Suddenly, as the down-wash from my rotor blades reached him, he keeled over. I landed, and one of my crewmen walked over to see if he was all right. Although apparently un-marked, the 'shepherd' turned out to be a dead passenger from the aircraft.

Roaming further afield towards the east, we encountered more tragic sights: bodies still strapped in a row of virtually intact seats and further isolated victims, some lying in the bottom of small craters pock-marking areas of softer ground. Their precise locations were recorded and plotted on our charts for the forensic teams to follow up. Interspersed with the bodies were large and small pieces of wreckage together with concentrations of personal belongings and baggage bearing mute testimony to the force of the destruc-tion. Many trees and hedgerows were bedecked with strips of silver foil and other remnants of the aircraft's trim in a cruel parody of Christmas decorations.

I continued flying east, plotting and logging all we found. Although the pieces of debris became noticeably smaller and lighter, we were still detect-ing a fairly well-defined trail, extending well beyond the dense forests of Kershope and Kielder, some 30 miles east of Lockerbie. Resulting from the pattern of disintegration described earlier, the eventual detailed report on the disaster by the Air Accidents Investigation Branch identified two separate wreckage trails, each extending eastwards from Lockerbie, with some debris even reaching the North Sea beyond Newcastle-upon-Tyne over 80 miles away and covering an estimated area of over 845 square miles. At the time, however, our radioed reports back to the control centre at Lockerbie of debris this far out were met with some scepticism and we were ordered to return and start lifting bodies back to Lockerbie Town Hall.

Returning to the field containing the nose of the aircraft, my crewmen commenced removal of the bodies from the cockpit. From my vantage point high in my cockpit I watched as they quickly and efficiently zipped each of them into body bags before loading them gently into my cabin. Not only was the careful handling of the bodies proper and decent, it was also vital to preserve any forensic pathological evidence that may have been present. This was a sad task but one that they had performed many times before in the course of their search and rescue duties. The sheer scale of this operation, however, was daunting. As I watched, I offered a silent prayer for each of them and their families. They had just loaded the third body, when we were ordered to leave those remaining in the field until full forensic recording of their locations had been completed. We landed back at Lockerbie where the bodies were transferred to a waiting ambulance for transfer to the temporary mortuary set up in the Town Hall. At this point we were diverted to Glasgow Airport to pick up an FBI team who had just arrived from the United States to assist with what had now become a murder inquiry. We then flew on to the RAF Maintenance Unit at Carlisle to refuel and to pick up a further supply of body bags.

On our return to our search area, we were concerned to note that no progress appeared to have been made in recovering any more bodies, while the weather had started to deteriorate and threatened to reduce the few remaining hours of daylight available. Suddenly, there was a burst of activity. RAF Chinooks from RAF Odiham in Hampshire had arrived on the scene and fresh police, drafted in from Glasgow, moved purposefully around the area, placing the bodies in the bags and loading them into the cavernous fuselages of the Chinooks. We continued to help by collecting casualties from the more remote and inaccessible areas.

* * *

As darkness fell on what was the shortest day of the year, all the search and rescue helicopters were ordered back to their respective bases to resume their standby commitments, leaving the Chinooks to complete the recovery tasks and ferry the investigation teams around the wreckage sites. We were included in that order and prepared for our flight back to Valley. Having carried out a couple of refuelling stops at Carlisle during the day, I estimated I had just sufficient fuel for the return trip to Valley. As we set off in the dark, it soon became apparent that the rapidly deteriorating weather would necessitate flying at very low level. I decided to pick up the coast on the south side of the Solway Firth and follow it down towards Blackpool, from where we would head straight across the sea to Anglesey and home. The second Valley Wessex helicopter followed some ten minutes behind us.

Our return flights were not without incident. Encountering lashing rain and winds much stronger than forecast, I had to make an unscheduled stop at the helicopter pad at Bangor Hospital and call for a refuelling tanker from

Valley to meet me there. While awaiting its arrival, Jock succumbed to influenza and sat in a corridor, clammy and shivering uncontrollably while a nurse plied him with hot tea and aspirin. In the meantime, Steve Garrod in the other Wessex had fared little better. Encountering even lower cloud, his navigation equipment out of action and his crew also suffering the onset of influenza, he had decided to seek temporary refuge at the British Aerospace airfield at Warton, near Preston. Creeping up to the bright lights of what he had taken to be the airfield, he was surprised to find himself crossing the perimeter of a nearby maximum security prison. The roar of his low over-shoot sparked off a full-scale alert when the staff suspected a break-out attempt.

It was now the evening of Thursday 22 December, but it felt like half a life-time since I had left home just over twenty-four hours before. My daughters had arrived for Christmas but what should have been a happy occasion was now a very muted affair. Now that I could unwind, the enormity of the horror that I had witnessed, coupled with the overwhelming sense of frustration and impotence at having been unable to render any assistance to any of the 270 victims, suddenly hit me.

I locked myself in the bathroom and wept.

CHAPTER TWENTY-NINE

POSTSCRIPT

Fatal accidents to RAF search and rescue helicopter personnel have been fortunately rare in operations, and even rarer during training. There is a particularly bitter irony in the death during training of someone who has put his life on the line so many times in the past to rescue others. Such a death was that of Master Air Loadmaster Peter 'Jock' Menmuir. Jock had been employed for many years on search and rescue flights all around the UK, and had earlier given particularly meritorious service at 'A' Flight, 202 Squadron at RAF Boulmer. There he had been involved in the rescue attempt on four men who had been thrown into the bitterly cold North Sea when their 14-foot open fishing boat capsized. The crew of an RNLI inshore lifeboat, which had gone to their aid, also required rescuing when it too overturned in the treacherous seas.

The extraordinary stamina and determination that Jock had shown during that prolonged and difficult operation was to make the manner of his death nine years later, almost to the day, of this very experienced and skilled winchman, instructor and unsung hero of RAF helicopter search and rescue, so very difficult for his friends and colleagues to understand.

* * *

Monday 12 February 1990 was a normal busy working day on the Search and Rescue Training Unit, at Valley. The usual mix of courses was being run – the long courses designed to equip qualified helicopter crews posted to search and rescue units with the requisite skills vital for their new role, and the short familiarisation course for all trainee RAF helicopter pilots to teach them the basic techniques they might be called upon to use at short notice, in whatever helicopter role they might find themselves. It was for one of these familiarisation courses that I briefed my crew on that fateful Monday afternoon. My student was Flying Officer Jonathan Dixon (later, as a group captain, to become one of the first RAF Search and Rescue Force Commanders). We were going to practise rescues from cliff situations. This was a labour-intensive instructional sortie, requiring not only me as the pilot instructor, but also a winch operator, a winchman, and also a survivor. Staff instructors would normally perform all these supporting roles, the survivor having the important task of presenting an exercise emergency situation carefully graded to the student pilot's developing skills. My survivor for this sortie was Jock Menmuir, supported by Master Signaller Jim Clark as winch operator and a newly qualified search and rescue navigator, Flying Officer Chris Palgrave, in the role of winchman.

Following a crew briefing, our Wessex helicopter was soon clattering out across the wide sweep of Trearddur Bay to our usual cliffs rescue training area on Holyhead Range. A weak sun shone on a sea scattered with white horses stirred by a brisk north-westerly breeze, perfect weather for the planned sortie. The exercise involved teaching and testing my pilot student in a variety of rescue situations on and close to the rugged cliffs, using Jock Menmuir as the distressed victim requiring rescue. The area I had selected for the final exercise on this sortie was a high cliff overlooking the sweeping panorama of Abraham's Bosom, a relatively sheltered bay, encompassed on its north-west side by the rocky feature on which was perched the iconic South Stack lighthouse. I landed in a field adjacent to the cliff top and, with a backward glance and cheery wave, Jock left the aircraft and disappeared from view down the grassy slope to reach the location for the next 'situation' near the cliff's base.

While waiting for Jock to get into position, I discussed various options for searching cliff locations with Jonathan before I gave him a simulated radio call.

'Message from Holyhead Coastguard – person seen falling over the cliff at Holyhead Range in the vicinity of Abraham's Bosom. Request immediate helicopter assistance!'

Jonathan quickly re-positioned at the start of the cliff facing Abraham's Bosom and set up a search, creeping to his right along the cliff edge. Suddenly, as we rounded a slight outcrop, I spotted Jock floating face-down near the water's edge, rising and falling on the swell. Simultaneously, Jim, the winch operator, who was kneeling in the cabin doorway, reported the sighting.

'Drowning casualty, near base of cliff, three o'clock, 50 yards!' At this stage, nothing appeared untoward. It was common practice for the survivor to take a deep breath and 'play dead' as he heard the helicopter approaching, thus presenting the student with a realistic scenario that emphasised the need to get the aircraft into a winching position quickly and safely, but without being rushed into making dangerous mistakes. As the crew completed their essential checks prior to winching, for the moment keeping the battering downwash from the rotors away from the casualty, Jim suddenly interrupted.

'Something's wrong! Jock's not moving!'

Again, in the training situation, it would have been normal for the survivor to have given a subtle indication that he was OK once he had seen the correct action initiated by the student. There was no movement from Jock. With the nearest part of the cliff now on my side of the aircraft, I took control of the Wessex.

'Let's get him out – fast! I'm happy with my clearance on the left and can come down 15 feet.' This indicated to Jim that he could devote all his attention to getting the winchman to the casualty without constantly having to check and reassure me of the main and tail rotor clearances from any obstructions. By allowing Jim to descend me a further 15 feet, we could significantly reduce the time taken for the winchman to reach Jock. Now hovering with the nose of the Wessex tucked tightly into a fold in the steep grassy slope in front of me and only inches from touching, and the rotor blades whirling just feet from the cliff face at my side, I followed Jim's calm instructions to maintain position over Jock's inert body. His patter was interspersed with Chris's progress in getting Jock into the rescue strop and a commentary on Jock's condition.

'Jock still hasn't moved … steady … this is not looking good … steady, height is good … survivor in the strop, winchman attempting resuscitation … steady … winching in … clear of the water … steady, height is good … at the cabin door … entering the cabin …. clear above and behind … clear up and away.' Without further ado, I pulled to the maximum power, angling the nose of the Wessex down to accelerate away as quickly as possible.

With the Wessex now shuddering at its maximum speed, I aimed straight for the airfield in the distance. While operating in our local area, we were monitored by Valley Air Traffic Control on a so-called 'quiet' frequency, which was only used to make periodic reports of our position for safety purposes. I now used this frequency.

'Mayday! Mayday! Mayday! This is Whisky Yankee Tango Zero Four inbound on low level transit from Holyhead Range direct to the Station Medical Centre with one drowning crew member.' By invoking the international distress call-sign, I was claiming absolute priority of movement wherever possible. The response I received, however, was not what I wanted to hear.

'Mayday Zero Four. Be advised that there is a low level Hawk formation aerobatic display practice in progress over the airfield. Call Tower.' As an Assistant Air Traffic Controller, he could neither give me clearance to continue, nor stop the display practice. Switching frequency to that of the airfield controller, my headset was instantly filled with the curt instructions of the formation display leader as they manoeuvred at low level above the airfield. Choosing my moment carefully, I transmitted.

'Mayday Zero Four inbound to Medical Centre, remaining at ground level, no confliction.' As I lifted to clear the roofs of the Station Married Quarters – I reasoned that any Hawk this low down would be in serious trouble.

Fortunately, the air traffic assistant had alerted the Station Medical Centre to our imminent arrival and I was relieved to see the staff waiting by its small landing pad. The moment I landed, eager hands reached out to place Jock on a stretcher and rush him inside. It was the last time I was to see him as he laid there totally limp and motionless.

While waiting at the Medical Centre, I called our Operations Room on another radio, requesting that the standby helicopter from 22 Squadron be scrambled to take Jock to hospital. Unlike my Wessex, kitted out in the training role, theirs had a far more comprehensive medical kit on board that would assist in Jock's care during his transfer to Bangor Hospital.

Jock lingered on a life-support system in the Intensive Care Unit at Bangor for a further three days. At the meteorological briefing held each morning, Chris Gibbons, the Squadron Commander, provided bulletins on Jock's losing battle before his life-support system was eventually switched off.

We said our farewells to our friend and colleague at his funeral in the tiny RAF church at Valley, packed to capacity, with many more standing outside. Standing by the side of Jock's coffin, draped in the Union Flag, I read a passage from the Bible, thankful that I had memorised it; I could not have read it with eyes blurred with tears. Later that week, a lone Wessex scattered Jock's ashes above the hills of Snowdonia.

I retired from the RAF a few months later after thirty years of service. It was a sad note on which to end my career.

Index

Note: For clarity, the use of unfamiliar abbreviations and acronyms in the text has been avoided. However, the following have been used to reduce cumbersome repetition:

FATOC – Forward Air Transport Operations Centre
SARTS – Search and Rescue Training Squadron
SARTU – Search and Rescue Training Unit